THE GOAL
OF THE
GOSPEL

THE GOAL
OF THE
GOSPEL

God's Purpose in Saving You

PHILIP M. BICKEL
&
ROBERT L. NORDLIE

Publishing House
St. Louis

To our brothers and sisters
at Immanuel Lutheran Church of Hillside, Illinois,
whose growing courage to obey God's will
led us into the Scriptures,
where the Holy Spirit taught us the truths
contained in this book

Unless otherwise noted, the Scripture quotations in this publication are from The Holy Bible: NEW INTERNATIONAL VERSION, © 1973, 1978, 1984 by the International Bible Society. Used by permission of Zondervan Bible Publishers.

Copyright © 1992 Concordia Publishing House
3558 S. Jefferson Avenue, St. Louis, MO 63118-3968
Manufactured in the United States of America

Library of Congress Cataloging in Publication Data

Bickel, Philip M., 1948-
    The goal of the gospel: God's purpose in saving you / Philip M. Bickel and Robert L.
    Nordlie.
        p.   cm.
        Includes bibliographical references.
        ISBN 0-570-04569-X
        1. Church renewal—Lutheran Church—Missouri Synod.   2. Evangelistic
work—Biblical teaching.   3. Bible. N.T. Romans—Criticism, interpretation, etc.   4.
Lutheran Church—Missouri Synod—Membership.   5. Lutheran Church—Membership. I. Nordlie, Robert L., 1949–   II. Title.
BX8061.M7B53   1992
269'.2—dc20   91-43170

---

1   2   3   4   5   6   7   8   9   10   VP   01   00   99   98   97   96   95   94   93   92

Contents

Foreword

Concordia Publishing House offers this book as an additional voice in an ongoing conversation. This conversation, first of all, is theological. That is to say, it originates with God who, when he speaks, causes things to happen (2 Peter 3:5), and who by his Son, Jesus Christ, pronounces every sinner who believes his promises fully righteous and completely acceptable before him.

And, God invites believers to join his conversation, to talk to him in love, and to respond in love to others. Nor is the decision to respond left to those who feel like doing so. Nevertheless, God's people don't always engage wholeheartedly in the conversation. Sometimes it seems as if they are nearly silent. What then? What motivates Christians to tell others of God's mighty deeds? What arouses congregations to speak his love?

That very question and concern sent the authors—both parish pastors at the time—to their Bibles looking for answers. What resulted, among other things, after two years of intense weekly study together, was the beginning of this book. Concordia offers it in order to contribute to the conversation the Lord has originated and invited us to join. *The Goal of the Gospel* is not the last word. It may challenge you, possibly provoke you and send you back to your Bibles. You may disagree with parts of it. It is not the final word, but part of the ongoing conversation, inviting your responses.

Hopefully, it will also help you to examine your participation in the Lord's conversation with a dying world. And, who knows, perhaps it will even challenge someone to write the next book in the ongoing conversation.

The Publisher

Part I

The Goal of the Gospel in the Scriptures

1

Oh, To Arouse the Sleeping Giant!

Seated at his desk, Pastor Ralph Kramer alternately fretted and prayed. Even though attendance at Good Shepherd was up again after the summer lull, the spiritual health of his flock appeared in jeopardy. The Pasarellas were filing for divorce. Natalie Taylor was slipping deeper into the New Age Movement. When Pastor Ralph had objected that the Youth Talent Night featured some heavy metal music with satanic themes, most of the parents had actually come to the defense of their children. And as usual, the congregation was much more concerned about making the annual sausage dinner a success than they were about the new evangelism program that had been kicked off two months ago and now appeared ready to kick the bucket.

"Lord," Ralph pleaded, "I feel like I have tried everything. What do I do next to try to wake up your people from their spiritual lethargy? Where can I ... "

Interrupted by a knock at his study door, Pastor Ralph hurriedly wiped the tears from his eyes and ran his fingers through his thinning hair that had become mussed in the turmoil of intercession. "Come in."

In walked Dave Schmidt, the president of Good Shepherd and the closest thing to a best friend Pastor Ralph had in the congregation. The minister's spirits rose momentarily, expecting Dave's sparkling personality to brighten the moment, but an uncustomary frown on Dave's face quelled his hope.

"Hello, Pastor Ralph. Do you have a moment?"

"I always do for you, Dave. What's troubling you?"

"I guess it's written all over my face, isn't it? I'm not sure what to call this feeling that's bugging me," Dave sighed. After a pause he proceeded, "I guess it's mostly disappointment. When I read my

Bible, when I hear you preach and teach, Pastor, I see so clearly what we here at Good Shepherd need to be accomplishing. There are hurting people to be loved and cared for. There are folks to be saved. And hardly anyone seems to care. Oh, they say they care, but if the saying never grows up into doing, what good is it?"

"So you're upset that we exhibit so little commitment to doing God's will." Pastor Ralph reiterated.

"Uh-huh."

"How does that make you feel?"

"It makes me angry at some of our people. But then I get even madder at myself, because I'm no Super Christian either. I've got enough inconsistencies of my own to worry about. So who am I to criticize others?"

"Yes, we all fall short of God's glory. I'm glad you recognize that. I understand your concern, Dave. You're a man who hungers and thirsts after righteousness. I'm just as hungry and thirsty as you are."

"What do you mean, Pastor?"

Pastor Ralph hesitated, wondering whether to hide his personal feelings or to speak from the heart and thus become vulnerable. The need to share his burden won out. "Dave, I've been in here the last hour praying and weeping. I'm troubled about the spiritual weakness and laziness of the people of God at Good Shepherd. They say that a pastor's best years at a parish begin after he has been there six years. Well, I've been here for nine, and my ministry doesn't seem to have made much impression at all on the lifestyles of the most of our people. Dave, I'm pushing 50. God willing, I may have about 20 more years to serve my Savior. When I look at the progress that the church—not just here, but around the world—has made in the 20-odd years of my ministry, I'm plenty disappointed. In two whole decades we've nudged ahead an inch. I'm afraid we'll only nudge ahead another inch in the next two decades. It is just not enough! Our glorious God deserves better than that."

"That's just how I feel!" Dave shouted excitedly. "It's the reason why I came in here dragging my jaw. People are dying of AIDS, and our only concern is whether to keep serving communion with the common cup. Half the churches in our denomination don't add a new convert in a year, and we don't seem to worry that we are in the wrong half. TV and the media bombard us with ungodly morals and materialism, and we soak it up like sponges, while complaining every time you preach over 18 minutes. Half the people on the face of this earth don't even know who Jesus Christ is and what he has done for them. And what do we do about it? We sit behind stained glass windows singing, 'Tell everyone what he has done,' but we don't seem to really mean it."

"Believe it or not, your depressing tirade encourages me a bit," Pastor Ralph chuckled. "At least now I know I'm not the only one who's frustrated."

"So what are you—I mean we—going to do about it? Why don't you really give it to them next Sunday, Pastor? A hard-hitting sermon might jolt a little guilt into them and get them rolling."

"Boy, sometimes I feel that I ought to do just that. But, Dave, you know that's not my style. I don't think it's the Bible's style either. I was taught, 'Just preach the Gospel, and everything else will take care of itself.' So that's what I do, preaching God's Law and Christ's salvation as best I can, and then I wait for the fruits of faith to appear."

"But why is the harvest of fruits so meager, Pastor?"

"I don't know, Dave. It appears that everything else doesn't just take care of itself. I surely don't want to become a legalistic preacher, browbeating with the Law and overlooking the Gospel. I wish I could find a way to preach obedience and witnessing and still be faithful to the Scriptures."

"Hey! That would be great."

We, the authors, know just how Dave and Pastor Ralph feel. We have been there too, wondering how to motivate people for dedicated Christian living without whipping them with the Law and losing sight of the Gospel. Back in June 1988, our church was passing through a valley of financial stewardship commitment. That particular crisis, when many people seemed unwilling to risk giving more to the Lord's work, led us to begin a Bible study together. We set out to study all the places in the Bible where the words "courage" and "courageous" appear. As we studied these words, another set of terms kept appearing: "obey" and "obedience." So when we had finished investigating "courage/courageous," we went on to tackle "obey/obedience." Following that, we were led one step further, to analyze closely one book of the Bible that stressed these themes.

All together, we spent about 15 months on this project, studying for about 90 minutes two mornings per week.

All of this Bible-study-in-duet has changed our style of ministry. In this book we wish to share our findings with you. At times we may say something that at first sounds bizarre or even wrong. But please bear with us. We do not pretend to have discovered new doctrines. Instead we have found in the Scriptures a different emphasis or balance between doctrines than we had ever seen before. In response to this, we have since been developing a new approach to teaching obedience and the Christian life in our church. We believe this new approach is more biblical than our previous, traditional practice.

Billy Graham and others have referred to the authors' denomination, The Lutheran Church—Missouri Synod, as a sleeping giant. Christians of other denominations may feel the same about their congregation or church body. To be a sleeping giant is frustrating. We could do so much, if only we would wake up, as the Word of God urges us to do:

> Wake up! Strengthen what remains and is about to die, for I have not found your deeds complete in the sight of my God (Rev 3:2).

> The hour has come for you to wake up from your slumber, because our salvation is nearer now than when we first believed. The night is nearly over; the day is almost here. So let us put aside the deeds of darkness and put on the armor of light (Rom 13:11–12).

Is there an antidote for ecclesiastical sleeping sickness? We firmly believe so! Not because of any ingenuity on our part, but solely due to the Holy Spirit's guidance during months of Bible study, we believe that we have discovered the antidote for ecclesiastical sleeping sickness, the alarm clock which can wake up sleeping giants.

If you and your church long to be aroused to action, read on.

The Goal of the Gospel

The Greek word *telos*,[1] which means goal, end, or outcome, is used regularly to show us what God wants to accomplish in our lives through the Gospel of Jesus Christ. For example, John writes, "But if anyone obeys his word, God's love is truly made complete in him" (1 Jn 2:5). What John means is that God's love, which he demonstrated in Christ our Savior, is made complete (*telos*) in us; that is, it accomplishes its purpose or reaches its goal, when the Spirit brings us to faith in Christ's death for us and therefore we learn to "obey" (trust, follow) God's word. That is his goal in redeeming us by the Gospel.

That has always been God's purpose in the Gospel promises which he has given to his people. James writes about Abraham, "You see that his faith and his actions were working together, and his faith was made complete by what he did" (James 2:22). James is telling us that Abraham's faith in God's promises was made complete (*telos*); that is, it reached its goal or accomplished its purpose when it expressed itself in action. In this case, in obedience to God's command, Abraham offered his son Isaac on the altar. Abraham's faith in God's Gospel promise enabled him to do that.

In Heb 12:2 Jesus is called "the author and perfecter of our faith." The word *perfecter* is a form of the word *telos*. We rejoice in having a Savior who through his Spirit authors our faith. To the same degree we should rejoice in Christ, the perfecter of our faith, who through his Spirit brings our faith to its goal (*telos*).

The outcome (*telos*) of the Gospel is radically different from the outcome (*telos*) of sin. In Rom 6:21–22 Paul writes,

> What benefit did you reap at that time from the things you are now ashamed of? Those things result (*telos*) in death! But now that you have been set free from sin and have become slaves to God, the benefit you reap leads to holiness, and the result (*telos*) is eternal life.

Yes, Paul does say that the goal or result (*telos*) of the Gospel is eternal life, but along the journey to heaven the benefit that you reap is holiness or sanctification, that is, learning to obey.

OBEDIENCE, MISSION, AND GLORY

Ultimately we will see that the goal of the Gospel has three facets. It includes (1) obedience to God's revealed will; (2) world evangelization through the proclamation of the Gospel; and (3) living to the glory of God. We will touch on all three themes repeatedly in this book, at times referring to each one as the goal of the Gospel. When doing so, we do not wish to imply that any one of these three facets is the only goal of the Gospel. Obedience, world evangelization, and the glory of God are too intimately linked to be treated as three separate goals.

In looking at the word *telos* we have already seen that obedience is the goal of the Gospel. The fact remains, however, that people can obey God's will only when they believe in Jesus Christ by the power of the Holy Spirit. Thus, if the goal of obedience is to be reached, the Gospel must be proclaimed, because God brings people to faith only through the Gospel. This adds the mission aspect to the goal of the Gospel. God saved us so that we may lead others to salvation by telling them the good news of Jesus Christ.

By our obedience (living in faith) and our mission, God is glorified. For his name's sake we obey his will. As David said, "He guides me in paths of righteousness for his name's sake" (Ps 23:3). It is for the glory of his name that we proclaim the Gospel to all nations. "Sing to the Lord, praise his name; proclaim his salvation day after day. Declare his glory among the nations" (Ps 96:2–3). Thus, glorifying God is also the goal of the Gospel.

Most often, Christians who are urged to let God be glorified in their lives respond positively. "Yes, I want my life to glorify God!" they say. Even the mission challenge excites most Christians. "Oh, I love to hear about missions. I'll often give a little extra for an important mission cause," they respond. But how do many Christians feel when they are confronted with God's call to obey His will?

The Four-Letter Word

To many people, obey is a "four-letter word," as dirty and nasty as they come.

Bill picked at his salad almost distastefully as he watched Melanie bite into her thick, juicy burger. "How do you do it?" he asked.

"Do what?" Melanie replied, as she wiped the corners of her mouth.

"How do you eat that huge burger for lunch and not gain an ounce? What do you do to keep in shape?"

"Oh, I jog a couple times a week. And I play volleyball every

Friday night. Hey, why don't you come with me tomorrow? We could use another tall guy."

"You know, I think I will. I used to play a lot of volleyball in college, but lately I haven't been doing much of anything besides working. Maybe that's why I'm having such a hard time keeping in shape," Bill said as he pulled in his stomach and took another bite of lettuce. "Where do you play?" he asked.

"At my church," replied Melanie. "We have a great time!"

"Sure, I'll bet you do," said Bill sarcastically. "I think I just changed my mind about volleyball."

"Why?" asked Melanie with surprise.

"I had plenty of religion crammed down my throat as a kid. I don't need any more of that stuff right now. I got sick and tired of all the rules you had to obey. No thanks!" said Bill emphatically.

Unfortunately, there are many people like Bill, even people who were brought up as Christians, who get a bad taste in their mouth when they hear the word *obey,* especially in connection with the church. Why? It may have something to do with the way in which Christianity was presented by the church in which they grew up. But another factor is our sinful nature. We have this stubborn streak in us that makes us want to go our own way and rebel against everything God would ask of us. And so we hate the word obey.

Why does obey sound like a four-letter word? Here is a list of synonyms for *obey* that are found in *Roget's International Thesaurus*: submit, comply, acquiesce, relent, succumb, resign oneself, knuckle under, lie down, and roll over. The list does not exactly conjure up pleasant thoughts. It makes us feel trapped, coerced, or forced to comply against our wishes. *Obey,* however, did not always have such connotations and is not at all what God has in mind when he asks us to obey his will. The obedience that God speaks of involves nothing but joy and blessing.

Actually, there is another four-letter word that we ought to hate instead of the word obey. That word is *sinn*. Okay, so that's not how it's spelled! But it should be! Then sinn would be a four-letter word. Sinn traps us, robs us of joy, and ultimately destroys us. Just as much as we hate the word sinn, we should love the word obey. One of the goals of this book is to lead Christians to appreciate, yes, even to love the word obey. That's certainly the picture we see in the Scriptures.

The Joy of Obedience

The Bible describes the will of God by using a number of very positive images. It tells us that, for those who have been redeemed, obedience is satisfying, joy-filled, and pleasurable.

To obey the will of God is satisfying. Jesus said, "My food is to do the will of him who sent me and to finish his work" (Jn 4:34). Thus Jesus describes the Father's will as "food," that which sustained him, indeed, that which was the very source of his life. That's the way we need to view the will of God, even as David did when he wrote, "The ordinances of the Lord are sure and altogether righteous. They are more precious than gold, than much pure gold; they are sweeter than honey, than honey from the comb" (Ps 19:9–10). Combining the images of gold and honey, David shows us that the Father's will nourishes and sustains us like a sumptuous feast and richly blesses us with the finest treasure.

To obey the will of God is a joy. Jesus saw every part of his obedience to the Father's will from the perspective of the joy it would ultimately bring. Thus, Heb 12:2 tells us to "fix our eyes on Jesus, the author and perfecter of our faith, who for the joy set before him endured the cross." So it was that Jesus, even on that occasion when he stared suffering and death square in the face, was able to pray, "My Father, if it is possible, may this cup be taken from me. Yet not as I will, but as you will" (Mt 26:39). Jesus saw the joy on the other side of the cross.

To obey the will of God is a pleasure. "You have made known to me the path of life; you fill me with joy in your presence, with eternal pleasures at your right hand," sings David in Ps 16:11. God is the source of every pleasure, of every good thing that is a part of our lives. His Spirit gives us faith in Jesus, and having this faith, we are able to see the will of God in a positive light. That is why Paul refers to "the obedience that comes from faith" (Rom 1:5). When we live in accord with his will we cannot help but be blessed by it. "God's will already has our good embedded in it, and obedience to such a will is to cooperate with an enormous power determined to bless us. God invites our involvement. The blessings do not come by fate, but by faith" (Mattson and Miller 1982, 27).

Unfortunately, most Christians in America today do not see obedience as something positive. Does that sound too critical? Perhaps

18

we need to see our brand of Christianity from the perspective of another culture.

Dr. Eugene Bunkowske, a former missionary and now professor of missions, relates a revealing story about a conversation he had with an Igbo man from Nigeria while delivering a series of lectures on missions at an American Christian university. After the lecture the man, whose name was Chinedu, came up to Dr. Bunkowske and said, "I need your help because I am getting terribly confused about Christianity." He continued, "I came from a very religious family, not Christian but animist. My father was a juju priest. Ten years ago we became Christians. We understood Christianity as a change of loyalty. That is, we had always believed that spiritual things were central and basic to everything that happened in life. For us to receive Christ was to change loyalty. It was to take the idols, witchcraft, juju power, and ancestor worship out of the spiritual center of our life and receive the triune God—Father, Son, and Holy Spirit—into the center of our life. This included repentance for our sins and full belief in Jesus as our Savior and friend. Now after being here at the university I am confused. I believe my family and I got it wrong. Christianity is not a change of loyalty but rather a change of . . . model."

Now Dr. Bunkowske was confused. He asked, "What do you mean?"

Chinedu answered, "I am getting the impression that 'true Christianity—American style' demands a new model of reality in which the spiritual things are taken out of the center and placed at the edge of life. . . . [T]he spiritual center . . . is replaced by SPECL."

"And what, Chinedu, do you mean by SPECL?" asked Dr. Bunkowske.

Chinedu replied, "SPECL, as I see it here at the university, is the real heart and center of true Christianity—American style. S stands for *Success,* which is the natural result of P which stands for *Progress.* Progress in terms of Christianity—American style is not very likely without E which stands for *Education.* Then finally to be a real Christian you show your progress, wealth, and success by *Collecting* (C) many things and by your *Leisure* (L) time activities" (Bunkowske 1989, 2–3).

Chinedu has quite an insight into Christianity—American style.

Loyalty to Jesus Christ is not at the center of most Christians' lives. If it were, obedience would follow naturally. Rather, it's as though Jesus floats on the edge of the Christian's life, like a helium balloon attached to a child's wrist. The balloon bobs overhead, but the child doesn't notice it until she wants to play with it. In the same way, the Christian who has Jesus on a string pulls him back into focus only in times of real crisis.

Why is this? Could it be because we have lost sight of the goal of the Gospel, that is, to *obey* everything that Christ has commanded us (Mt 28:20)? We have come to think that our Christian faith relates only to a heavenly goal. It is not the center of our lives here and now. Instead, success in collecting things and enjoying our leisure takes center stage while we live here on earth. Frills and thrills have replaced the obedience that comes from faith. But these things that pass away will never bring us lasting joy. Knowing Christ, trusting in him, and obeying his good and gracious will bring the greatest joy there could ever be.

Seeing the Big Picture

The good news of salvation by grace through faith in Jesus Christ is the heart and core of our Christian faith. There is no more important doctrine than the pure Gospel of Christ which teaches that we are saved by grace alone, without any merit of our own. It is central to everything we believe, and every other doctrine must be seen in the context of the Gospel.

Because of this heavy emphasis on the Gospel, we have tended to view most other doctrines as peripheral. This does not mean that we think of them as unimportant or non-essential. It only means that we have relegated them to a position of minor importance in comparison to the Gospel itself. Perhaps this is why we have lost sight of the goal of the Gospel.

Sometimes you can't see the forest for the trees. Maybe that has happened to us in this instance. The Gospel, like a huge sequoia, towers majestically over all the other trees of the forest. Its majesty so captivates us that we tend to lose sight of the forest and see only that singular tree. When that happens, we need to step back and try to recapture the big picture. We need to remember that there are other trees in the forest of doctrines besides the one towering sequoia. In addition to the Gospel itself, we need to see the goal of the Gospel.

OBEDIENCE HAS ALWAYS BEEN GOD'S GOAL

To see the big picture is to realize that the Gospel of Jesus Christ has a goal. To understand that goal, let's look at what God's will was at the time of creation, what it will be at the end of time, and, therefore, what it must be in the present. This is what we mean by the big picture.

To get that big picture we need to start at the beginning, back before the Gospel had ever been revealed, before it was even necessary. The Scriptures tell us that "God created man in his own image" (Gen 1:27). This means that the first couple, Adam and Eve, were like God, holy and righteous. They lived at the very center of God's will and had an intimate knowledge of the Holy One. It was God's plan that they should be fruitful and multiply and fill the earth with a thousand generations of holy people devoted to doing the will of God. With such people God could maintain a loving, joy-filled relationship in which he would shower them with his abundant blessings and receive from them their highest praise, to the glory of his name. What would this world be like if God's original plan had been carried out by Adam and Eve?

Imagine the perfect world God intended: Every person able to be in relationships that are perfect in every aspect, marked only by love; our human resources, that is, our God-given energies, abilities and interests, used to their fullest extent, without any exploitation or abuse of individuals, and without exploitation of the resources of the earth or the environment. Under such conditions mankind's ingenuity and creativity could forge an amazing technology without dehumanizing or depersonalizing society. Wealth could be shared freely by all, without the greed of capitalism or the oppression of totalitarianism. Art forms would truly glorify God and bring pleasure to everyone.

Adam and Eve failed when they succumbed to the devil's temptation. Now because we as heirs of Adam and Eve are unable to obey God's will perfectly, the lost possibilities stagger our imagination. When you begin to imagine the perfect world, you begin to understand that perfect obedience to God's will equals paradise.

21

Clearly, obedience was not an afterthought. It was God's goal and purpose in creating humanity.

When Adam and Eve chose disobedience, they made not only a moral choice, but also an existential one, that is, a choice with real-life consequences for their future existence. Had they chosen to obey God's command, they would have continued to exist in a condition of perfect joy, knowing only good all their lives. However, when they chose to disobey, they entered an existence marked by evil and great suffering as a result of their rebellion. In this state they would know blessings only by God's grace and mercy.

OBEDIENCE AND THE WORD OF GOD

Like Adam and Eve, we too are sinful and rebellious. As a result, we experience much sorrow and suffering. We can know the blessings of obedience only by the grace of God through faith in Jesus Christ. Only as the Holy Spirit empowers us by the Gospel, only as he guides us by God's word, can we begin to obey God's will. That's why God's Word is so important to the goal of obedience. On our own, we simply cannot muster the strength to do God's will. We don't even have the desire to do so, as the following story illustrates.

Pastor Mike did not score any brownie points with some of the members of Bethel congregation when he asked them to limit their "coffee hour" to fifteen minutes and spend the rest of the time between services studying the Bible. Only a few of them understood that Bible study enables us to move towards the goal of obedience. Bill and Marge, who were among those disturbed by Pastor Mike's plan, were chatting at coffee hour one Sunday morning with Ed and JoAnn.

"What's wrong with a little friendly conversation at church on a Sunday morning? That's what I want to know!" Bill asked rather heatedly, stirring his coffee with some nervous agitation.

"Yeah!" Marge chimed in, "I've got nothing against Bible study, but we've had a lot of fun during coffee hour over the last few years. Why do we have to give it up?"

"Pastor Mike isn't asking us to give up our conversation time entirely," replied Ed. "I think he just wants us to keep a balance."

"I think there's more to it than balance," JoAnn added. "It has to do with the purpose of our church. In fact, I believe it has to do with our purpose as Christians."

"What do you mean by that?" asked Marge.

"Ask yourself, why does our church exist? Is it just to be a social club, a place for friends to get together?" challenged JoAnn.

"No," said Bill, "we all know that. We come here to listen to a sermon, to sing and pray. We all go to one service or the other. None of us comes here on Sunday morning just to sit and chat!"

"That's just the point," replied JoAnn. "If we think our only purpose as Christians is to go to church, then we don't really understand the Bible. We need to dig deeper."

"I think JoAnn has a point," said Ed. "I used to leave my Christianity at the door of the church when I went home on Sunday morning. During the rest of the week I didn't really practice what I heard preached. Then, about six months ago, one of my friends invited JoAnn and me to a neighborhood Bible study group that meets Tuesday nights at his house. It wasn't long before I realized that there was more to being a Christian than going to church on Sunday. God wants me to obey him in the choices I make every day of the week. I started to think a whole lot more seriously about how I treat my family and how I talk at work. It's made a real difference in my life."

Bill looked at Ed cynically. "I've got enough to think about without having to worry about more rules all the time."

"Oh, I'm not thinking about rules. I'm thinking about God and how he feels when I do certain things. I look at what he's done for me in Christ, and I want to make him happy," Ed explained.

"That's what Bible study did for you?" Marge asked.

"I guess it doesn't sound so bad when you explain it that way," Bill commented.

"It's really helped me look at my relationship with God in a completely different light. My faith means more to me now than it ever did before," said Ed.

"That's why I said that Bible study has a lot to do with our purpose in life as Christians," JoAnn added. "Aren't we supposed to be honoring and serving God all the time? The more we study the Bible the better we will understand how we can do that, and the more we will want to please and obey God."

"Are you two asking the question, 'How can we do God's will if we don't understand it?' " Marge wondered.

"Understand it and want to do it!" Ed answered. "Bible study can help us do both."

Before we can know the joy and blessings of obedience, the Holy Spirit must work through God's Word to give us faith and, along with it, the longing and strength to obey God's will.

Summing Up the Goal

God wants to restore each of us to that loving, joy-filled relationship with him for which he created us in the beginning. He wants us to experience the blessings that he has in store for everyone who obeys his will. This is his plan, and he will not be thwarted in it. He has redeemed us in order to restore us to his image, so that we may live at the very center of his will, experiencing his perfect goodness. This is the goal of the Gospel.

Most Christians tend to see heaven, eternal life with God, as the goal of the Gospel. Certainly, that is our ultimate goal. But ask yourself, "What will we be like when we reach that goal?" Then we will become perfectly obedient to the will of God. Since this was God's plan for mankind at the time of creation, and it is his goal for us at the end of time, it must also be his desire for us in the present.

The goal of obedience is not just a future goal. God wants to see our restoration to his image begin now. True, our restoration will not be complete until we reach heaven, because the old sinful nature continues to cling to us as long as we are in the flesh. Nevertheless, God cares as much about our obedience now as in the future. His Gospel enables us to strive to live according to his will, both now and eternally. This is the goal of the Gospel.

God wanted Adam and Eve to glorify him in Eden. Throughout eternity we will glorify him in heaven. As his people here on earth learn to obey Christ's commands, God is glorified in the present. When we do his will, we honor him before men and bring glory to his name. Since we are able to do this only through faith in the Gospel of Jesus Christ, glorifying God is also the goal of the Gospel.

To achieve these goals among all people, the Gospel must be proclaimed to the ends of the earth. People everywhere need to hear the message of redemption in Christ Jesus so that they can trust in him and be moved to obey his will by the power of the Holy Spirit. When this happens, people all over the world will be glorifying God. The Gospel has been shared with us, then, so that we will share it with others. God's goal in bringing us to faith is that we will share our faith with as many other people as possible. This is our mission as Christ's church. This is the goal of the Gospel.

The goal of the Gospel, then, is to accomplish everything which God intended to accomplish in the beginning. This will happen perfectly in heaven, but it begins here and now, as Christians pursue the goal of the Gospel.

Look Ahead

In the next three chapters, we will study various parts of the Bible, looking for the goal of the Gospel. This overview of the Bible is the result of the authors' word study on *courage* and *obedience*. We will begin in the Old Testament and move on to the teachings of Jesus and the apostles. It is our hope that you will come to see the goals of obedience, missions, and the glory of God as clearly as we have—and make those goals your own.

Digging Deeper

Each chapter of this book will conclude with a section called "Digging Deeper." It will contain questions designed to help you comprehend and process the material contained in that chapter. Please consider these questions on your own; or, better yet, in a small discussion group.

1. Have you ever shared any of Pastor Ralph's or Dave Schmidt's frustrations with regard to your own local church? What signs of spiritual indifference or lethargy do you find there? What positive signs of life and growth do you recognize? How does each make you feel?

2. Summarize in your own words the three aspects of the goal of the Gospel: obedience, world evangelization, and the glorification of God.

3. According to this chapter, what are some of the positive images the Scriptures use to portray obedience? Can you think of any

others that the biblical writers use, other than those to which the authors referred? How do such images make you feel about obeying God's will?

4. What do you think of Chinedu's analysis of *true Christianity–American style* (Success, Progress, Education, Collecting, and Leisure)? Is there any validity to what he says? How closely does his analysis come to describing your brand of Christianity? How would you describe true Christianity–American Style?

5. What do the authors mean by "the big picture" when talking about the Gospel and the goal of the Gospel? Explain it in your own words.

6. Why is the Bible the key to achieving the goal of obedience?

7. How do you feel about the idea of "the goal of the Gospel?"

____ "It's just something the authors cooked up."

____ "It's a threat to the pure Gospel."

____ "It's an impossible dream."

____ "It's an exciting idea."

____ "It seems to be Biblical."

____ "I'm still thinking about it."

____ Other_____

Explain your choice.

Note

1. The Greek word *telos* actually appears in several different forms and derivatives in the Scriptures. The simplest and root form of all the others is the noun *telos* which means *end* or *goal*. The verb form is *teleō* which means *complete, accomplish,* or *fulfill*. In addition, this word is used as an adjective meaning *having attained the purpose,* as an adverb meaning *completely,* or *perfectly,* and in various derivatives like *teleiotes,* meaning *perfecter*. To simplify the matter in writing for lay people, the authors have chosen to refer to any form of this root word as *telos,* though we are aware of its various forms and meanings.

2

Obedience in the Old Testament

In our treatment of the Old Testament, we will concentrate on (1) God's promises and warnings in Deuteronomy 28–30; (2) texts that link the themes of obedience and the nations; (3) God's charge to Joshua to be strong and courageous; and (4) the intense desire of the author of Psalm 119 to obey and glorify God. These four examples do not by any means comprise all the teaching on godly living to be found in the Old Testament, but they will help us gain a clear understanding of Jehovah's concern with obedience during the centuries before the Savior's entrance onto the stage of human history.

Obedience: A Matter of Life or Death

Deuteronomy is a great book of the Bible, worthy of repeated readings. Its most crucial section includes chapters 27–30. These chapters are central to the history of the Jewish people, because they predict so many ills which later befell them. For this reason, many other parts of the Old Testament harken back to Deuteronomy 27–30. If the generations of Jews following had listened to this word of God, they would have been spared much suffering. If our own generation would heed these chapters, we as God's people today also could avoid much suffering and futility, for these chapters teach us that faith and accompanying obedience are no small matter. They are literally matters of life or death. Whether you individually believe and obey God's word *is* a matter of life or death for you. Whether your church as a unit believes and obeys God's word is a matter of life or death for your congregation.

The events recorded in Deuteronomy 27–30 occur at the close of the 40 years of wandering in the desert. Through his prophet

Moses, the Lord wished to prepare a new generation to enter the promised land. Therefore, in these chapters Moses calls Israel—and us—to faith and obedience. Israel's obedience was critically important, because this nation was to be a magnet drawing all the nations of the world to trust and follow the living God who would some day send his Savior into the world (Deut 18:15).

Options and Consequences

Deuteronomy 28 reveals how the Lord treats his people with compassion, just as a parent warns his/her own children. Before we dig into that chapter, however, let us consider an example of how a parent ought to properly guide and discipline a child.

Coffee breaks seem to stretch out longer on Friday afternoons, especially when the conversation turns serious. That's what happened when Kristen opened up to Dee about a domestic problem that was bothering her.

"I dread the thought of being trapped at home with my son, Jason, all weekend," muttered Kristen.

"What do you mean, 'trapped'?" Dee asked.

"I grounded him yesterday because he rode his bike home from the bowling alley after dark. It just isn't safe for a 12-year-old to be out alone at night, not to mention riding a bicycle in the dark. That's why I had to teach him a lesson."

"Has he done this before?"

"No, not in the dark. He always rides home at 6 p.m. when his league finishes. But, you know, last Sunday we switched off Daylight Savings Time; so when he came out of the alley it was pitch dark. You would think he would have had the sense to call me up so I could come and get him. But no! He just biked home as though he didn't have a care in the world."

"Maybe he didn't have a care in the world," offered Dee.

"Huh?"

"What I mean, Kristen, is that he probably didn't think anything of it."

"He should have known of the danger."

"Did you warn him that it would be dark this week?"

"No, it hadn't occurred to me," Kristen admitted.

"And have you spoken to him about the dangers of coming home from the bowling alley at night?"

"No, because he's always come home before dusk. Oh, Dee, do you think I made a mistake by being so hard on him?"

"Kristen, I don't want to get on your case, because I know you're a good mother. But perhaps Jason did not obey because you failed to warn him about possible dangers which had never occurred to him."

"I think you're right," Kristen conceded. "I guess in this case I'm as much at fault as he is. I not only didn't warn him, but I didn't tell him what the consequences would be if he disobeyed. To a kid, being grounded is a disaster; and he didn't even see it coming. I suppose I also could have encouraged him to do the right thing by talking about the positive consequences of making a wise choice."

"That sounds like a good idea."

"Even though I'll have to eat some crow tonight, I'm sure looking forward to this weekend more favorably than I was before we had this chat. Thanks a lot, Dee."

"That's what friends are for."

Blessings and Curses

Wise parents provide their children with thorough instructions before a difficult situation arises. They reveal both the benefits of good conduct and the dire consequences of disobedience. In Deuteronomy 28, God, who is the wisest Father, informed the children of Israel of these very things. It is an imposing chapter, 68 verses long. The Lord began by revealing what would be the blessed consequences of faithful obedience. We invite you to turn to Deut 28:1–14 in your Bible and bask in the many blessings of obedience which God was prepared to bestow on his Old Testament people.

The Lord promised that if their faith resulted in obedience, absolutely wonderful things would happen! They would be the greatest nation on the face of the earth. Israel was called to be such a nation, blessed by God, yet still living humbly before the Lord and avoiding by the Spirit's power the arrogance that often accompanies success. Through them, his plan of universal salvation would be put into effect when Messiah came. Today the church, a non-geographical nation with citizens all over the earth, is called to live before the world as the holy people of God because Messiah has come. If the church consistently displayed a lifestyle of holiness and love, what a world of difference it would make in the proclamation of God's name!

The first part of Deuteronomy 28 painted a picture of blessing for the obedient. However, the rest of the chapter is like a photographic negative. In starkly parallel terms, the Lord lists the curses of disobedience. Turn to Deut 28:15–68. As you read, please do not conclude, "How cruel God is for holding these disasters over the heads of the children of Israel." Rather say, "Praise the Lord that in his kindness he warns his foolish children ahead of time, so that they can avoid all these woes." These are the wise and kindly warnings of a loving Father who never wants to see his children rebel and fall to this level of depravity.

God could not have been more clear or more compassionate in his treatment of Israel. Like a caring parent he revealed his great concern about obedience. He didn't just preach the Gospel and let everything else take care of itself. Instead, he specifically named the blessings of obedience and warned his children about the consequences of disobedience.

Unfortunately, the people repeatedly experienced these curses during the days of Israel's judges and kings, culminating in the exiles forced upon them by Assyria and Babylon. Daniel referred to these very warnings of the Lord found in Deuteronomy 28: "Therefore, the curses and sworn judgments written in the Law of Moses ... have been poured out on us, because we have sinned against You" (Dan 9:11). Similarly, 2 Kings, Jeremiah, and other prophets constantly allude to Deuteronomy 28.

After God had gone to such pains to tell them of the blessings of obedience and the curses of disobedience, how could the Jews be so foolish as to fall away from him, nonetheless, and disobey? A better question is, Will we be so foolish ourselves? Why do you think God put these chapters in the Bible? He knew that not only would the Jews be apt to go astray, but so would his New Testament people. There are a thousand ways that we disobey our Savior God. We like to think that our sins are of minor consequence, yet they can bring curses as mournful as those listed in Deuteronomy 28. Paying lip service to God is not enough. He is looking for the real thing.

What about us who have already failed God? Is there any hope? Yes, in Deut 30:1–10 the Lord outlines the path of restoration. If we admit our guilt and repent, turning from the sin that stands in opposition to him, he will gladly forgive and restore us. "The Lord your God will circumcise your hearts and the hearts of your descendants, so that you may love him with all your heart and with all your soul, and live" (Deut 30:6). How merciful the Lord is! He who requires us to return to him supplies us with the spiritual strength which enables us to return.

Life or Death

Children's author Richard Scarry wrote a story about building a highway between Busy Town and Workville. The mayors of the two cities come into the construction office to propose their building project to the road engineer. On the wall of the road engineer's office hangs a diagram of the two kinds of roads his crews could construct. One is smooth, flat, and straight. The second is bumpy, hilly, and curvy.

Reading this page with children is a delight, because they grasp the pure silliness of the choice. Only a fool would choose the crooked, dangerous highway.

In essence, the Lord does the same in the closing chapters of Deuteronomy. His portrayal of blessings is like the picture of the straight highway. His litany of curses resembles the picture of the unsafe road. The choice is so clear that Moses sums up the whole matter in these words:

> See, I have set before you today life and prosperity, death and destruction . . . I have set before you life and death, blessings and curses. Now choose life, so that you and your children may live and that you may love the Lord your God, listen to his voice, and hold fast to him. For the Lord is your life (Deut 30:15, 19–20).

The alternatives are crucial. Everyone, even a non-Christian, covets life, prosperity, and happiness. Everyone wants to escape death and destruction. In essence, the Lord is saying, "I have shown you the way to obtain all the happiness you can desire and to avoid all misery. I have attracted you with the pleasantries of obedience, and I have compelled you by the fearful results of disobedience. Choose life, and it will be yours, for I am your life. However, if you don't want me as your life, then of your own accord you have chosen death and destruction to your own hurt."

We are not unlike the Jews in Deuteronomy. The Lord called them to conquer the promised land. Today He calls us to enter into battle with his enemies in our efforts to lead people to life in Christ, adding blood-bought men, women, and children to his kingdom. Often, however, we hold back, fearful whether the Lord can really provide for this campaign of courageous obedience for a dying world. In light of this situation, the material in Deuteronomy 27–30 is no small matter to us. What could our Father say to be more persuasive, more rational, more prudent, more affectionate? Obedience *flowing from faith* is a matter of life or death.

Courage: Faith to Obey

When the clatter of lunch dishes in the church kitchen had subsided, the 26 teenagers sat down for Bible study and prayer. This spiritual meal would prepare them for the major task of the day: to canvass a new subdivision and share their faith where the opportunity might appear. Needless to say, many of the young people were jittery about the assignment.

Randy, their head counselor, calmly helped them to verbalize their apprehensions. Eventually, a host of witnessing fears were recorded on an overhead transparency: doors slammed in your face; people yelling at you; the door being answered by someone you know from school; being confronted with a tough question; accusations of being a Jehovah's Witness; doubting that the Holy Spirit could ever convert someone through your paltry witness; drawing a blank and not knowing what to say next; being bitten by a dog; and so on.

Then Randy asked a key question, "These things that we fear might happen—do they ever actually occur?"

After a moment of reflection, Michelle, a senior at Montgomery High, replied, "You know, I've participated in five canvasses, and no one has ever yelled at me or slammed the door. Some people aren't particularly interested in talking, but they are not unkind as long as you're polite to them."

Brent, a fourth-string player on the Central High football team, added, "I used to be so terrified that someone would see me that I wished I could wear a mask so no one would know who I was." This comment aroused a wave of laughter before Brent continued, "Then last year disaster struck. I knocked at a door and who answered? None other than Suzanne Queen-of-the-Clique Walters. I about died! What a relief when her mom came to the door and Suzanne left. Although I was really 'shook,' I shared the Gospel with Mrs. Walters, and she seemed to be somewhat interested—which was a surprise to me. Even so, I thought I had committed social suicide, because Suzanne was sure to think that I was the biggest dork on earth."

"Hey, you've convinced me never to go knock on doors," Chris interrupted.

"But that's not all I wanted to say, man," Brent replied. "A week later I was studying in a quiet corner of the library, and guess who sits down right across from me. It's Suzanne. She whispers to me, 'Brent, I was so surprised to see you at my house the other day. I sure was glad that my mom talked with you, because I wouldn't have known what to say. But I want you to know that I stayed close enough to hear the whole conversation. And . . . '

"Believe it or not, her eyes became a little teary. Then she went on, 'As you talked about Jesus and how he loves and forgives you, the certainty in your voice was so real and sincere. I knew you had something I wished I could have. Mom and I talked about your visit later on, and we decided to start going to our church again. We've been back two Sundays now, and the Bible is making more sense to me now than it ever did before. Thanks, Brent, for having the courage to come talk to my mom and me.' "

As Brent finished his story, the decibel level was zero, and that is a miracle at a youth event.

Finally, Michelle verbalized what they were all thinking, "If God can work like that, what are we afraid of?"

"You're right," Chris confirmed. Stepping up to the overhead projector, he erased the whole list of intimidating fears. "Since these problems hardly ever materialize, why should we be cowards about sharing the greatest news on earth?"

With renewed boldness and courage the 26 young Christians paired off and spread out into the new subdivision to claim the victories which the Lord had prepared for them that day (Eph 2:10).

Be Strong and Courageous

Like Brent, the Old Testament leader Joshua also learned what courage is. Shortly after Moses addressed the people in Deuteronomy 27–30, the Lord gave Joshua a more dangerous assignment than we have received. He would be going to war where he could lose his life; and yet he responded with courageous obedience. Why? Because, along with the command, the Lord spoke this promise to him:

> Be strong and courageous, because you will lead these people to inherit the land I swore to their forefathers to give them. Be strong and very courageous. Be careful to obey all the law my servant Moses gave you . . . . Meditate on it day and night, so that you may be careful to do everything written in it. Then you will be prosperous and successful. Have I not commanded you? Be strong and courageous. Do not be terrified; do not be discouraged, for the Lord your God will be with you wherever you go (Josh 1:6–9).

Wouldn't it be great to have a pep talk like this every time you faced a challenge? The Lord had this story recorded so that you could refer back to it whenever you feel short on courage.

What is courage? Memoirs of battle illustrate how soldiers wrestle with their fears to attain courage. In the Pulitzer prize-winning book *Profiles in Courage,* President John F. Kennedy defines the term in a political sense. However, if you want to know what God means when he says "Be strong and courageous," you have to go to the Bible.

A thorough biblical study of the words *courage* and *courageous* reveals that courage is faith to trust God and to obey His commands. Usually we speak of faith strictly in regard to believing God's promises, particularly his promises of forgiveness and salvation. Nevertheless, it is also proper to speak of having faith in the Lord's commands, as the psalmist says, "I have put my hope in your laws . . . . I believe in your commandments" (Ps 119:43, 66). Courageous faith is a proper response to God's decrees, because every command contains a latent promise. The Word of God speaks of the promise aspect of commandments:

> Be careful to obey all these regulations I am giving you, so that

34

it may always go well with you and your children after you, because you will be doing what is good and right in the eyes of the Lord your God (Deut 12:28).

"Honor your father and your mother"—which is the first commandment with a promise—"that it may go well with you and that you may enjoy long life on the earth" (Eph 6:2–3).

Every command carries a latent promise, because through it God is telling us, "This way will be good and right for you. It is the safe way to go. The results will be a joy for you." Thinking back to the fall into sin, we see that this was the very issue at stake there in the Garden of Eden: Could the will of God be trusted to lead us into a life of joy and pleasure? On that occasion, Adam and Eve answered in the negative, but God's redeemed children can daily declare to the world that the Lord's commands can be trusted. We do so by means of our courageous obedience to his word.

Fearing No One But God

A dramatic example of courageous obedience is found in C. S. Lewis's fantasy, *The Silver Chair.* The heroes are two children named Eustace Scrubb and Jill Pole, and a web-footed character named Puddleglum the Marshwiggle. Throughout most of the novel Puddleglum is a devout pessimist, putting the worst construction on every situation. Then, at the climax of the story, Puddleglum displays the kind of courage of which Joshua would have been proud. Here is the situation:

The great lion Aslan, who represents Christ in this semi-allegorical tale, gives Jill Pole four commands. In the succeeding chapters she, along with Eustace and Puddleglum, fails to obey Aslan's first three orders. The fourth command sounds simple enough. When someone asks them to do something in the name of Aslan, they are to do whatever that person requests. However, when a dangerous, crazed knight urges them in the name of Aslan to set him free from his bonds, it appears that if they obey, the knight will surely slaughter them. Here is their conversation at that climactic point:

"Once and for all," said the prisoner, "I adjure you to set me free ... by the great Lion, by Aslan himself, I charge you ...."

"Oh!" cried the three travellers as though they had been hurt. "It's the Sign," said Puddleglum. "It was the *words* of the Sign," said Scrubb more cautiously . . . .

"Oh, if only we knew!" said Jill.

"I think we do know," said Puddleglum.

"Do you mean you think everything will come right if we do untie him?" said Scrubb.

"I don't know about that," said Puddleglum. "You see, Aslan didn't tell Pole what would happen. He only told her what to do" (Lewis 1953, 145–46).

We have seen that God's commands contain the latent promise "that it may go well with you." Often, however, as in the case above, obedience appears to be risky business. The Lord doesn't tell us precisely how things will turn out. He only tells us what to do. At such times we, like Puddleglum, must respect the trustworthiness of the one who has given the command.

Thus in the Bible, courage means respecting or fearing no one but God. "This is the one I esteem: he who is humble and contrite in spirit, and trembles at my word" (Is 66:2). When faced with a choice between doing good or doing wrong, it is so easy to quake fretfully before the imagined problems that *might* assail us if we obey God. In the case of witnessing, we can all list a horde of fears, as the 26 youth did before they went canvassing. Yet the only thing that we need fear is God himself. Only his word should cause us to tremble. Martin Luther understood the centrality of this fact when in his Small Catechism he began his explanation of each of the Ten Commandments, "We should fear and love God . . . ."

To obey God requires courage, that is, faith in the latent promises included in every command of the Lord. Such courage is possible only when we know God as a friend and Father, whom we have come to know through trusting in our Savior, Jesus Christ. Then God's holy commands *encourage* us to overcome all kinds of fears that *discourage* us from living according to the Lord's will.

The Obedience–Mission Connection

Old First Church stands on a prominent corner in New York City. Once upon a time it was the very geographic and spiritual heart of a northern European neighborhood. Then, as is the pattern in American cities, the neighborhood changed—first to southern European, then to black, and now it is in transition again. With the previous waves of new people, the Christians of Old First were reluctant to accept change, hesitant to reach out with the Gospel, and unwilling to adapt to new cultures. As a result the membership of Old First has dwindled from 2,000 at its prime to 117 today, with an average age of 66. The members live in 13 different zip codes, since only ten percent still reside within a two-mile radius of the church.

Having failed in the past to adapt to new mission fields in its back yard, today Old First faces its greatest challenge ever. Moving into the old residences and tenements are a people of which the folks at Old First never dreamed. In the morning, olivewood-skinned men board the buses headed for factories and shops. Women hooded in black walk under the shadow of Old First on their way to the market. On the roof of that market, a billboard proclaims, "Read God's final revelation—the Qur'an."

After all these years of virtually ignoring the Muslim world, we now find that God in his wisdom is bringing Muslims into our very neighborhoods. No longer can we claim that we did not realize that men, women, and children are dying without the grace which Christ alone can provide. How will churches like Old First, in both city and suburb, respond—with courage or with fear?

Prophecies to the Nations

The Old Testament intimately links obedience and outreach to the nations. As we heard in Deuteronomy, the people of Israel were to attract the nations to Jehovah by means of their godly living. The Old Testament is, in part, the history of Israel; but this does not mean that God's concern was only with that one nation. The Lord repeatedly expressed interest in other nations and peoples. Again and again he demonstrated his concern for all people. The prophets were continually given messages directed at specific nations. For instance, Isaiah 13–23 contains messages for Babylon, Philistia, Moab, Damascus, Ethiopia, Egypt, Dumah, Arabia, and Tyre. Likewise, Ezekiel 25–32 speaks God's word concerning Ammon, Moab, Edom, Philistia, Tyre, and Egypt. The book of Daniel reveals God's

37

concern for all the peoples ruled by the Babylonian Empire and later by the empire of the Medes and Persians. These passages are only the beginning of the list of Old Testament texts that reveal God's love for the nations. In particular, these sections demonstrate that the Lord is disturbed by the disobedience of the nations. Repeatedly he calls them on the carpet for their evil deeds, which spring from their fundamental disobedience of his rule over them.

Certainly, the story of the prophet Jonah impresses us with God's love for a disobedient land. When Jonah made a beeline west to avoid going to Nineveh in the east, the Lord supplied a great fish to rescue his prophet and transport him back in the right direction. While Jonah would just as soon have seen Nineveh fried to a crisp by divine judgment, the Divine One longed for them to repent from their disobedient ways and know his salvation. In spite of the infamous wickedness and idolatry of Nineveh, the long-suffering Jehovah sent that great and evil city a prophet to call them to repentance. Most astoundingly of all, when the Ninevites finally repented, the Lord forgave them! Mercy is available for all the nations of the earth, even in the Old Testament.

Concern for Foreigners

God's love for the earth's peoples in general was to be exhibited in particular by Israel's treatment of individual foreigners. Repeated Old Testament commands to the Jews bring home this fact:

> Do not mistreat an alien or oppress him, for you were aliens in Egypt (Ex 22:21).

> The alien living with you must be treated as one of your native-born. Love him as yourself, for you were aliens in Egypt. I am the Lord your God (Lev 19:34).

> Assemble the people—men, women and children, and the aliens living in your towns—so they can listen and learn to fear the Lord your God and follow carefully all the words of this law (Deut 31:12).

To treat foreign residents in such a loving manner would be radical behavior in that day or in any day. The stranger in a strange land often has limited rights and privileges and becomes the target of taunts, mistreatment, and oppression. This was not to be the case in Israel. "Love him as yourself" (Lev 19:34) reminds us of Jesus' command to love our neighbor as ourself. Evidently, the foreigner among us is to be viewed as a neighbor, not as a nuisance or a non-entity. Furthermore, Deut 31:12 reveals that sojourners are not to be left out of the sphere of our evangelistic outreach. Just as aliens in Israel were to be taught the words of God's Old Testament law, so today we are to share God's Law and Gospel with the foreigners among us, so that they too may hear, believe, and be saved.

The opportunities for such ministry lie all around us. We merely need to take advantage of them. The Lord is internationalizing our communities, bringing us new neighbors from the ends of the earth. Over 300,000 international students live in the U.S. Many of them do not know Christ and would gladly accept an invitation to spend a Sunday morning and afternoon with us. If you do not have these opportunities nearby, your church, wherever it is, can take on the joyful responsibility of resettling refugees.

Clearly, the Lord's call to obedience is closely linked with his concern that all nations hear his word and be saved. We have seen evidence of this in the prophecies directed to various nations; in the story of Jonah, missionary to Nineveh; and in God's commands concerning aliens living among his people. God's heartfelt interest in the many peoples of the earth did not commence when Jesus spoke the Great Commission (Mt 28:18–20). It has been his passion from the beginning. In a world fraught with oppression and bigotry, he called the Jews and he calls us today to love the nations. Generalized, obligatory goodwill will not do. The Lord seeks from us obedience that will result in our touching other people with his love. The book of Ruth depicts what occurred when a Jew named Boaz put these laws into practice through his kind treatment of the Moabitess Ruth. Such kindness was to demonstrate to all the world that God was surely among these people who accorded friendship, mercy, and justice to outsiders.

Like a blacksmith fashioning a mighty chain at his anvil, the Lord has forged together the call to obedience and his love for the nations as key links in his plan, never to be separated.

Messianic Mission Prophecies

The messianic prophecies of the Old Testament also illustrate the obedience-mission connection. In each of these prophecies God

39

reveals some detail of the Savior's life long before it occurred. We ought not fail to recognize, as well, that from Genesis to Malachi some of the prophecies of the coming Savior also make mention of obedience and the nations (Lk 24:44–47). Let's look at a few.

Dan 7:27 states, "Then the sovereignty, power, and greatness of the kingdoms under the heavens will be handed over to the saints, the people of the Most High. His kingdom will be an everlasting kingdom, and all rulers will worship and obey him." The global emphasis of this verse is obvious. The rulers who worship and obey the Most High are "saints," people who are made holy by the blood of the Lamb and by the Spirit's power live in a holy manner, as much as is possible this side of heaven.

Zeph 3:9–10 is an often overlooked prophecy concerning what will occur when Messiah has come: "Then I will purify the lips of the peoples, that all of them may call on the name of the Lord and serve him shoulder to shoulder. From beyond the rivers of Cush my worshipers, my scattered people, will bring me offerings." Peoples with purified lips (provided by God's Son, Heb 1:3) will come from beyond the rivers of Cush. Cush is Ethiopia. This is a prophecy about the Gospel taking hold in the southern half of Africa. Today the growing number of believers in that region can look to this text (plus Ps 68:31; 87:4; and Isaiah 18) as evidence of the Lord's ongoing concern for them and their people. The obedience-mission connection is portrayed most graphically in the phrase, "that all of them may call on the name of the Lord and serve him shoulder to shoulder" (Zeph 3:9). Calling on his name refers to saving faith. Serving him equals obedience. No matter where in the world we come from, we can serve our Savior God shoulder to shoulder as fellow citizens of Christ's kingdom, setting aside cultural differences and reaching out to a dying world.

Mal 1:11 foretells, " 'My name will be great among the nations, from the rising to the setting of the sun. In every place incense and pure offerings will be brought to my name, because my name will be great among the nations,' says the Lord Almighty." The global mission emphasis of this verse is self-evident. The obedience theme appears in the concept of incense and pure offerings being brought to his name. We are reminded of the several places in Scripture where believers offer a wide range of sacrifices in response to the one perfect sacrifice offered by the Lamb of God who takes away the sin of the world (Ps 4:5; 27:6; 50:14,15; 51:17; 116:17; Rom 6:12–14; 12:1–2; Phil 4:18; Heb 11:4; 13:15, 16; 1 Pet 2:5; and Rev 5:8).

The Gospel According to Jacob

The three messianic prophecies we have looked at thus far are all from the latter part of the Old Testament. The very first occurrence of the word *obedience* in the New International Version appears way back in Gen 49:10: "The scepter will not depart from Judah, nor the ruler's staff from between his feet, until he comes to whom it belongs (or "until Shiloh comes") and the obedience of the nations is his." This verse could be called "The Gospel According to Jacob," for in it old Jacob prophesies that from the descendants of his son Judah the Savior will arise. The Coming One will rule. He will be called Shiloh, the Man of Peace. What a fitting title for Jesus, about whom the angels declared, "On earth peace to men on whom his favor rests" (Lk 2:14)!

We dare not overlook the last phrase in the prophecy, "and the obedience of the nations is his." Ever since the fall of the human race into sin, and especially since the tower of Babel fiasco, the nations have been drifting further and further from their Creator. How the Lord longs to see the peoples of the world give him homage, accept his rule over them, and gladly do his will, so that their days may be free of strife and overflowing with blessing! In the "Gospel According to Jacob," the Lord reveals his plan to reverse people's drifting from him, by means of the Man of Peace, whose ministry on earth will transform the nations to a state of joyous obedience. Clearly, Gen 49:10 links obedience and world mission.

Shiloh has come. He rules now at the right hand of God the Father. For us, his subjects, there remains the joyous mission of bringing his light to the many peoples of the earth until, as Jacob foretold, the obedience of all the nations is his.

Psalm 119: To Hunger and Thirst after Righteousness

Every Thursday afternoon you can find Lydia, Claire, and Harriet crocheting blankets for their church's world relief organization. As Social Security-pensioned widows, this is a good, nonmonetary way for them to contribute to the work of their Lord. One day, as they stopped to rest their tired fingers and have a cup of tea, the conversation turned to their favorite psalms.

After reciting many treasured verses, Lydia ventured to include a criticism. "For the life of me, there is one psalm I really can't understand, Psalm 119. Remember, that's the long psalm."

"I seem to recall some excellent verses in it, Lydia, dear," chimed in Claire. "For instance, verse 11: 'I have hidden your word in my heart that I might not sin against you.' "

Harriet added, "And how about verse 105? 'Your word is a lamp to my feet and a light for my path.' Isn't that just beautiful?"

"It surely is a classic," Lydia agreed as she set her teacup in its saucer. "Most Christians know only those verses, and I have no squabble with them. But in the rest of the psalm the writer strikes me as an arrogant fellow who thinks he can obey God's laws perfectly." Pulling her Bible out of her crochet bag, she leafed through the pages to Psalm 119 and then continued, "For instance, verse 44 says, 'I will always obey your law, for ever and ever.' "

"Hmmm," mused Harriet. "Now that you mention it, Lydia, I do remember feeling a little uneasy sometimes when I've read Psalm 119. We are saved by grace, not works; so why does the psalmist make such a big deal about obedience?"

"It sounds like we have a mystery on our hands, ladies," Claire observed. "What do you say we set aside our craft work for a while and take a good long look at Psalm 119 together?"

"Yes, let's!" they agreed.

A Most Amazing Chapter

Anyway you look at it, Psalm 119 is unique. Here are some characteristics that qualify it for "Ripley's Believe it or Not." First, it is the Bible's longest chapter, weighing in at 176 verses. In fact, it is longer than 14 entire books in the Bible!

Second, Psalm 119 is an acrostic poem, that is, an alphabetic poem, because each succeeding set of eight verses begins with the next letter of the Hebrew alphabet. That explains the strange-sounding titles before each section, like "Aleph, Beth, and Gimel." Those are the letters Jewish children recite as they begin to learn Hebrew.

Third, every verse (except 90, 121, 122, and 132) mentions the

Word of God under synonyms like law, testimony, judgments, statutes, commandments, precepts, word, ordinances, and ways. Thus the theme of the psalm is recognized to be the merits of the Word of the Lord.

In addition, there is a fourth significant characteristic of which most people are unaware. Psalm 119 uses the words *obey* and *obedience* more than any other chapter of the Bible. Of the 257 times the New International Version of the Bible uses these two words, 20 of them are in Psalm 119. This is an amazing concentration: one out of every 13 occurrences is located in this chapter. Even when *obey* is not used, the concept of obedience is implied in almost every verse.

Obviously, this is one of the key sections about obedience in the whole Bible. We cannot gain a complete view of obedience without taking a good look at Psalm 119.

Understanding Mr. 119

To avoid overusing the word *psalmist,* let us call the author of this psalm "Mr. 119." Our friend Lydia was troubled by Mr. 119 because, in her opinion, he seemed to be an arrogant man who failed to recognize that we are saved by faith, not by our works. Perhaps Lydia is not the only believer who has felt that way. Consider these words, for example: "I have kept my feet from every evil path so that I might obey your word. I have not departed from your laws, for you yourself have taught me" (Ps 119:101–2).

However, as Lydia and her cronies dug into the psalm, they could have seen that Mr. 119 really does understand grace. "My soul faints with longing for your salvation, but I have put my hope in your word" (v. 81). Clearly, he recognizes that God's salvation is ours only by faith. Furthermore, the repeated use of the phrase "preserve my life" (vv. 154, 156, 159) shows that Mr. 119 believes that salvation comes only by God's merciful power to save. The final verse closes the entire psalm with a note of humble repentance: "I have strayed like a lost sheep. Seek your servant, for I have not forgotten your commands" (v. 176). Surely, the writer recognizes that he is lost, just like the sheep in Jesus' parables. Stray sheep do not find their way home by themselves. They remain lost until the Good Shepherd rescues them.

But, then, we wonder, how does he dare say, "I will always obey your law, for ever and ever" (v. 44)? Here is the answer: These are the words of a person who so fears, loves, and trusts God that he longs to obey him with perfect faithfulness. This is the way we who know the forgiveness of Christ ought to talk. This should be our attitude of submission to the God who has saved us. As we dig deeper into the psalm, ask yourself honestly, "Is this how I think about God's will? Or are some attitude adjustments in order?"

Mr. 119 sees the commandments as liberating, not restricting or burdensome. "I run in the path of your commands, for you have set my heart free" (v. 32). Only those who are in shape can run. The flabby soon become winded and either quit the race or drag along. Similarly, weak Christians do not have the heart for obedience because they are spiritually out of shape. Christ has set our hearts free by his salvation so we can regularly be blessed with runner's high as we run in the path of his commandments.

To know what pleases God and to do it is the psalmist's greatest thrill. At least 12 times he states his delight in God's laws. Perhaps his most poetic expression of this thought is v. 54: "Your decrees are the theme of my song wherever I lodge." God's commandments make him want to sing. They bring him delight no matter where he is. Think about it. Is this how you feel when you consider the Lord's wise commands?

Mr. 119 does not advocate blind obedience. His willingness to comply springs from his personal knowledge of the wise and loving Lord who gives the commandments.

> You are good, and what you do is good; teach me your decrees. Your hands made me and formed me; give me understanding to learn your commands. To all perfection I see a limit; but your commands are boundless. I hate double-minded men, but I love your law. Long ago I learned from your statutes that you established them to last forever (Ps 119:68, 73, 96, 113, 152).

He bases his confidence on the Giver of the laws. The Lord is good. He is the perfect Creator. The Lord is not double-minded; he and his will endure forever. Therefore, he can be trusted, both when he promises forgiveness and salvation and also when he promises blessing through his commandments.

Mr. 119 is resolute in his determination to follow God's will. It is his heart's desire. "I have hidden your word in my heart that I might not sin against you" (v. 11). This is the reason for memorizing Scripture—not to get a grade in school, but for help and strength to avoid sinning against the God who loves me.

While the world seeks after the inferior values of wealth and trivial vanities, Mr. 119 declares, "Turn my heart toward your statutes and not toward selfish gain. Turn my eyes away from worthless things; renew my life according to your word" (vv. 36–37). He is not trying to obey God by using his own puny power, or he would not plead, "Turn my heart . . . turn my eyes." He trusts in the Lord to bring about the obedience he longs for.

The more you look at this chapter, the more you respect the intensity and resolve of its author. "Your promises have been thoroughly tested, and your servant loves them" (v. 140). How can we test God's laws? Only by doing them can we ever discover if their latent blessings will become a reality. When we test God's laws, we grow to love them, too (Rom 12:1–2).

Mr. 119 is not ashamed to get emotional about obedience. "Streams of tears flow from my eyes, for your law is not obeyed" (v. 136). His own sins cause him to weep before the Lord. The sins of other believers fill him with sorrow. And the rebellion of the world brings tears to his eyes. No matter who is the source of the disobedience, he knows that this is not as the Creator originally intended it to be, nor is it what the Lord deserves after all his kindnesses to us.

Psalm 119 People

Well, what do you make of the author of Psalm 119? Unfortunately, too many Christians see him as odd, fanatical, or perhaps even crazy. Could it perhaps be that we are the ones who are abnormal? Listen to this fable.

Once there was a village where everyone lived together in peace and merriment. Resenting their happiness, an evil sorcerer poisoned the town well with a potion that drove to insanity all who drank from it. In a matter of days, everyone but the king of that village had drunk of the bewitched water. Now the ruler of a host of crazy people, the king was roundly berated by the populace, for they, being insane, took him for a madman. Although the king held out for days, finally he too went to the well and drank, overcome by the harassment of his crazed subjects.

Similarly, lukewarm Christians imagine that the devout and dedicated believers among them are the loony ones. Seeing this tendency, Mr. 119 warns us in 176 different ways, "Don't drink from the polluted well of sin! Instead drink from the pure spring of God's truth, and by his power we will live out his truth before the lost world."

What do you make of Mr. 119? John Wesley was once asked how he attracted large crowds to hear his preaching. He answered, "All you have to do is set yourself on fire, and people will come to watch you burn." In Ps. 119 we are privileged to read the heartfelt expressions of a man who is fired up for the Lord. No one has described Mr. 119 better than Jesus when he said, "Blessed are those who hunger and thirst for righteousness, for they will be filled" (Mt 5:6). Don't you agree? Having analyzed Mr. 119 more closely, we can see that he is not arrogant and self-righteous, as our crocheter, Lydia, suspected. He is simply a forgiven believer, and because he is a forgiven sinner he has a burning hunger and thirst for righteousness in his daily life.

Imagine what your church and denomination would be like if it were filled with Psalm 119 people. Would it be any different? You bet it would, because Jesus promised that those who hunger and thirst for righteousness will be filled and blessed. How the church would be revived if we humbled ourselves before the Lord's holy commands and became Psalm 119 Christians!

"Open my eyes that I may see wonderful things in your law" (v. 18). We have surely seen wonderful things concerning the Old Testament's treatment of obedience. As our loving Father, the Lord both encourages us with blessings and warns us with the negative consequences of disobedience. He calls us, as he did Joshua, to be strong and courageous, to trust boldly that his ways will surely lead us to the blessings he has promised. We have seen the link between obedience and God's concern for the nations. He desires all people to be saved. He wants the light of our faith and works to shine before all people. Thus, the Old Testament is filled with constant messages from God to revive the people to a life of faith and obedience.

Among these passages Psalm 119 stands as one of the most

amazingly powerful. Were we to respond wholeheartedly to these Scriptures, both we as individuals and our churches would be revived for service to the world.

How does one begin a revival? The best advice we have ever heard is this: (1) Go into a room by yourself to pray for revival; (2) With a piece of chalk draw a circle on the floor; (3) Step into the circle; and (4) Plead with the Lord to begin the revival—inside that circle. You could do it with your Bible open to Psalm 119, praying it before the Lord.

Digging Deeper

1. Read Deut 28:1–14. Picture a community or nation like the one described in these verses. Which blessings of obedience are particularly pleasing to you? Express these in modern terms.
2. Now read Deut 28:15–68. Picture the devastation described here. Which curses of disobedience are particularly tragic to you? Express these in modern terms.
3. If you are a parent, recall the times when you have had to warn kids of dangers: playing in the street, drug abuse, premarital sex, etc. How was your experience similar to that of the Lord in Deuteronomy 28? What motivated you? What motivated the Lord? Were you as detailed and clear as the Lord was?
4. Read Deut 30:15–20. When have you ever faced a moral choice that meant life and death? What did you decide? On what did you base your decision?
5. While on vacation a young Christian couple spent a few days in the home of non-Christian friends. The first evening the friends offered them the chance to go to a movie and heighten the experience by smoking marijuana. The Christians politely refused the offer, even though they knew they appeared to be killjoys. Later in their visit, the Holy Spirit opened a door for the believers to have a lengthy conversation with their friends regarding the need to trust Christ as Savior and Lord. What kind of witness would these Christians have given if they had earlier accepted the marijuana and later tried to speak the Gospel? How does this true story parallel Israel's role before the nations of the world?

6. Debate the validity of this statement from the chapter: "Courage is faith to trust God and obey his commands.

7. Go through the Ten Commandments (Ex 20:1–17), asking yourself: What are the latent promises, benefits, and liberties God offers us in each one?

8. Recall an example of courage to obey, an example either from your life or from your church.

9. When you or your church are reluctant to obey God, what words do you use to describe (and rationalize) your decision? Do you say your decision is "practical," "prudent," or "realistic"? How would your opinion of your decision change if you identified it as "cowardly"?

10. What role does courage play in personal witnessing? Where does courage come from? See 2 Tim 1:7–8.

11. When you are facing a major moral decision, would you feel secure with the attitude expressed by the character Puddleglum: "God didn't tell me what would happen. He only told me what to do"?

12. What do you think of this statement: "Don't doubt in the dark what God told you in the light"?

13. To what degree are you surprised at the emphasis on obedience and on the nations in the Old Testament? Are you surprised at the presence of these themes in the messianic prophecies? (You may wish to refresh your memory by referring to the chapter.)

14. Consider the laws concerning the treatment of aliens in Ex 22:21; Lev 19:34; and Deut 31:12. What modern applications of these commands are near at hand for you and your church to put into practice? Be specific. Name the individuals whom you can touch with God's love.

15. In your personal devotions set aside several days to study Psalm 119. As you read, keep in mind Jesus' words, "Blessed are those who hunger and thirst for righteousness, for they will be filled" (Mt 5:6).

16. What do you make of Mr. 119? What would occur if your church were full of Psalm 119 people? These changes will have to begin with one person. Could it be you?

3

Jesus and Obedience

God cares about obedience.
Jesus Christ is the Son of God.
Jesus cares about obedience.

The logic is clear; and having seen God's emphasis on obedience in the Old Testament, we shouldn't have any trouble following that logic. Yet many Christians may still have a problem with the statement "Jesus cares about obedience." It's not that they don't believe it, but somehow it just doesn't sound quite right.

A heavy emphasis on obedience in the Old Testament is to be expected. After all, wasn't it there that God gave the Law? You would expect God to talk a lot about obedience in the Old Testament.

But Jesus is our Savior. What he really cares about is our salvation. Isn't that what he was willing to die for? Isn't that what the Gospel is all about? And isn't the Gospel revealed in the New Testament? Surely we would not expect Jesus or the apostles to put the same emphasis on obedience as God did in the Old Testament. Unfortunately, too many Christians are under the false impression that the Old Testament is primarily Law, while the New Testament is almost exclusively Gospel. The truth is, however, that the Holy Spirit has provided a proper balance of Law and Gospel throughout the Scriptures.

Yes, Jesus is our Savior; and through him we have the free gift of eternal life. However, Jesus is not only interested in passing out free tickets to heaven. He also has much to say about the lives we should live by faith in him. He is concerned about obedience. We should not be surprised by this. Jesus himself told us, "Do not think that I have come to abolish the Law or the Prophets; I have not come to abolish them but to fulfill them" (Mt 5:17). In what sense did Jesus mean that he came to fulfill the Law? In the context of this passage it is obvious that he wants people to look beneath the surface of the commandments to their underlying principles. He wants people to realize that it's not enough to conform outwardly to the letter of the Law; one's mind must be conformed to its spirit. But that's not all Jesus meant when he said that he came to fulfill the Law.

Jesus also came to fulfill the Law by obeying it. He is concerned that we also obey it precisely because he cares about our salvation. By his active obedience to God's Law, he fulfilled the Law for us and thus was able to offer the perfect sacrifice for our sins. Jesus' obedience is essential for our salvation!

Jesus' Obedience Fulfills the Law

Two evangelism callers named Steve and Tom had been chatting comfortably with the Fergusons for about ten minutes when Steve noticed the framed photo of a sky diver hanging on a wall near the living room fireplace.

"Is that you sky diving, Mike?" Steve wondered out loud.

"No. Actually, it's Sally."

Surprised, Tom and Steve began to talk with Sally in an animated fashion about the thrills of such a sport.

After a few minutes Mike Ferguson spoke up. "I can't bring myself to watch Sally jump. It just seems so dangerous," he admitted. "I know she packs her own chute and everything, but there are so many factors involved in a jump. I'm always afraid that she won't come home some Saturday. Maybe that's why I've been bugging Sally for us to find a church."

"I guess I can understand that," said Tom, "but none of us knows when we might not come home again. There's not one of us who has any guarantees for tomorrow."

"I suppose that's true," replied Mike.

At this point Steve posed a key question. "Mike, suppose you were to die tonight and stand before God. If he asked you, 'Why should I let you into heaven?' What do you think you would say?"

"Boy, that's a tough one!" He thought in silence for a few moments before answering. "I guess the only thing I could say is, 'I did my best.' I've tried to be a decent sort of guy. I treat Sally right. I work hard on my job. I try to be honest. I guess that's all anyone can ask of you, that you do your best, right?"

"Doing your best is certainly important, but what if your best isn't good enough?" continued Steve.

"Why wouldn't it be?" Mike's voice registered surprise.

"Mike, you told me you play piano."

"Well, I play at it. I took lessons as a kid, but I was never really serious about it."

"Suppose you were asked to play with the New York Philharmonic at Carnegie Hall. What would you say?"

"Are you kidding? I'd tell them no. I'm not good enough for that!"

"But what if you did your best? Wouldn't that be good enough?"

"I think I get your point. My best may not be good enough for God either."

"That is my point," replied Steve. "Our best is never good enough for God because God is perfect and we are sinners. Nevertheless, there is someone whose best was good enough. That was Jesus Christ. His best was good enough because he is the perfect Son of God. He obeyed God's Law perfectly as we cannot. And he did it for us."

"What do you mean?" Mike asked. "I can remember hearing as a kid in Sunday school that Jesus died for us, but now you're saying that he obeyed God's Law for us?"

Steve tried to clarify these two ideas. "If Jesus hadn't obeyed God's Law perfectly, then his death wouldn't have done us any good. He couldn't offer the perfect sacrifice for our sins if he hadn't lived the perfect life first. Since he was perfectly obedient, he could take our sins on himself and give us his perfect righteousness as a free gift. We only have to trust in him to receive that gift as our own."

"I'm still not sure what this has to do with me trying to do my best," Mike commented.

Tom attempted to pull it all together for him. "What we're trying to say is this: Since my best isn't good enough, Jesus' best can be mine, if I trust in him."

"Exactly," added Steve. "What do you think of that, Mike?"

All of a sudden a flash of understanding appeared in Mike's eyes and a smile swept across his face. "I'd say that's pretty good news," he replied.

When Jesus said that he came to fulfill the Law, he also meant that, by keeping the Law perfectly on our behalf, he would satisfy all the requirements for righteousness the Law places on us. He obeyed God in every way, even as a child. Jesus' perfect obedience to God's Law began formally at the time of his circumcision, when he was only eight days old. He submitted to the law of Moses, and his innocent blood was shed for the first time. As a youth he submitted to the authority of his parents when they told him to leave the temple and come home with them to Nazareth. Luke tells us, "He was obedient to them" (Lk 2:51).

Jesus was often accused by the Pharisees of failing to obey the Law, but their charges were false. Although he did not submit to their man-made regulations, he was perfectly obedient to God's Law. He even set the standard higher than most people ever imagined it could be, when he went to the heart of the commandments and showed us, for example, that to hate your neighbor is to commit murder in your heart.

Jesus' perfect obedience took him all the way to the cross where, to complete the Father's plan for our salvation, he willingly suffered and died to pay the price for our sins. He told his disciples, "The world must learn that I love the Father and I do *exactly* what the Father has commanded me!" (Jn 14:31; emphasis ours). This was the ultimate in perfect obedience.

Because of Jesus' perfect obedience, we can be saved even though we have not kept God's Law perfectly as he demands. If it were up to us to fulfill the Law, we would surely be lost. There's not one of us who has obeyed the will of God so that we can stand before him without guilt and shame. We are all guilty, but Christ is innocent—and that's enough! A song by Bob Kauflin of the singing group "Glad" illustrates beautifully this truth about Jesus' obedience:

> There's not one who has perfectly obeyed God's law.
> There's not one who has tried to follow God at all.
> There's not one who's half obeyed
> His simplest commands.
>
> There's not one who understands.
> No one was willing to believe.
> No one was worthy to receive.
>
> There's not one who has done the very best they could.
> There's not one who has had a single thought that's good.
> There's not one who's lived on earth that God could not
>   condemn.
> There's not one He would defend.

No one was willing to believe.
No one was worthy to receive.

But God showed His love for us
    while we went our selfish way.
He gave up His Son for us, and He paid the debt
    no man could pay.
And now there is One.

There is One who fulfilled the Father's just demands.
There is One who became the hope for every man.
There is One who rose above every sin this world has known.
There is One who stands alone (Kauflin 1989).

Through faith in him, his innocence becomes our innocence, and his righteousness our righteousness. Evangelism prospect Mike Ferguson finally understood.

Two Sides of Obedience

The cost of obedience and the blessings of obedience are like two sides of a coin. Jesus learned about both as he lived among us on earth. The writer to the Hebrews elaborates on the cost of Jesus' obedience in Heb 5:7–9.

> During the days of Jesus' life on earth, he offered up prayers and petitions with loud cries and tears to the one who could save him from death, and he was heard because of his reverent submission. Although he was a son, he learned obedience from what he suffered and, once made perfect, he became the source of eternal salvation for all who obey him.

Jesus learned that the cost of obedience can be extremely high. As we have already seen, God promises blessings in connection with obedience. Yet we all know that doesn't mean that the road of obedience is always the easiest or most attractive path to follow. Our sinful nature regards obedience as a miserable, painful sacrifice. That makes obedience seem costly even though it is a blessing. We also face opposition from the world and the prince of this world, the devil. They make it as difficult and unpleasant as possible for us to follow the will of God. Jesus experienced this firsthand, and he warned us about it:

If the world hates you, keep in mind that it hated me first. If you belonged to the world, it would love you as its own. As it is, you do not belong to the world, but I have chosen you out of the world. That is why the world hates you. Remember the words I spoke to you: "No servant is greater than his master." If they persecuted me, they will persecute you also (Jn 15:18–20a).

We, like the Master, will experience the cost of obedience whenever we try to follow Jesus.

But Jesus also learned about the blessings of obedience. The Father provided angels to minister to him after his victory over temptation when he obeyed God in the wilderness. When he had set his course for Jerusalem to offer himself for our sins, Jesus heard the Father's affirming commendation, "This is my Son, whom I love; with him I am well pleased. Listen to him" (Mt 17:5). Jesus told us that if we obediently carry out God's will as his servants, we too can expect to hear the Father's gracious words of commendation, "Well done, good and faithful servant.... Come and share your master's happiness" (Mt 25:23).

Jesus understands both the cost and the blessings of obedience. That's why he is in such an excellent position to teach us about obedience. We follow a God who obeys! We carry a false picture of Christ if we imagine that he is unconcerned whether or not his followers learn to do God's will. He wants us to experience both the blessings and the cost of obedience.

Faith Demonstrated by Obedience

Ed and Norm walked out of the banquet hall and into the hotel lobby together.

"Gary had a powerful message this morning, didn't he, Ed?"

"He sure did!" Ed replied. "I haven't been to the Business Men's Prayer Breakfast in months. I'm glad you invited me."

"Well, truthfully, I had another motive in asking you to come this morning. Can we sit down and talk for a few minutes, Ed?"

"Sure, Norm, what's on your mind?" The two men sat down on a sofa in the lobby.

"Ed, ever since you hired my firm as your accountant, I've become increasingly concerned about some of your company's accounting practices."

"Why's that?" Ed asked, moving to the edge of his seat in a slightly uncomfortable manner.

"Look, we've known each other for almost five years now. We're both Christians. That's why it bothers me that some of your accounting practices are highly questionable. In certain areas you make the picture look better than it really is to increase your company's borrowing ability, and in other areas you're making it look worse than it really is to avoid tax liability. It's not right. You can't have it both ways. You need a uniform system of accounting that will give an honest picture of where your business really stands. At first I thought it might be a lack of communication within your organization; but the longer I study the situation, the more it becomes clear that this is deliberate, and it's something you must be aware of personally."

"Sure I'm aware of it, Norm. Hey, you know how competitive my field is right now. I've got to use every trick I can think of to stay ahead of the pack."

"But how do you fit that into your faith life, Ed?"

"What do you mean, 'How do I fit it in?' That's what Christianity is all about. Jesus died for my sins. He knows I'm a sinner. He came into this world so that I can be forgiven. So I don't worry about it if I have to fudge a few numbers here or there."

"But you don't have to."

"If I want to come out on top, I do."

"Is that what's most important, Ed, coming out on top?"

"Look, Norm, I don't see what the big deal is. No matter how hard I try, I'm never going to be perfect. Jesus is always going to have to forgive me for something."

"So you might as well make it worthwhile? You make it sound as if you've got Jesus over a barrel."

"Aw, come on, Norm, lighten up."

"Why do you think Jesus died for your sins, Ed? Do you think he did it so that you could just go on sinning? Don't you think he had something better in mind for you?"

"What do you mean?" Ed wondered aloud.

"I think the reason Jesus died and rose again was to free me from sin. True, he wanted to take away the guilt of my sin by offering me forgiveness. But he also wanted to free me from the power of sin by giving me strength to obey his will. If I don't want to be free

55

from sin's control, then I don't really want the forgiveness Jesus is offering me either."

"Hmmm," Ed mused. "And if I don't want that forgiveness, then his death on the cross won't do me any good, will it? Norm, are you trying to remind me that I have to demonstrate repentance if I want to be forgiven?"

"Yes, Ed, I am. Jesus wants to forgive you, but he also wants you to obey, to be guided by his will."

"Well, you've given me some tough things to think about, Norm."

"And I'll be praying for you, Ed. Oh-oh, I've got a 9:30 appointment with a client. I'm going to have to hurry to make it. I'll call you in a couple of days and see where the Lord's been leading you, okay?"

"Okay. And thanks, Norm."

Repentance coupled with faith was a constant theme of Jesus' teaching. It is the first of his sermons Mark recorded in his gospel. "The time has come. The kingdom of God is near. Repent and believe the good news" (Mk 1:15). Jesus not only wants us to believe in him; he also wants us to obey him. At the close of the Sermon on the Mount he said, "Therefore everyone who hears these words of mine *and puts them into practice* is like a wise man who built his house on the rock." Just hearing Jesus' words is not enough. "But everyone who hears these words of mine *and does not put them into practice* is like a foolish man who built his house on sand" (Mt 7:24, 26; emphasis ours). When one woman told Jesus that his mother was blessed to have him for her son, he replied: "Blessed rather are those who hear the word of God and obey it" (Lk 11:28). Notice that Jesus did not say, "Blessed rather are those who hear the word of God and believe it."

Faith is demonstrated by obedience. That's why Jesus cares about obedience. His final charge to his disciples in the Great Commission exhibits his concern for obedience very clearly. He told his disciples to go and make disciples of all nations baptizing "and teaching them to obey everything I have commanded you" (Mt 28:20).

"Jesus did not simply command the 11 to proclaim the Gospel or even to bring people to the point of conversion through the Gospel. Rather, he commanded discipling, bringing people to faith and obedience, incorporating them as functioning members of his body through the proclamation of the Gospel" (Rudnick 1984, 38).

Notice again that Jesus did not say "and teaching them to *believe* everything I have commanded you." That's not to say that faith is unimportant. Faith is the foundation. It enables us to obey. Obedience is faith in action. It reveals inward faith, and it is what Christ wants to see in our lives.

Mere words professing faith are not enough. Ed, the businessman with questionable accounting practices, thought that Jesus was content with lip service. He felt that if he professed faith and went to church, he could go on living as he pleased in other areas of his life, and Jesus would have to forgive him. That's not the kind of Savior we find in Christ, however.

Jesus, the Church Consultant

In recent years it has become very common for congregations to hire church consultants to help them resolve problems, overcome obstacles, and strengthen and improve their ministry. In the book of Revelation, Jesus Christ, the greatest church consultant of all times, gives his advice to seven different churches.

He repeats one phrase in five of the seven letters addressed to them: "I know your deeds." Jesus is concerned about what these Christians are doing (or not doing). Christians have always been very concerned about orthodoxy, or right doctrine. Here, our divine church consultant makes clear that orthopractice,[1] or right living, is just as important as orthodoxy. In speaking to these churches he condemns false teachers by name, discrediting the Nicolaitans and those who follow the teachings of Balaam and Jezebel. He also makes clear that these false teachings lead to false practices, such as participation in idolatrous rituals and sexual immorality.

Jesus demands a high level of commitment from these Christians as he consults with them about their congregational life. In two of the letters he condemns weak commitment. He commends the church in Ephesus for its deeds, hard work, and perseverance— nevertheless adding, "Yet I hold this against you: You have forsaken your first love. Remember the height from which you have fallen! Repent and do the things you did at first" (Rev 2:4–5a). Jesus tells them to renew their commitment to him or he will remove their lampstand from its place.

In the letter to the church of Laodicea we find out that there is something that makes Jesus nauseous: lukewarm Christians. He minces no words: "I know your deeds, that you are neither cold nor hot. I wish you were either one or the other! So, because you are lukewarm—neither hot nor cold—I am about to spit you out of my mouth" (Rev 3:15–16). Jesus is not content with spiritual apathy. He wants action!

Jesus' next words to the Laodiceans are especially apropos for twentieth century Christians in North America: "You say, 'I am rich; I have acquired wealth and do not need a thing.' But you do not realize that you are wretched, pitiful, poor, blind and naked" (Rev 3:17). This is often the case with contemporary believers. We have become content with the riches of this world. We are so well off in this life that we find it difficult to set our minds on the things of heaven. As a result we may become apathetic about obeying Christ's commands or carrying out his Great Commission, and Jesus tells us that makes him want to vomit. We are not overstating the case. This is the implication of the Greek word that Jesus uses for the phrase "spit you out of my mouth."

In another powerful section he addresses the church in Sardis: "I know your deeds; you have a reputation of being alive, but you are dead. Wake up! Strengthen what remains and is about to die, for I have not found your deeds complete in the sight of my God. Remember, therefore, what you have received and heard; obey it, and repent" (Rev 3:2–3). Jesus' words ring true for far too many Christians today. But, can you imagine any modern church consultant getting away with telling your church such severe yet honest truths?

Throughout this section of Revelation, Jesus warns Christians about the consequences of failing to repent and obey his commands. He tells the church in Pergamum, "Repent therefore! Otherwise I will come to you and will fight against them with the sword of my mouth" (Rev 2:16). Christ was telling them that the Law would become a sharp, double-edged sword to rip their false righteousness to shreds if they did not repent.

At the same time the Lord promises rich rewards to those who will listen to him and obey his word. Many different promises and rewards of grace are offered "to him who overcomes." "I will give the right to eat from the tree of life" (Rev 2:7). "He will not be hurt at all by the second death" (Rev 2:11). "Be faithful, even to the point of death and I will give you the crown of life" (Rev 2:10). In speaking this way, Jesus was doing the same thing which his Father did with the children of Israel in Deuteronomy 27–30. Jesus' consequences and rewards parallel the blessings and curses that God laid out for the Israelites as they entered the promised land.

From the example of this church consultant we can learn much about what kind of preaching the church needs today. Christ analyzes the life and deeds of the Christians of these seven churches. He repeatedly calls them to repentance and obedience. That's what we need to be doing in the church today. Unfortunately many of us don't want to be told that repentance and obedience are what the Christian life is all about. But the church needs to hear just that.

Jesus' Marching Orders

When Jesus serves as consultant to his church, he doesn't mince any words. He shows himself to be our Lord who expects his church to obey his will and carry out the mission he has committed to us. The church is not a comfortable society of friendly people who enjoy each other's company at potlucks and bake sales. The church is not simply ours to enjoy, like a neighborly country club. Robert Kolb reminds us,

> The church is indeed his. Many North Americans view their local congregation as a free association of individuals who want and like to be together in their own little group. Yet the church does not belong to its members; they, rather, as individuals and as a congregation, belong to the church's Lord and are directed by his Word (Kolb 1984, 180).

Unfortunately, that's not always how Christians see it. By grace, through faith in Jesus Christ, we are justified. Having been redeemed, by the Spirit's power we can overcome and do his will to the end, as our church consultant ordered (Revelation 2 and 3). His command is not only that we obey his will in our own lives. No, our God cares not only about the obedience of those who are already a part of Christ's church, as Jesus has shown us in the book of Revelation. He is also concerned about the obedience of the nations. Jesus Christ came to achieve that goal, as we saw in "the Gospel According to Jacob" in Gen 49:10.

For this to be accomplished, however, the Gospel of Jesus Christ must be proclaimed the world over, so that people might come to faith and be saved. Without such justifying faith, living obediently is utterly impossible. The obedience of the nations cannot be achieved without the proclamation of the Gospel. In fact, in 63 out of 127 occurrences, the word *Gospel* appears either in verb form, meaning *preach the Gospel,* or with another verb meaning *proclaim.* Since the New Testament emphasizes proclamation in at least 50 percent of the times when the word *Gospel* is used, it is therefore safe to conclude that the worldwide proclamation of the good news of Jesus Christ is another part of the goal of the Gospel. These are our marching orders from our Commander in Chief!

This comes out very clearly in a section of Scripture which is much more familiar to us than is the Gospel According to Jacob. That section is Jesus' Great Commission in Mt 28:18–20. In fact, when viewed side by side with Gen 49:10, the Great Commission almost appears to be Jesus' commentary on the Gospel According to Jacob and how it would be fulfilled.

"The *scepter* will not depart from Judah nor the *ruler's staff* from between his feet, until he comes to whom it belongs and the *obedience* of the *nations* is his."	"All *authority* in heaven and on earth has been given to me. Therefore, go and *make disciples of all nations*, baptizing them in the name of the Father and of the Son and of the Holy Spirit, and teaching them to *obey* everything I have commanded you."

Notice what Jesus stressed when he commanded us to go and make disciples. He accented his *authority*. He urged us to go to *all nations*, and he emphasized *obedience* to his commands. Jesus could have said, "Go and make disciples of all nations, baptizing them . . . and teaching them to *believe* everything I have *taught* you," but he didn't. By doing so he would have emphasized the Gospel without the goal of obedience. Instead he chose words which showed the close connection between the Gospel and its goal, between obedience and missions.

Bearing the Cross

Satan hates the church and is waging an all out war against "those who obey God's commandments and hold to the testimony of Jesus" (Rev 12:17). Because of the devil's enmity, being a Christian is not easy. Following Jesus' marching orders will mean labor, work, toil, trouble, and difficulty. It includes bearing the cross. After listening in on Christ's consultation with the churches in Revelation, we cannot help but realize that. Yes, being a Christian is hard work, but you've got forever to rest! "Blessed are the dead who die in the Lord . . . . they will rest from their labor, for their deeds will follow them" (Rev 14:13).

Unfortunately, too many Christians are resting now! Too many Christians fall asleep before they die. Instead, we ought to be asking ourselves, "How shall I labor for my Savior today?" That may sound strange, since the Savior has said, "Come to me, all you who labor and are heavy laden, and I will give you rest" (Mt 11:28–30). But when we come to faith in Jesus, we exchange one burden for another. The first is the crushing burden of our sin which will destroy us. Jesus frees us from that and says, "Take my yoke upon you and learn from me, for my yoke is easy and my burden is light." The burden which Jesus calls us to carry is the cross. Bearing the cross is a common theme in Jesus' teaching, but it is also commonly misunderstood.

Emily, Jan, and Sheila were sitting together around Jan's kitchen table at their weekly "Prayer Partners" meeting. Emily read from Mk 8:34: " 'If anyone would come after me, he must deny himself and take up his cross and follow me.' What do you think Jesus means by this?" she asked the other two women.

"Well, we all have our cross to bear, don't we?" asked Jan.

"Yes, but what do you think Jesus means when he says we have to bear the cross?"

"I can't help but think of Esther Johnson," Jan replied. "She is so crippled from arthritis that she can hardly walk. She's in constant pain, seven days a week, 365 days a year. I can't imagine how she keeps going. I certainly wouldn't want to bear her cross."

"Do you really think that's what Jesus had in mind when he asked us to take up the cross and follow him?" Emily asked.

"Well, not only that," continued, Jan. "I mean, your cross could

61

be heart trouble or cancer." Then she quickly expanded the list. "Think about all the pain our friend, Anne, felt when her daughter got pregnant. That was certainly a heavy burden on her. And what about someone like Sandy Martin, whose husband is an alcoholic?"

"I'm not sure these are the kinds of things Jesus had in mind when he talked about bearing the cross. Listen to the rest of this section in Mark 8." Emily read on. "For whoever wants to save his life will lose it, but whoever loses his life for me and for the gospel will save it. What good is it for a man to gain the whole world, yet forfeit his soul? If anyone is ashamed of me and my words in this adulterous and sinful generation, the Son of man will be ashamed of him when he comes in his Father's glory with the holy angels (Mk 8:35–38).

"It doesn't sound to me like Jesus is talking about ordinary troubles when he says we should lose our life for him, or never be ashamed of him," Emily concluded.

Up to this point Sheila had been silent. Now she began to understand. "I think you're right, Emily. I think bearing the cross involves something more than daily trials. Think of what the cross was used for."

"Jesus died on it," said Emily.

"That's right, and we have to use the cross to die as well."

"What do you mean, Sheila?" asked Jan.

"We are all sinners, and if we're going to be able to follow Jesus, we first have to put to death our old sinful nature in order to be able to do his will. We have to die to sin."

"So, is Jesus talking about repentance when he says, 'Take up the cross and follow me'?" asked Emily.

"That's at least part of it," Sheila answered.

Repentance, or dying to sin, is a big part of what Jesus meant when he spoke of bearing the cross. Al Menconi directs a ministry which points out the dangers of secular rock music to Christian young people and introduces them to the alternative of Christian rock music. In a recent letter to supporters of his ministry he wrote:

"I had a chance to speak to a church youth group recently. I began playing the first few notes of 'Living in Sin' [by Bon Jovi], then stopped the tape and asked the kids if they could identify the song.

"I was shocked. This #1 hit song is blatantly against the moral values you and I and our churches are trying to teach our children, yet these Christian young people knew it immediately. And not only did they know it, they expressed open affection for the performers! . . .

"The young people in this youth group would barely sing a note of the youth choruses earlier, but could sing along with every note from the most perverted songs imaginable. Yet, when I asked if they loved Jesus, most responded with a resounding 'Yes.' It was obvious they didn't have the slightest idea what Jesus meant when he told us to take up our cross and follow him" (Menconi 1990).

Just like these young people, many Christians don't understand that bearing the cross means dying to the sinful things that intrude into our lives as Christians. For young people, that may mean "dying" to some of their secular rock music. For others it may mean "dying" to their favorite soap opera or porn magazine.

Let's go back to the conversation continuing in Jan's kitchen.

"I think there's even more than dying to sin in carrying the cross," Sheila went on.

"Like what?" Emily wanted to know.

"Bearing the cross really talks about the sacrifices, the suffering, and the persecution a Christian bears for the sake of the Gospel. Sometimes when we are obedient to Christ, the world will hate us. And sometimes following Jesus requires sacrifice."

"You know what? I just thought of a good example of that," offered Jan. "I was talking with my neighbor last week. Their son-in-law has been studying medicine for several years now. He just agreed to serve as a medical missionary in Nepal. He and their daughter and two grandchildren will be over there for five years. They may not get to see them at all during that time. I told her I wouldn't have been able to stand that; but she said she was glad they were going. She said the Gospel was needed so desperately there, and even though she would love to have her daughter and grandchildren live with her, she knew that her son-in-law would need the support of his family to do the Lord's work. She also said she knew God would go with them, and protect them, and give her patience until they return. I was really impressed with how strong her faith was!"

"You're right, Jan, that really is a good example of bearing the cross. In fact, Jesus talked about something just like that. Look at Lk 14:26–27," suggested Sheila.

"I'll read it," volunteered Emily. " 'If anyone comes to me and does not hate his father and mother, his wife and children, his brothers and sisters—yes, even his own life—he cannot be my disciple. And anyone who does not carry his cross and follow me cannot be my disciple.' Wow, you're right. That sounds just like Jan's neighbor. She was willing to give up her family for the sake of Christ."

"But I also think your original example of crossbearing was a good one, Jan," added Sheila.

"Why?" Jan questioned. "After what we've discovered, I really don't think it fits anymore. I can sympathize with Esther Johnson, but I guess arthritis doesn't really qualify as bearing the cross."

"I think that depends on how you bear it," said Sheila.

"What do you mean?" asked Emily.

"Think of Esther Johnson's attitude in the face of all her pain and suffering."

"I think I see what you're getting at," Jan reflected. "In spite of her pain, Esther never complains. She always seems to be cheerful."

"She's dying to herself by denying herself pity," Sheila explained.

"Whenever I ask her how she's doing, she always has the same answer. 'Well, I just thank the Lord that he's given me strength for one more day.' And she's always doing something for someone else in spite of her condition, when she's the one other people should be helping."

"So you see," Sheila concluded, "faith can turn even ordinary troubles into a cross which we bear for the sake of the Gospel. It all depends on faith."

Discipleship

A willingness to die to self and bear the cross seems all too uncommon among Christians nowadays. Sometimes, like the teens Al Menconi spoke of, we think we can love the world and Jesus at the same time. Like Ed, the businessman with unethical accounting methods, we expect Jesus to forgive us without repentance. Some Christians seem to have the attitude, "I like to sin and God likes to forgive sin; isn't that a nice arrangement?" The Christian who has this attitude does not understand discipleship. He thinks one can be a Christian without being a disciple of Jesus Christ. In reality, there is no difference between the two. Jesus made this plain when he gave us the Great Commission. He didn't say, "Go and save all nations, then make a few of them my disciples." Jesus said, "Go and make disciples of all nations, baptizing . . . and teaching them to obey everything I have commanded you." Discipleship and salvation are inseparable. Christians can't be satisfied simply to soak up the Gospel and forget about its goal.

Straw Man

Some readers may ask, "Aren't you creating a straw man in describing a Christian with this attitude? Aren't you just setting up a phony position so that you can knock it down? No Christians really believe that willful sin and the Christian life are fully compatible, do they?"

Perhaps Christians do not profess such beliefs, but if you examine the lives and commitment of numerous professed Christians, you will find many such straw men among them. That's exactly what a weak Christian is: a straw man. Paul wrote,

> If any man builds on this foundation using gold, silver, costly stones, wood, hay or *straw,* his work will be shown for what it is, because the day will bring it to light. It will be revealed with fire, and the fire will test the quality of each man's work. If what he has built survives, he will receive his reward. If it is burned up, he will suffer loss; he himself will be saved, but only as one escaping through the flames (1 Cor 3:12–15; emphasis ours).

> The lives of too many believers with a lukewarm commitment to Christ produce nothing but straw. Obedience is scarce, witness is absent, and God is not glorified.

Think about the Christians you know. How many people in your church think being a Christian and being a disciple of Christ are two different things? How about your own life? What materials are you using to build on the foundation of the Gospel? Is your Christian life a house of straw because you are unwilling to bear the cross? Is it nothing more than a bale of hay because you want Jesus Christ to be merely your Savior but not the Lord of your life? If so, you too may be saved "only as one escaping through the flames." Jesus issued an even stronger warning against some who profess allegiance to him while living in rebellion against him. He said, "Not everyone who says to me, 'Lord, Lord,' will enter the Kingdom of Heaven, but only he who does the will of my Father in heaven" (Mt 7:21).

Christians need to heed these words of warning. Proclaiming the pure Gospel of Christ's death for our sins is crucial, but we must never forget the goal of the Gospel. Jesus certainly didn't omit the Gospel's goal when teaching his own disciples. John recorded for us the discourse which Jesus shared with his disciples on the night of the Last Supper. This section clearly shows how Jesus preached both the Gospel and the goal of the Gospel.

Jesus' Discourse on the Goal of the Gospel

In Jn 14:1, Jesus begins his discourse with this beautiful Gospel: "Do not let your hearts be troubled. Trust in God; trust also in me." In fact, all through John 14–17 Jesus shares many wonderful Gospel promises with his disciples. At the same time, however, he repeatedly reminds them of the goal of the Gospel by calling them to obey his command. Jesus tells his disciples, "If you love me, you will obey what I command" (Jn 14:15). "Whoever has my commands and obeys them, he is the one who loves me" (Jn 14:21).

Jesus even warns the disciples about the dangers of disobedience.

> He who does not love me will not obey my teaching (Jn 14:24).

> I am the true vine, and my Father is the gardener. He cuts off every branch in me that bears no fruit, while every branch that does bear fruit he prunes so that it will be even more fruitful" (Jn 15:1–2).

> I am the vine; you are the branches. If a man remains in me and I in him, he will bear much fruit; apart from me you can do nothing. If anyone does not remain in me, he is like a branch that is thrown away and withers; such branches are picked up, thrown into the fire and burned (Jn 15:5–6).

Here again Jesus is doing just as God the Father did in Deuteronomy 28 when he warned the Israelites against disobedience.

If Jesus was bold enough to issue this warning, we must be, too. If he urged his own disciples to be obedient, we need to do the same. We can't assume anything. Jesus never said to his disciples, "I love you," and expected obedience to be the result. He told them to obey and gave them the commands he expected them to follow. Jesus' teaching makes it plain that sanctification doesn't simply "take care of itself" when the Gospel is preached.

Jesus also talked about the connection between obedience and missions. He told his disciples, "You did not choose me, but I chose you and appointed you to go and bear fruit—fruit that will last" (Jn 15:16). What is the fruit Jesus was speaking of? His "High Priestly Prayer" in Jn 17:15–20 makes that plain. There he said to his heavenly Father,

> My prayer is not that you take them out of the world but that you protect them from the evil one. They are not of the world, even as I am not of it. Sanctify them by the truth; your word is truth. As you sent me into the world, I have sent them into the world, For them I sanctify myself, that they too may be truly sanctified. My prayer is not for them alone. I pray also for those who will believe in me through their message.

When Jesus said, "For them I sanctify myself," he was talking about his death on the cross. Jesus sanctified himself and us by obeying his Father. Likewise in Jn 14:31 he said, "The world must learn that I love the Father and that I do exactly what my Father has commanded me." Jesus sets us the example of obedience. We follow an obedient God and Savior who calls us to bear much fruit. The fruit that lasts are the souls saved for eternal life by our witness. That's what Jesus meant when he prayed, "I pray also for those who will believe in me through their message." This is the fruit Jesus wants all of his disciples to bear, not only his first disciples, but also those today, including you and me.

By our obedience we witness to our faith in Christ and so win others for Christ. Our lives become a vibrant witness for the Gospel when we do the will of God in our daily lives. Many Christians say that they try to witness by their good example, by their obedience. But what they usually mean by this is not doing the "don'ts," avoiding those things prohibited in God's commandments. This is only half of what Jesus is talking about. In Jn 15:12–15 Jesus told his disciples,

> My command is this: Love each other as I have loved you. Greater love has no one than this, that he lay down his life for his friends.

You are my friends if you do what I command. I no longer call you servants, because a servant does not know his master's business. Instead, I have called you friends, for everything that I learned from my Father I have made known to you.

Here Jesus is teaching "friendship evangelism." Who are our friends? Anyone we choose to love. Paul tells us that all the people in the world were God's enemies (Rom 5:10), but Christ chose to die for all, treating us as his friends. He demonstrated his friendship by laying down his life. Now Jesus is asking us to love others as he has loved us. Like a two-sided coin, this is the other half of witnessing by our example. It is not only not doing the don'ts, but also witnessing by love, that is, by doing the do's. This means laying down our lives, losing our lives for others, so that they might know the love of Jesus.

By obedience and love we will bear much fruit. We demonstrate to others our love for God by doing what Jesus did. If I am to win others for Christ, I must be obedient to him. But obedience grows out of God's love in me, and my love must reach out in kindness to meet the needs of others in order to win them to Christ. In this way our love reflects to others Christ's love for them and for us.

Notice that Jesus calls his disciples friends, not servants. That's because we know his business. And what is his business? Christ's business, according to John 15, is obeying the Father and loving His friends. When we understand what Christ's business is and remain in his love by obeying his command to love others, then we can become "branch offices." After all, Jesus said, "I am the vine and you are the branches" (Jn 15:5).

In this discourse to his disciples Jesus also spoke about glorifying God. He made it clear how we glorify God. "I have brought you glory on earth by completing the work you gave me to do" (Jn 17:4). Our obedience as God's redeemed people results in glory for our Savior God. And, as a reward of grace, God shares his glory with us. Jesus prayed, "Father, I want those you have given me to be with me where I am, and to see my glory, the glory you have given me because you loved me before the creation of the world" (Jn 17:24).

Ask Whatever You Wish

One thread that runs through Jesus' discourse in John 14–17 is easy to miss. It appears in isolated passages, and often it is misinterpreted because most people don't see it as a part of Jesus' whole teaching about the goal of the Gospel. This thread is Jesus' promise, repeated four times in these chapters, "*Ask me for anything* in my name, and I will do it" (Jn 14:13–14; 15:7–8, 16; 16:23–24; our emphasis).

What an incredible promise this is! But too many have not believed the promise because they didn't understand its context. They thought this promise applied in general to anything a Christian might ask for. It doesn't. Look at each of these references carefully *in context*. This promise applies to the goal of the Gospel. Do you need strength for obedience? Ask and you will receive. Do you need power to witness? Ask and you will receive. Do you need love to reach out to someone in need? Ask and you will receive. Do you need help to glorify the Father in your life? Ask and you will receive. In fact, Jesus' promise goes far beyond what we can imagine. Only those who know the Master's business and want to spread his joy will be crazy enough and visionary enough to "ask whatever you wish."

Digging Deeper

1. Which statement are you more comfortable with: "Jesus loves me" or, "Jesus wants me to obey?" Why?
2. Review on pages 50 to 53 the different ways in which Jesus came to "fulfill the Law":
   a. To fill the Law full of meaning by going beyond the letter of the Law, that is, the surface meaning of the commandment, to the spirit of the Law.
   b. To obey the Law perfectly on our behalf.
   c. To energize and equip his disciples to obey the Law in their daily lives.

   Talk about what each of these means for your life as a disciple of Jesus. Can you think of any other ways in which Jesus fulfilled the Law?
3. Why is our best not good enough to satisfy God? How does Jesus' best become our own?
4. What are the "two sides of obedience?" that the chapter discusses? What are some of the blessings that may come from obedience to God's Law? What are some of the difficulties that may come from obedience to God's Law?

5. How do you think your congregation would react if a church consultant came and said the kinds of things that Jesus said about the seven churches in Asia Minor? Which of his messages do you believe apply to your church? Which do you personally need to hear? (See Rev 2–3.)

6. What are the church's marching orders (See Mt 28:18–20; Mk 16:15–16; Lk 24:45–49; Jn 20:21–23; and Acts 1:8)? How seriously have you taken these orders? How seriously does your church take them? How seriously does our Commander in Chief take them? Why?

7. What does Jesus really mean when he says, "Take up your cross and follow me?"

8. What does the word *Christian* mean? What does the word *disciple* mean? Are being a Christian and being a disciple of Christ two different things?

9. Take a look at Jesus' prayer promises in Jn 14:13–14; 15:7–8, 16; and 16:23–24. Study the context to determine what kinds of petitions Jesus is encouraging us to ask.

10. Make a list of verses in John 14–17 where you think Jesus is talking about each of the following aspects of the goal of the Gospel:
    a. obedience/sanctification
    b. mission/proclamation
    c. glorifying God.

Note

1. The authors are not using the term "orthopractice" with all of the liberation-theology baggage that has been attached to it. Rather, we use the term with the same attitude as that expressed in Luther's Morning Prayer, "I pray that you would keep me this day also from sin and every evil, that all my doings and life may please you."

4

The Apostles and Obedience

In chapter 2 we saw an overview of the Old Testament teaching about obedience and the goal of the Gospel. In chapter 3 we learned that Jesus also cares deeply about the obedience of his followers. In this chapter we will go on to see that the apostles are just as concerned about obedience as their Master was. They carefully emphasize both the Gospel and its goal throughout their letters.

Gospel Myopia

That Sunday morning when Jim and Cathy came down to the coffee and fellowship time following worship, they noticed something was different. Instead of the usual small talk about kids, sports, or the weather, all their friends were talking about the Bible. Then they noticed the card standing in the middle of each table. It read, "Share your favorite Bible passage with someone at the table."

"So what's yours, Jim?" asked Wayne as Jim was taking his seat.

"Wait a minute; I didn't even get time to think about it yet," Jim protested.

"Good; then it really will be your favorite," quipped Wayne.

"I know my favorite," Cathy volunteered. "Eph 2:8–9, 'For it is by grace you have been saved, through faith—and this not from yourselves, it is the gift of God—not by works, so that no one can boast.'"

"Hey, you stole mine," Jim complained melodramatically.

"Sure," Wayne joked. "It's the only one you know, right Jim?"

"No way! Just give me a minute to come up with another," Jim appealed in feigned desperation.

"Well, one of my favorites is 1 Jn 1:9," Sue offered. "'If we confess our sins, he is faithful and just and will forgive us our sins and purify us from all unrighteousness.' "

"That's too easy," Wayne objected. "We use that one in church all the time."

"We're still waiting, Jim," Tom prodded with a smile on his face.

"Okay, I've got one, but I have to look it up," Jim replied.

"Yeah, right," Wayne joked, "and how long is it going to take you to find it?"

"No, no, it won't take long," said Jim, flipping through his Bible. "I know it's right near the beginning of 1 Peter. Let's see, 1 Pet 1:18–19, 'For you know that it was not with perishable things, such as silver or gold that you were redeemed from the empty way of life handed down to you from your forefathers, but with the precious blood of Christ, a lamb without blemish or defect.' " Jim looked thoughtfully at the Bible for a moment. "You know, that's interesting."

"What's interesting?" asked Jan.

"All of us chose great Gospel verses as our favorites, probably passages we memorized years ago."

"So?" remarked Tom. "That's natural."

"Yeah, but when I memorized this passage, I didn't notice the section it's in. I didn't pay any attention to what came before or after it. These two verses are great Gospel—Christ redeemed us with his blood. But look at the heading of the section." Jim pointed to his Bible.

"Be holy," read Jan. "Wow, that is interesting. I wouldn't have expected that."

"Me either," remarked Wayne. "We've got a few minutes before Bible class starts. Why don't we look up the other passages we shared and see what comes before and after them?"

What this group of friends found as they looked up their favorite Bible passages surprised them. Perhaps it will surprise you as well.

Take for example the Ephesians 2 passage that Cathy shared. Many believers can quote verses 8 and 9, but far fewer know verse 10 by heart: "For we are God's workmanship, created in Christ Jesus to do good works, which God prepared in advance for us to do." Eph 2:10 presents us with God's purpose in saving us by grace through faith. It is the goal of the Gospel, and it follows right on the heels of one of the most beautiful Gospel passages of all.

Sue referred to 1 Jn 1:9. In the Lutheran liturgy, it is used to call God's people to confession. It reminds us of God's promise that if we will heartily confess our sins, he will graciously forgive them. But, there is more in this section than beautiful Gospel. Listen to the admonition which John gives just three verses earlier. "If we claim to have fellowship with him yet walk in the darkness, we lie and do not live by the truth."

Jim's passage from 1 Pet 1:18–19 is probably the best example. Listen to the words of the five verses that immediately precede the verses he shared.

"Therefore, prepare your minds for action; be self controlled, set your hope fully on the grace to be given you when Jesus Christ is revealed. As obedient children, do not conform to the evil desires you had when you lived in ignorance. But just as he who called you is holy, so be holy in all you do, for it is written: 'Be holy, because I am holy.' Since you call on a Father who judges each man's work impartially, live your lives as strangers here in reverent fear."

"That's really something," Jim remarked. "In each case we really zeroed in on the Gospel itself, without bothering to see what God wanted to tell us along with the Gospel."

"Yeah, it's like we've got selective vision or something so that we see only the Gospel," Wayne added.

"Myopia," Sue joined in.

"My what?" Tom asked.

"Myopia," Sue continued. "Being near sighted. You can see what's right in front of you, but you can't see anything at a distance. It's like we can see the Gospel, but we can't see beyond it."

"True," remarked Wayne as he flipped through his Bible. "How many people do you know who claim James 2:17 as their favorite Bible passage?"

"What does it say?" asked Jan.

" 'In the same way, faith by itself, if it is not accompanied by action, is dead,' " read Wayne.

"I see what you mean," Cathy concluded.

It does seem as though some Christians have a case of "Gospel myopia." We have a tendency to lift great Gospel verses right out of a sanctification section without seeing beyond them. Thus, we fail to see them in their proper context.

In this chapter we will put on our "goal-of-the-Gospel glasses" so that we will see not only the Gospel but also the goal of the Gospel. As a result, we will plainly recognize that the apostles did not suffer from Gospel myopia. We will learn to appreciate how clearly and consistently they connected the goal of the Gospel with the Gospel itself. Perhaps from them we can learn to do the same, not only in our doctrine but, even more importantly, in our daily lives.

James

Ever since the Reformation, Protestant Christians have had a hard time reconciling James's practical emphasis on Christian living with the teaching of salvation by grace through faith in Jesus Christ, which is so prominent in Paul's epistles. James does make it clear that justification by faith is the backdrop for everything he says in his letter. For example, he reminds his readers that God "chose to give us birth through the word of truth, that we might be a kind of firstfruits of all he created" (James 1:18).

Probably the most troublesome passage in James is found in the second chapter.

> You foolish man, do you want evidence that faith without deeds is useless? Was not our ancestor Abraham considered righteous for what he did when he offered his son Isaac on the altar? You see that his faith and his actions were working together, and his faith was made complete by what he did. And the scripture was fulfilled that says, "Abraham believed God, and it was credited to him as righteousness," and he was called God's friend. You see that a person is justified by what he does and not by faith alone (James 2:20–24).

At first glance these words may cause some Christians to stumble. But can we accuse James of bad theology at this point? No, indeed, not when we compare what he says with what God himself said in other Scriptures. Note the opening words of James 2:23: "And the scripture *was fulfilled* that says, 'Abraham believed God, and it was credited to him as righteousness' " (emphasis ours). This accords perfectly with what the Lord said to Abraham when he stayed his hand from harming Isaac: "Do not do anything to him. *Now I know* that you fear God, because you have not withheld from me your son, your only son" (Gen 22:12; emphasis ours). Abraham's actions did indeed fulfill God's word accounting him righteous, because they demonstrated even to Almighty God himself the sincerity of Abraham's faith.

At the close of v. 23 James says, "And he was called God's friend." What James says here is no different from what Jesus said to his disciples in Jn 15:14: "You are my friends, if you do what I command." We demonstrate our friendship, our love for God, by our obedience to his commands.

Note that James refers to Genesis 15 where Abraham's faith is credited to him as righteousness. God declared Abraham righteous apart from and without his obedience. Trusting God's friendship and love, Abraham obeyed and thus "did indeed fulfill God's word accounting him righteous" (James 2:2–24). So faith was fulfilled in obedience, even if justification was declared without obedience.

James 2:22 is really the key here: "You see that his faith and his actions were working together, and his faith was made complete by what he did." Here again we have that word *telos* that we talked about in chapter 1. Abraham's faith was made complete—it reached its goal—when it was perfectly obedient to God's command, when his faith and actions were working together. That's precisely the point! We need to keep the Gospel and its goal united at all times. They must be working together. Justification and sanctification are inseparable. James is right. Faith without works is dead, and faith without works cannot justify, for it is not saving faith.

The truth is that James speaks no differently from any of the other apostles. In light of what we will see in the writings of Peter, Paul, John, and the letter to the Hebrews, your reaction to James 2 will probably be, "No big deal; it's just more of the same."

Paul

Perhaps a good place to begin in Paul's letters is at 2 Tim 3:15–17. Here, Paul writes about,

the holy Scriptures, which are able to make you wise for salvation through faith in Christ Jesus. All Scripture is God-breathed and is useful for teaching, rebuking, correcting, and training in righ-

teousness, so that the man of God may be thoroughly equipped
for every good work.

Paul emphasizes that God gave us the Bible to bring about both
our justification—to make us "wise for salvation through faith In
Christ Jesus"—and our sanctification—that we "may be thoroughly
equipped for every good work."

Even though we are saints of God by faith in Jesus Christ, we
need the admonition of God's holy Word. Why? Because we are
sinner/saints who still struggle with sin every day.[1] Unfortunately,
we have developed such an easy, almost lackadaisical brand of Christianity that we rarely hear a word of rebuke or correction. We need
both the sweet savor of the Gospel and the sharp sting of the Law,
even after we have come to faith, so that we can continue to mature
and progress in Christian living.

Galatians

Paul's classic dissertation in which he opposes salvation by works
is the epistle to the Galatians. Yet, even in this fundamental treatise
on justification by faith, Paul devotes two full chapters to the subject
of sanctification. His transition is interesting. In Gal 5:4–6 he sums
up what he has been saying to the Galatians.

> You who are trying to be justified by law have been alienated from
> Christ; you have fallen away from grace. But by faith we eagerly
> await through the Spirit the righteousness for which we hope. For
> in Christ Jesus neither circumcision nor uncircumcision has any
> value. The only thing that counts is faith expressing itself through
> love.

Works of the Law count for nothing. They do not save. "The
only thing that counts is faith," and that's exactly where many Christians would have stopped after arguing against works righteousness
for four chapters. But not Paul. He adds a final, crucial phrase that
links the Gospel and its goal together. "The only thing that counts
is faith *expressing itself through love*" (emphasis ours). Though Paul
is clearly striving to destroy works righteousness, he does not fail
to emphasize obedience to Christ's command.

Paul goes on to emphasize the freedom that Christians have in
Christ and, in some of the strongest terms imaginable, he warns the

Galatians against sacrificing it to anyone. Then, in the very next paragraph, he issues this warning:

> You, my brothers, were called to be free. But do not use your freedom to indulge the sinful nature; rather serve one another in love. The entire law is summed up in a single command: "Love your neighbor as yourself" (Gal 5:13–14).

Paul then continues with stern warnings against the acts of the sinful nature and a beautiful promise of the fruits of the Spirit. Thus he conscientiously adds sanctification to justification, even when he is warning people against works righteousness.

Paul's method may seem strange to some Christians. Those coming from an evangelical background, with a strong emphasis on justification by faith, may think that Paul is laying too much stress on good works. This is not the case.

The classic Lutheran author on Christian doctrine, Franz Pieper, gives exactly the same advice to pastors.

> In urging the members of their churches to become "rich in good works," pastors should not be deterred from doing this boldly and resolutely, without any fear or faltering, by the thought that this insistence on good works might crowd out of its central position the doctrine of justification without works. Only if he does not know the Scriptural doctrine of justification by faith will he be timid in asking for a multitude of good works. It is therefore impossible to teach a doctrine of sanctification and good works in accord with Scripture without at the same time teaching justification (Pieper 1953, Vol. III, 48).

It's plain that Pieper urges pastors to do exactly as Paul does in Galatians.

2 Corinthians

In a speech to a national convention of the Evangelical Press Association, pollster George Gallup, Jr., noted that too many Americans are shallow believers who fail to link religion and daily life. He said,

> We want the fruits of religion, but not the obligations. We revere the Bible, but don't read it. We believe the Ten Commandments to be valid rules for living, although we can't name them. We believe in God, but this God is often a totally affirming one. He

does not command our total allegiance (Gallup 1990, p. 4).

Could it be that God does not command our total allegiance because we have taken to heart only the Gospel itself, while forgetting the goal of the Gospel? In 2 Cor 2:9 Paul tells the church in Corinth that he had written them previously to see if they would "stand the test and be obedient in everything." He wanted to see if they would follow orders, in this case his order to excommunicate an immoral brother.

A soldier proves that he is ready for combat by immediate and unquestioning obedience to commands from a superior. Whether we realize it or not, Christians are at war, and the enemy is Satan. Could it be that so many churches are losing the battle because they are filled with insubordinate troops who have not learned the importance of obedience? How many of our "soldiers" are ready for spiritual combat, that is, ready to obey the Commander's orders?

In 2 Cor 9:6–15 Paul begins to sound strikingly like another apostle. In these verses he carefully connects the Gospel with its goal, mentioning not only obedience, but also the glory of God. The key section is vv. 13–15.

> Because of the service by which you have proved yourselves, men will praise God for the obedience that accompanies your confession of the Gospel of Christ, and for your generosity in sharing with them and with everyone else. And in their prayers for you their hearts will go out to you, because of the surpassing grace God has given you. Thanks be to God for his indescribable gift!

This sounds like James 2, right in the epistles of Paul! He too tells us that obedience accompanies our confession of the Gospel, that we prove our faith by the service which we perform. The loving service that we offer to others is irrefutable evidence of the genuineness of our faith. This is precisely what James said in his epistle. When Paul in his letters talks about the "obedience of faith," he has more in mind than that we simply believe. Faith without obedience is meaningless; it is dead.

Titus

Probably the clearest example of Paul's combined use of the Gospel and sanctification is in Titus 2–3. Here Paul shows us how the good news of Christ provides the motivation to do God's will. Paul writes,

> For the grace of God that brings salvation has appeared to all men. It teaches us to say "No" to ungodliness and worldly passions, and to live self-controlled, upright and godly lives in this present age, while we wait for the blessed hope—the glorious appearing of our great God and Savior, Jesus Christ, who gave himself for us to redeem us from all wickedness and to purify for himself a people that are his very own, eager to do what is good (Titus 2:11–14).

The phrase "It teaches us to say 'No' " sounds strangely familiar in today's world.

Sue and Sharon rounded the corner to the school parking lot just a few minutes before the P.T.A. committee meeting was scheduled to begin.

"I'm glad we're planning this Say-No-to-Drugs workshop next month," Sue commented. "Did you hear that they arrested a drug dealer just two blocks from the school, over on Sycamore Street?"

"Uh-huh," Sharon replied. "That's scary. At least there are still a few people who care. Look!" she added as she pointed to the street corner across from the school parking lot. There stood a young man wearing a black T-shirt boldly emblazoned with the slogan, "Say No to Drugs."

"That's great. I hope we'll see a lot of our kids from school wearing those shirts after the workshop. We better hurry or we'll be late," said Sue as she stepped out of the car and moved quickly toward the school entrance.

Plans for the workshop went smoothly. An hour later, when the two women were walking back to the car, they noticed several police cars with their lights flashing—on the same corner where they had seen the young man before the meeting.

"Look!" Sue called out. "They're putting that man with the Say-No-to-Drugs shirt into a squad car. Do you suppose they're arresting him?"

"I don't know, but there goes the police car with him in it. Want to see if we can find out what happened?"

"Sure," said Sue. Together they walked over to the corner and asked the nearest police officer what had taken place.

"He sold some crack to an undercover officer," was the officer's reply.

"Right here, across the street from our school?" Sharon asked with a note of fear in her voice.

"But he was wearing a Say-No-to-Drugs shirt!" said Sue in a tone that betrayed her shock.

"We see a lot of street dealers wearing those T-shirts," the officer added. "I guess they think it's a good cover."

Empty words; even sarcasm. That's all the Say-No-to-Drugs slogan is without the proper motivation behind it. In this section of Titus, Paul supplies what is lacking in many of today's secular Say-No-to-Drugs campaigns. God's grace in Jesus Christ, who has redeemed us from sin and death and purchased us to love and serve him, furnishes the reason and the power for us to say no to drugs or any other sinful influence that may confront us.

Paul also highlights the mission aspect of the goal of the Gospel in Titus 3 by telling us why our obedience is so important. It is crucial to an effective witness. We must set an example for others. "Remind the people to be subject to rulers and authorities, to be obedient, to be ready to do whatever is good, to slander no one, to be peaceable and considerate, and to show true humility toward all men" (Titus 3:1–2).

Too often in our Christian teaching and preaching we have presented the Gospel motivation, but we have not added the command that can be completed because of the motivation. Paul tells us to do differently. "I want you to stress these things, so that those who have trusted in God may be careful to devote themselves to doing what is good" (Titus 3:8).

Here in Titus 2–3, Paul artfully weaves obedience to God's Law together with Gospel motivation. If you want to see an interesting demonstration of this, try using colored pencil markings in your Bible throughout this section—red for Gospel, green for sanctification or obedience. You will see the "plaid" passages of Paul emerge as he frequently moves from the Gospel itself to the goal of the Gospel, which is our sanctification and obedience to God's commands.

Philippians

Have you been to the Rocky Mountains? If you are coming from the east driving westward across the plains, gradually the mountain peaks begin to appear on the horizon, almost as if they were growing up out of the ground. When you get to the foothills, the beauty of the snow-capped pinnacles is breathtaking—at first. Then, after a few days of driving through the passes and valleys, rounding a corner to glimpse yet one more peak, you begin to feel, "Oh yeah, another mountain. So what?" Perhaps that's how you are beginning to feel about the many examples of Gospel myopia you have been seeing. At first it is startling to see how the apostles weave together the Gospel with its goal. After a while, it's not so surprising. Bear with us, however, as we share a few more examples. Repeated exposure to the emphasis on the goal of the Gospel will help us overcome our Gospel myopia.

The way we commonly use Phil 2:6–11 furnishes another example of Gospel myopia. The complete context includes Phil 1:27–2:18 and speaks of contending for the Gospel, suffering for Christ, maintaining the unity of church, the obedience of faith, and Gospel proclamation. Please take time now to read the whole context in your Bible. Out of this whole section we usually focus only upon the portion that tells us what Christ has done for us. We like to read Phil 2:6–11 because this Gospel text is like apples of gold in a setting of silver, the setting being obedience and the way we work out our salvation so that we may shine like stars in the universe.

In particular, many evangelical Christians have been troubled by Paul's admonition in Phil 2:12–13:

> Therefore, my dear friends, as you have always obeyed—not only
> in my presence, but now much more in my absence—continue
> to work out your salvation in fear and trembling, for it is God
> who works in you to will and to act according to his good purpose.

Paul is simply telling us to let our faith (James 2:22) express itself through love (Gal 5:6). By our obedience we flesh out our salvation. We make it a working reality.

Paul's admonition to work out our salvation is preceded by grace that flows into sanctification and flows out to evangelism.

> Do everything without complaining or arguing, so that you may

81

become blameless and pure, children of God without fault in a
crooked and depraved generation, in which you shine like stars
in the universe as you hold out the word of life (Phil 2:14–16a).

Many Christians have so compartmentalized the concepts of justification and sanctification that their interrelationship is lost. It's as
though we have placed them in separate, hermetically sealed jars.
In the act of justification, God declares us righteous because of what
Jesus has done for us—not because of what we do. Sanctification is
the daily obedience to God's will that flows from our justifying faith
in the Gospel of Jesus Christ. But until we use the Gospel power
of Word and Sacrament to motivate sanctification (obedience), the
church can't grow. If Christians aren't working out their salvation,
they can't shine like stars in the universe.

This thought leads us back to the earlier verses of Philippians
2, which strongly indict the complacent affluence so typical of much
American Christianity. Paul says, "Do nothing out of selfish ambition
or vain conceit, but in humility consider others better than yourselves. Each of you should look not only to your own interests, but
also to the interests of *others*" (Phil 2:3–4; emphasis ours). How far
does Paul's "others" extend, only to our fellow church members or
to the whole world? When Paul tells us that "every knee should
bow" and that we should "shine like stars in the universe," he is
trying to convince us that we should be looking out for the interests
of the whole world!

Our Savior Jesus Christ certainly considered others better than
himself and looked not only to his own interest but to the interests
of the whole world. Missionaries follow their Savior's lead. Paul's
description of Christ in Phil 2:5–8 could really be applied to almost
all missionaries, men and women who humble themselves and lay
their lives on the line so that others will finally bend the knee before
Christ.

Sarah was excited about going to church Sunday evening. She
had always been intrigued by missions, and the guest pastor that
evening had been serving as a missionary to Ghana in West Africa.
As she drove into the church parking lot, she was disappointed by
the small number of cars. "People are just too busy with their own
lives to care about missions," she thought with some disgust.

While Sarah listened intently to the pastor's presentation on the challenge of becoming a missionary, a feeling of excitement flowed through her. Yet, she was troubled at the same time. At first she couldn't put her finger on the reason for her discomfort. Later that evening, however, after she got home, she sat down at the kitchen table and took out a piece of paper. On it she began to list all of the things she would have to give up and all the adjustments she would have to make in her lifestyle if she were going to become a missionary.

The list seemed almost overwhelming: selling most of her furnishings, her car, giving up many of her personal belongings. There would be no more concerts or trips to the museums which she frequently enjoyed. Then, her after-concert dinners came to mind, and she thought of the new foods she would have to adjust to and the many favorite foods she would have to give up. The faces of family and friends she would leave behind filled her mind.

The list grew steadily longer until Sarah felt she couldn't go on. Then she remembered the Bible passage about Jesus to which the missionary had referred: "Who being in very nature God, did not consider equality with God something to be grasped, but made himself nothing" (Phil 2:6–7). She recounted everything Jesus had been willing to give up for her, considering others better than himself. Then Sarah remembered how she had been so quick to condemn the people from her church who didn't even bother to come and hear the missionary. She felt almost hypocritical. Quietly she wept. Finally, she prayed that Jesus would give her the strength to let go of all that she was grasping so desperately so that she could be free to serve him in his kingdom.

Too few of us have been willing to follow Christ's example and make such sacrifices. Too often Christians in America have considered our affluence something to be grasped. We're not putting our wealth where it can do the most eternal good. As long as our churches are content to do only the minimum of maintenance ministry, then we really don't consider others, that is, the lost, better than ourselves.

Carefully read through Phil 1:27–2:18 and you will be convinced that, just as Jesus hit all the key notes of the goal of the Gospel in John 14–17—obedience, mission, and the glory of God—so Paul does here.

Is this heavy emphasis on the goal of the Gospel too much to handle? Are you feeling a little overwhelmed? Consider the example of a man who was a respected leader in his church. Everyone in the congregation looked up to him because he always took the initiative in doing the Lord's work. His faith seemed extraordinary. His outspokenness on behalf of Christ was remarkable. Everyone who knew him expected him to be steadfast in the faith under every circumstance.

One day, however, he found himself in a difficult situation where he was called to stand alone, to be different from those around him who were unbelieving and worldly. Standing up for his faith on this occasion might even cause him to suffer persecution. What did this man do? Was he strong and courageous, as his fellow congregation members expected he would be? No. Sadly, he caved in to the pressure and denied his faith. What a miserable end to such a promising beginning!

Yet, that was not the end of this man's story, for God did not cast him off. Instead, the Lord forgave this man, restored him to his position of leadership in the church, and used him mightily for the sake of the Gospel. Yes, God is merciful to restore his fallen children. He continues to love us, forgive us, and renew us even when our faith fails to achieve its goal.

The man in this example was Peter. That's right, Simon Peter, Jesus' disciple. Next we shall see what this same man has to say about the goal of the Gospel.

Peter

Peter tips us off to his position immediately. He writes to God's elect, "chosen . . . by the sanctifying work of the Spirit for obedience to Jesus Christ and sprinkling by his blood" (1 Pet 1:2). This is a key verse! Peter tells us that sanctification is an integral part of salvation. It's not an addendum that we can take or leave as we see fit. The Lord has chosen us both to justify us by the "sprinkling by his blood" and to sanctify us for "obedience to Jesus Christ."

Peter wrote to Christians facing persecution, but his letter not only speaks about suffering as a Christian; it also stresses holiness.

> Therefore, prepare your minds for action; be self-controlled; set
> your hope fully on the grace to be given you when Jesus Christ

is revealed. As obedient children, do not conform to the evil desires you had when you lived in ignorance. But just as he who called you is holy, so be holy in all you do; for it is written: "Be holy, because I am holy (1 Pet 1:13–16).

Following the same plan God had for his people Israel, Peter calls Christians to be a people set apart. "Live your lives as strangers here in reverent fear" (1 Pet 1:17). Fear of whom? Certainly not of our persecutors, but of God. There is no contradiction between faith in God and fear of God. Even though we know God's love in Christ Jesus, we are to fear him, respect him, as sovereign Lord of all. We are to "do what is right and . . . not give way to fear" (1 Pet 3:6). Peter tells us to have courage saying, "Do not fear what they fear; do not be frightened" (1 Pet 3:14).

How may we gain this sort of courage that will enable us to be obedient to Christ in the face of opposition, even when it means that we must be distinctly different from unbelievers or stand alone? Peter supplies the answer: "But in your hearts set apart Christ as Lord" (1 Pet 3:15). Only as Christ reigns supreme in our hearts and lives, only as we fear him more than we fear anyone or anything else, will we be able to be a people set apart for him. In all of this, Peter speaks from experience, having learned the hard way.

And what is the purpose of this holy living and suffering for the sake of Christ? It is to "declare the praises of him who called you out of darkness into his wonderful light" (1 Pet 2:9). It is so that you might "always be prepared to give an answer to everyone who asks you to give the reason for the hope that you have" (1 Pet 3:15).

1 Peter 2 jumps back and forth between justification and sanctification. Christians love to quote 1 Pet 1:18–19 and verses 23–25. However, the context shows us that Peter is here using the Law to guide and the Gospel to motivate the obedience of those who have been redeemed. Note Peter's words:

As obedient children, do not conform to the evil desires you had when you lived in ignorance. But just as he who called you is holy, so be holy in all you do; for it is written: "Be holy, because I am holy."

Since you call on a Father who judges each man's work impartially, live your lives as strangers here in reverent fear. For you know that it was not with perishable things such as silver or gold that you were redeemed from the empty way of life handed down to you from your forefather, but with the precious blood of Christ, a lamb without blemish or defect. . . .

Now that you have purified yourselves by obeying the truth so that you have sincere love for your brothers, love one another deeply, from the heart. For you have been born again, not of perishable seed, but of imperishable, through the living and enduring word of God (1 Pet 1:14–19, 22–23).

Most often when we hear the admonition "be holy," we think that must be the Law used as a mirror to show us our sin, for we are not holy. But Peter shows us that the Law can rightly be used by believers as a guide and rule to lead us in the paths of holiness, even if we cannot follow that Law perfectly this side of heaven.

Spiritual Unemployment

When Chuck walked into his office that morning, nothing seemed unusual at all. He started into his workday with enthusiasm, just as he had for 18 years at the same company. It was only 9:30 in the morning, however, when the company president summoned him to his office. He was apologetic, saying the times were very difficult. The company had to consolidate its operations. Many, many people had to go. Chuck's hard work had been deeply appreciated. Nevertheless, the severance paycheck and the pink slip in Chuck's hand were very real.

As Chuck cleaned out his desk, he couldn't believe it was happening. The drive home seemed briefer than ever, knowing he would have to tell his wife the bad news. What would he do? Where could he go? "I'm 53 years old," Chuck thought. "How can I start over now?"

Chuck's wife, Miriam, was very supportive. As they ate lunch together, she tried to encourage Chuck in every way. He began his search for a new job that same afternoon. Days turned into weeks, however, with no sign of work. At first there were plenty of odd jobs around the house to keep him busy, but as the weeks wore on, Chuck grew increasingly depressed. He began to wonder whether he was worth anything to anyone. He felt unproductive and useless.

Unemployment can have devastating effects on a person's spirit. In his second letter, Peter deals with the issue of spiritual unemployment. Although we are saved by faith alone, Peter says there's more to being a Christian than having faith. Sometimes Christians have been reluctant to talk about adding anything to faith. Peter is not afraid to do so. Consider his words:

> For this very reason, make every effort to add to your faith goodness; and to goodness, knowledge; and to knowledge, self-control; and to self-control, perseverance; and to perseverance, godliness; and to godliness, brotherly kindness; and to brotherly kindness, love. For if you possess these qualities in increasing measure, they will keep you from being *ineffective and unproductive* in your knowledge of our Lord Jesus Christ. But if anyone does not have them, he is *nearsighted* and blind, and has forgotten that he has been cleansed from his past sins (2 Pet 1:5–9; emphasis ours).

When you are unemployed, you may feel like Chuck did: ineffective and unproductive. You may begin to have doubts about your worth as a person. Peter says the same thing can happen spiritually. You are spiritually unemployed when you fail to add the fruit of faith to faith itself. You are spiritually unemployed when you suffer from "Gospel myopia," nearsightedness that prevents you from seeing the goal of the Gospel as well as the Gospel itself.

When you are spiritually unemployed you may begin to have doubts about who you are and where you stand in relation to God. How may we overcome such doubts? Peter says,

> Therefore, my brothers, be all the more eager to make your calling and election sure. For if you do these things, you will never fall, and you will receive a rich welcome into the eternal kingdom of our Lord and Savior Jesus Christ (2 Pet 1:10–11).

When we are making progress in our sanctification, when we "possess these qualities in increasing measure," then we will have confidence about our calling and election.

It is God who calls, trains, equips, motivates, and employs us in his kingdom. This is his goal in redeeming us by grace through faith in Jesus Christ.

Hebrews

A trip to the National Pro Football Hall of Fame in Canton, Ohio, is an exciting treat for any football fan. There you can catch glimpses of the greatness of football heroes George Hallas, Vince Lombardi, Johnny Unitas, Bart Starr, Mike Ditka, O. J. Simpson, and hundreds more. The record of their accomplishments is displayed there to thrill the armchair quarterback and to motivate the budding star.

In many ways, Hebrews 11 is like the Football Hall of Fame. In order to understand what Hebrews says about faith and obedience, we need to focus on this chapter, which perhaps we should call "The Hall of Faith." In this great faith chapter the writer catalogs the *works* of those who believed. Why? To understand, we need to look at his definition of faith at the beginning of the chapter. He writes:

> Now faith is the substance of things hoped for, and the evidence of things not seen. . . . Through faith we understand that the worlds were formed by the word of God (Heb 11:1–3 KJV).

The substance of what God has created is evidence of his existence. God's real estate shows us that God is real. Similarly, the substance of our obedience is evidence of our faith in God. The reality of my obedience shows that my faith is real (Collins 1988, 2–3).

The Hebrews 11 catalog names saints like Abel, Enoch, Noah, Abraham, Isaac, Jacob, and Moses. Of them the writer states, "Therefore, God is not ashamed to be called their God" (Heb 11:16). The Lord was pleased to have them as his representatives on earth.

Sadly, this is not always the case. Paul had to warn his fellow Jews, "As it is written: 'God's name is blasphemed among the Gentiles because of you.' " (Rom 2:24). How sad it is to see the same thing happening in the secular media today as it portrays Christianity as a life of hypocrisy rather than a life of faith because of the unholiness of so many prominent Christians!

When God says he is not ashamed to be called our God, he is talking about how we represent his name among the nations. Heb 11:16 has to do with the mission aspect of the goal of the Gospel. Abraham and others represented God so well that he was not ashamed to be known as their God. Yet how often has God had to say, "Don't drag me into this," when believers acted contrary to His will? Hebrews tells us that "Both the one who makes men holy and those who are made holy are of the same family. So Jesus is not ashamed to call them brothers" (Heb 2:11). If we live out our faith in a life of holiness, Jesus will not have to be ashamed to call us his brothers and sisters.

Hebrews 11 concludes, "These were all commended for their faith, yet none of them received what had been promised. God had planned something better for us so that only together with us would they be made perfect" (Heb 11:39–40). That "something better" God has planned for us was the sacrifice of Christ on the cross for our sins and for the sins of the whole world, even the sins of those who had lived before that time. Obedience will never make you perfect. Only Christ will make you perfect.

Our works of faith need to be added to the catalog displayed here in the "Hall of Faith" of Hebrews 11. Then, together with those saints of old, we will be "made perfect" in a different sense by the "Author and Perfecter" of our faith. Then our faith—our trust in Christ's gift of perfect righteousness—will generate our response. Thus our faith will have reached its goal and become the obedience of faith. But remember that it is faith that first puts us into the Hall of Faith (Heb 11:40); our works follow from that faith.

John

Before we conclude our survey of the apostles' statements about obedience and sanctification, we must look at John's epistles. Do you remember Paul's "plaid" passages? Well, if Paul weaved justi-fication and sanctification, it seems that John has put them through a blender.

Try reading through the entire first epistle of John using the "plaid approach," marking Bible verses—red for salvation and green for sanctification. In John's letters you will often find it quite a chal-lenge to distinguish the Law from the Gospel, sanctification from salvation. For example,

> Dear friends, if our hearts do not condemn us, we have confidence
> before God and receive from him anything we ask, because we
> obey his commands and do what pleases him. And this is his

command: to believe in the name of his Son, Jesus Christ, and to
love one another as he commanded us. Those who obey his commands live in him, and he in them. And this is how we know that
he lives in us: We know it by the Spirit he gave us (1 Jn 3:21–24).

Could you clearly label each verse or phrase as either Law or
Gospel? If you are able to do so, when you have finished the entire
epistle, you will want to ask Martin Luther for a doctor's degree,
which he said should be awarded to anyone who can rightly separate
Law and Gospel. In his epistles John carefully blends the two to
enable us to achieve the goal of the Gospel.

Compared to John's epistle, James's treatment of faith and works
is a piece of cake. However, we don't complain about John, because
he frequently makes crystal clear Gospel statements, but we, with
our Gospel myopia, lift them out of context. So we fail to take
seriously what John teaches about the goal of the Gospel.

A key verse in John's first epistle is 1 Jn 2:4–5. "The man who
says, 'I know him,' but does not do what he commands is a liar, and
the truth is not in him. But if anyone obeys his word, God's love is
truly made complete in him." Once again we have that important
word *telos*, here translated *complete*. John is telling us that the love
which God has shown us in Christ reaches its goal when it enables
us to obey God's will. Too often we have been content to know that
God saved us because he loved us. That's certainly true, but that's
not all there is to it. We must also realize that he saved us because
he wants us to obey him. He wants us to be in an intimate relationship with him so that we may be guided by him, and we can't
be in relationship if we are at odds with him.

John says, "This is love for God: to obey his commands" (1 Jn
5:3). In his second epistle he says essentially the same thing. "And
this is love: that we walk in obedience to his commands" (2 Jn 6).
Faith is a necessary requirement for obedience, and obedience is
a necessary result of faith.[2] The two are completely intertwined. If
we are to be obedient, we must love God. John tells us, "We love
because he first loved us" (1 Jn 4:19). Until we know God's love in
Jesus Christ and trust in him, we cannot obey his will. Obedience
without faith is impossible, and faith without obedience cannot possibly be alive, as James says. Ultimately, obedience is love and love

90

is obedience, according to John's theology. The Gospel and its goal could never be more closely connected!

John also speaks of confidence regarding our calling, as Peter did in 2 Pet 1:10–11. John writes,

> We know we have come to know him if we obey his commands (1 Jn 2:3).

> Dear children, let us not love with words or tongue but with actions and in truth. This then is how we know that we belong to the truth, and how we set our hearts at rest in his presence whenever our hearts condemn us (1 Jn 3:18–20).

Do you want concrete evidence of your salvation? Look at your life. Are you obedient to Christ's command to love?

If so, you can be confident. Are you disobedient? Then you may well harbor some doubts and should examine your faith and life more carefully. To reassure ourselves about salvation, we can use the same evidence today as Christ will use on Judgment Day. When our faith and actions are working together, the Gospel is achieving its goal in our lives and we have nothing to fear. And what about those times when we truly desire to obey and still fail miserably? At such times where can we look? We look to the cross.

As we come to the close of our examination of the apostles' teaching on obedience, we may be tempted to ask ourselves, "How did all these fellows end up with the same unexpected theological bent?" They all think that obedience, mission, and glorifying God flow from the Gospel. Could it be the influence of Jesus, since the thread of his teaching seems to run through all their letters? Could it be the influence of God's Spirit, who prompted these men to take pen in hand and gave them the words to put down on paper? Shouldn't we expect the Spirit to be "hung up" on sanctification and obedience? After all, his first name is "Holy."

Digging Deeper

1. Make a list of ten of your favorite Bible passages, whether from the epistles, the gospels, or the Old Testament.
2. Classify each passage as either

    P = Promise of God, good news, Gospel, or

THE GOAL OF THE GOSPEL

C = Command of God, something we should do, Law.

How many passages did you choose in each category before you classified them?

3. Look up each of these Bible passages which you classified as a "P," or promise of God, and read them in their larger context. Are they closely connected to some aspect of the goal of the Gospel? Make a note of your findings.

4. Share the results of your study with other members of your Bible study group, if you are part of one. On the basis of your own study, decide if you are suffering from a case of "Gospel myopia." If yes, how serious is it?

_____ Don't have the disease.

_____ A mild case; I usually see the goal of the Gospel.

_____ A moderate case; I occasionally see the goal.

_____ A severe case; I only seem to see the Gospel itself, and miss the goal.

5. How have you felt in the past about the epistle of James? Did his emphasis on works bother you at all? How do you feel about it now, after reading about the apostles and obedience?

6. Read 2 Thess 1:11–12. What aspect of the goal of the Gospel is Paul emphasizing here? What do you think he means when he says "that the name of our Lord Jesus may be glorified in you, and you in him"? How can we glorify the name of Jesus? From whom alone can we receive glory?

7. How can Christians urge fellow believers to obey the will of God and perform good works, while also avoiding the danger of promoting works righteousness? What clues or techniques to help you do you find in the letters of the apostles?

8. How aware are the members of your church of the war we are engaged in against Satan and his evil forces? How ready for battle are the "troops" in your local congregation? How many "rebels" are there? What makes them rebels? How many "deserters" are there? What makes them deserters? How would you characterize your own readiness for combat? Read Eph 6:10–18 to find out how we can be prepared for the war.

9. Why is "just say no" insufficient to help people overcome the temptation to abuse drugs, alcohol, nicotine, sex, even food?

What does Paul share in Titus 2–3 that provides adequate strength and motivation?

10. Read Phil 2:5–11. Think of Jesus as a missionary. What are some of the things he was willing to give up to save us from our sins? What all did he have to adjust to? How did Jesus feel about himself? How did he feel about others? What were the results of his efforts for us? For himself? How can such an understanding of Jesus provide motivation for more of us to consider work as missionaries?

11. How would you rank yourself on Peter's scale of spiritual productivity? (See 2 Pet 1:5–9.) How much of each of the following have you added to your faith?

	Much	A little	Almost none
goodness	_____	_____	_____
knowledge	_____	_____	_____
self-control	_____	_____	_____
perseverance	_____	_____	_____
godliness	_____	_____	_____
brotherly kindness	_____	_____	_____
love	_____	_____	_____

Based on your evaluation would you consider yourself
_____ fully employed, working at full capacity
_____ working full-time but not always as productively as I should be
_____ only working part-time
_____ just doing an occasional odd job for the Lord
_____ unemployed, ineffective, and unproductive

12. Did you try the "plaid approach" with Titus 2–3? If not, please take time to do so now, making salvation phrases red and sanctification phrases green. When you have finished Titus 2–3, try the same thing in 1 John.

13. Compare your "plaid passages" of Paul and your colorized version of 1 John with the other members of your Bible study group, if you are part of one. How often did you agree about what should be red and what should be green? Did this approach help you realize why we must never separate the Gospel from its goal? Discuss your thoughts.

Notes

1. Have you ever considered our English expression "sinner/saint"? It is the opposite of the Latin *simil justus et peccator,* meaning "at the same time saint and sinner." Is it possible that by putting the word *sinner* first in English, we have allowed this phrase to become nothing more than an excuse for sin, saying, "Oh, yes, we are sinners, but that's okay because we have been declared saints through faith in Jesus Christ"? We have indeed been declared righteous by grace through faith, but this must never become an alibi for sin. Wouldn't it be better to view ourselves as *saint/sinners?* In phrasing it that way, we emphasize the fact that we are being transformed by God to live righteously (2 Cor 3:18), even though we cannot not do so perfectly because we are still sinners.

2. The necessity of good works is a debate that goes back to the time of the Reformation. The Lutheran confessions make it plain that, while good works are not necessary for salvation, evangelical Christians do not deny the necessity of good works or obedience on the part of the believer.

   "Good works should be done because God has commanded them and in order to exercise our faith, to give testimony, and to render thanks. For these reasons good works must necessarily be done" (Tappert 1959, 133).

   "Of course good works are necessary. We say that eternal life is promised to the justified, but those who walk according to the flesh can retain neither faith nor righteousness. We are justified for this very purpose, that being righteous, we might begin to do good works and obey God's Law" (Tappert 1959, 160).

5

Sanctiphobia

In chapters 1 to 4 we have seen that God has saved us so that we are enabled to obey his will, evangelize the world, and glorify his name. As we authors studied the Bible's teaching about obedience, we were alternately amazed and confused—amazed to see how important obedience is in God's plan, but confused because many of our traditional assumptions and practices were being called into question. We found ourselves asking questions like these: If this is true, then how are we to preach and teach? How are we to offer people the free gift of life in an evangelistic conversation if we are supposed to tell them that Christ wants everyone to take up his cross and follow him?

Realizing that similar concerns may be running through your mind, in this chapter we will share with you the practical and theological applications that we have had to hammer out on the anvil of our pastoral ministry experience. First, we will diagnose some maladies that appear in the Lord's church when his Gospel and its goal are not properly balanced and emphasized. Secondly, we will share some remedies that we hope will lead to teaching the whole counsel of God in a healthy manner. We do not pretend to have all the answers. This chapter simply reflects what the Spirit has taught us thus far through the Word.

A Balanced Spiritual Diet

Family devotions were a tradition at the Monroe home. Every evening after dinner Kevin Monroe would lead his family in songs, Scripture lessons, a devotional reading, discussion, and prayers. For years the Monroes had been using a devotional booklet which they appreciated for its comforting emphasis on God's mercy in Jesus Christ.

Then one evening after their family worship time, Kevin's wife,

Brenda, expressed a concern that had been growing in her heart.

"I'm not sure, but I think that we need a change of pace in our devotions."

"Oh, really?" Kevin said. "What do you have in mind?"

"I don't feel like I'm being challenged by these devotional readings. Almost every day they remind us once again that Jesus is our Savior and that our sins are forgiven through faith in him."

Kevin asked, "So what's wrong with that? It sounds good to me."

"It is good, Dear. We do need to be reminded constantly of those precious truths; but it seems that the readings rarely go beyond reminding us that we are saved. It's sort of like we are always being pointed back to square one in the Christian life but are not given much encouragement or guidance about all the steps that come after that."

"I've got an idea. Charlie, who attends the Community Church, uses a different booklet. I'll ask him for a copy, and we can try that for a while."

Charlie's devotional booklet was an instant success at the Monroes, because Kevin and Brenda appreciated its consistent challenge to put their Christian faith into practice. After a year, however, they grew tired of this booklet, too.

One day Kevin admitted, "You know, Brenda, I loved these messages at first; but lately, they've been leaving me burdened with their continual stress on all the things that I ought to be doing as a Christian. After a while, the weight just gets too heavy."

"You know, I've sensed the same thing. In fact, sometimes I miss our old booklet. I hunger for its comforting reminders that we are saved by grace, not by works."

"Hunger, huh?" Kevin mused. "Maybe our problem has been spiritual malnutrition."

"What do you mean? We feed on the word regularly at home and at church," his wife observed.

"Yes, we do; but is the diet balanced? There are four food groups aren't there? To stay healthy everyone needs regular intake of grains, meats, dairy products, plus fruits and veggies. Maybe it's the same with spiritual food. Perhaps we need both Gospel assurance and spiritual challenges in order to have a balanced Christian diet."

"I see," Brenda agreed. "First, we had the Gospel and hungered for themes on Christian living. Then we feasted on those themes

96

for a while; and now we are experiencing Gospel deficiency."

"That's a good way to put it."

"You know what we ought to do? In order to have a well-balanced spiritual diet, let's use them both."

That is just what they did, and the two devotional booklets proved to be more beneficial together than either had been separately.

Gospel Deficiency

The Monroes made an important discovery. The biblical doctrines of justification and sanctification are both treasures of God's grace, which he provides for our good. How we prize the good news that Jesus Christ died so that we might stand before the Holy God as justified, forgiven sinners! Like treasure stored in a jeweled chest, we love to gaze upon the riches that are ours through Christ our Savior.

On the other hand, the doctrine of sanctification is also a treasure of God's grace, which he provides for our good. We should be gazing regularly upon this fortune too, in order to be reminded how God, in his grace, equips and empowers us to live in this world as his saints, his justified ones, his ambassadors to a dying world.

He has given us both gifts, justification and sanctification, to cherish, believe, and put into practice in our lives. The failure to value either treasure brings negative results. If we fail to repeat the Gospel message and concentrate only on how we ought to live as Christians, we will suffer from Gospel deficiency, as Brenda termed it. It is as real as a vitamin deficiency, leaving individual Christians and the body of Christ weak, disheartened, and without much motivation.

Gospel deficiency is not the only danger, however. Just as easily we can fall into the opposite malady of fearing to challenge people to live courageously for their Lord. This disease we could call "sanctiphobia." Surprisingly enough, sanctiphobia often occurs when people are diligently striving to defend the Gospel against false teaching.

Both Gospel deficiency and sanctiphobia are common Christian sicknesses. Do you recognize either in your Christian setting? Consider the preaching and teaching content of your church leaders.

Consider the content of your own conversations about God's word. Do you detect signs of Gospel deficiency or sanctiphobia? Is there a healthy biblical balance between salvation and obedience? Are both justification and sanctification cherished as treasures from our loving God? Or does one of the two fail to receive its due emphasis?

Factors Contributing to Sanctiphobia

Sanctiphobia does not originate in a vacuum. Several false teachings have caused Christians to skirt around the subject of obedience. The Christian life is like hiking along a narrow ridge with dangerous chasms on both sides of the trail. Overreacting to any of these false teachings can cause us to fall off the trail on one side or the other. Let us briefly discuss the dangers along our Christian path that cause sanctiphobia.

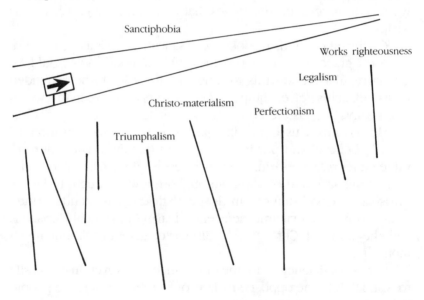

Works Righteousness

With his Bible in hand Bill LaSalle walked into the intensive care unit. After a briefing at the nurses' station, he concluded that this would likely be his last visit with Aunt Mildred this side of eternity. He was relieved, however, to find she was conscious in spite of the maze of plastic tubes. For a few minutes they discussed the many joyful times they had shared together over the years. Then, sensing the seriousness of the situation, Bill ventured to speak of spiritual matters.

"One memory that sticks in my mind, Aunt Mildred, is driving over to West Branch for church on Sunday mornings. I really liked Pastor Franklin."

"What a fine preacher he was! He was the one who got us to start going to church regularly."

"I remember him preaching about being ready to go to heaven." Bill cleared his throat and continued. "So what do you think, Aunt Mildred? Are you ready to go to heaven?"

"Oh, for sure, Bill. Don't you worry. After all, I've been a faithful church member now for twenty years. I was Sunday school superintendent for six years and served on the building committee when we added on the school. I've done my best all these years, and I'm sure the Lord will recognize that."

Like a blow to the solar plexus, her words left Bill breathless for a moment. He had assumed that she believed in the saving grace of the Triune God. He had come tonight only to reaffirm her faith in Christ. However, her list of self-confident works revealed a much more critical need. Silently, he debated with himself, "What should I do? I could pretend that she's just confused and hope that she really does know Christ as her Savior, in spite of what she just said. But if she doesn't, how can I remain silent? Here I thought all I had to do was read a couple Bible verses to her, but now I see I need to share the very basic meaning of Law and Gospel with her."

And so, with intensive care, Bill took Aunt Mildred's hand and began to share with her how to be truly ready to go to heaven.

Works righteousness is a deadly peril, because the eternal destiny of people is at stake. Church membership does not save; nor does a stockpile of good works, no matter how impressive they may appear in the eyes of humans. We must always take with utmost seriousness Paul's warning, "You who are trying to be justified by law have been alienated from Christ; you have fallen away from grace" (Gal 5:4). Therefore, the last thing Christians want to do is to teach or imply that people can be saved by their puny attempts to please God by their good works. However, the desire to avoid the works righteousness chasm sometimes causes Christians to avoid speaking clearly about sanctification and obedience. This is sanctiphobia.

In order to avoid either works righteousness or sanctiphobia, we must maintain a proper balance. On the one hand, we must oppose works righteousness. On the other hand, we dare not fail to teach the whole Bible, which makes clear that true, saving faith in Christ will result in righteous works (Jn 15:5; James 2:14–26).

Legalism

Some churches impose a long list of rules on their members. "Christians don't dance! Christians don't drink! Christians don't smoke! Christians don't listen to rock music of any kind!" Sometimes the list features dos as well as don'ts. "Christians must speak in tongues! Christians must tithe!" And the list goes on.

Although these churches may teach that salvation is by grace, their long list of rules often so overshadows the Gospel message that their members assume that their works play a significant role in their salvation. For example, one time I [Phil] received a phone call from a man who belonged to a Pentecostal church. He was deeply disturbed by a nagging fear that he would not be saved. When I inquired about his beliefs, he gave a very sincere confession of faith in Christ as his Savior.

Perplexed, I asked him, "Since you know and believe the Gospel, why do you fear that you might be lost?"

"Here is my problem, Pastor," he explained. "I have been taught that smoking is a grievous sin. I used to smoke profusely, but with God's help I have given up that habit almost entirely. However—and here is my anxiety—once in a while I fall to the urge to light a cigarette. Those few minutes that I smoke, I live in dread terror. For if Christ should return in that very moment, wouldn't I be lost forever?"

How dare people enslave Christian brothers and sisters with such legalistic burdens! I tried to share with him the freedom that we have in Christ—not a freedom to sin (Gal 5:13) but a freedom to live without fear of condemnation (1 Jn 4:18).

The worthy desire to escape legalism can lead to sanctiphobia. Noting the danger of legalism, we may mistakenly choose never to discuss the Law, the dos and don'ts that God actually does require of us. In order to avoid both legalism and sanctiphobia, we need a proper balance. On the one hand, we must oppose the elevation of human rules to divine status (Mt 15:6–9). We must oppose portraying Christianity as a list of laws to keep rather than as a Savior to trust as we live in our new-found freedom as redeemed sinners. On the other hand, we must allow God's Law to do its proper work among believers: (1) Showing us our sin as a mirror reveals our blemishes, so that we will daily repent and confess our sins; and (2) Showing us the path of God's will as a guide leads travelers, so that we may walk in righteousness.

Perfectionism

Perfectionism appears within Christian fellowships that teach a doctrine of holiness. Moral perfection, they claim, can be attained in this present life, because God has equipped and empowered us to rise above all temptation and sin. Thus, perfectionists cast aside the reality that Christians are sinner/saints, declaring that the sinner can be overcome and the saint can rule supreme, without fault.

Where do perfectionistic holiness people find the biblical rationale for their position? They do so by a selective use of the Scriptures. Texts such as Psalm 119 that encourage us to hunger and thirst for righteousness are viewed as overruling other verses that describe our weakness. They assume that the goal, the ideal, is a reality. Even more important, verses that speak of the Holy Spirit's work of empowering us for righteous living are interpreted as absolute promises of perfection in our dally lives. An example is 1 Jn 3:9, which reads, "No one who is born of God will continue to sin, because God's seed remains in him; he cannot go on sinning, because he has been born of God."

In response, we who disagree with perfectionism point out that John is talking about being delivered from *continuing* or *going on* in sin, rather than from never sinning again. The full deliverance from sin awaits us in heaven. If we take into account the whole counsel of God regarding sanctification, the sinner/saint model is the correct doctrinal conclusion. Perfectionism causes havoc when believers who think they can be perfect fall into sin. Their unrealistic

101

expectations can lead them to doubt their salvation and to question the power of God.

Once again, in trying to avoid perfectionism, it is easy to over-react and develop symptoms of sanctiphobia.

As we said before, to avoid both perfectionism and sanctiphobia, we need to maintain a proper balance, recognizing that Christians are going to be sinner/saints until their transfer to heaven. On the one hand, we dare never deny that God is morally perfect and desires perfection of us. We are God's saints. "Be holy, because I am holy" (1 Pet 1:16). And, praise God, he who calls us to holiness gives us his Holy Spirit. We cannot selectively omit these truths from our teaching. On the other hand, the Bible honestly describes the failures of saint after saint. "The spirit is willing, but the body is weak" (Mt 26:41). This is not a plausible excuse for continuing in sin. Rather, the passage calls for the realism of recognizing that, while God has *declared* us righteous because of Christ, we are not yet what we shall be, namely, sinless (1 Jn 3:2). Although we may not like having to live with the tension of being sinner/saints, the Scriptures and our own experiences show that we are just that for the present.

Christo-Materialism

Stan clicked the remote to turn on his favorite televangelist. Once in a while he would go to church with his wife, when she got around to it; but usually he was content to worship here before the electronic altar.

"God wants to bless you," emphasized the preacher with a thump of his Bible and a broad smile. "All you have to do is support our ministry as the Lord directs you, and he will cause the blessings of heaven to shower down upon you. There is no surer deal than this, my friends. The Lord calls you to obey. And when you do, he will not fail to bring to you and your family the health and security that you need."

"Sounds like good business to me," agreed Stan as he reached for his checkbook.

This is an example of the "Health and Wealth" message being proclaimed regularly both over the airwaves and in churches: "God's promises say thus. You perform your part of the bargain by obeying, and he will surely keep his end of the deal. It's a sure thing! You can't miss!" Christians from underdeveloped nations recognize this teaching for what it is—false doctrine. Only in America, which is so hung up on youthfulness and materialism, would health-and-wealth succeed at wedging its way into Christian preaching. We often shake a finger at Latin American churches because of Christo-paganism among their ranks. Meanwhile, here in North America, Christo-materialism is thriving, misleading folks like Stan, our television churchgoer. The health-and-wealth preachers claim that life will always be rosy for Christians. And if not, then the problem must lie with me: I failed to believe enough, or give enough, or pray hard enough. Notice how the focus ends up on me rather than on the Lord, where it belongs.

So, do we want to shun health-and-wealth doctrine? Like the plague! However, don't lurch too far out of harm's way, or you will step off the biblical path on the opposite side and wind up with sanctiphobia. In order to avoid both Christo-materialism and sanctiphobia, what do we need? You guessed it: a proper balance of biblical truths. On the one hand, God does promise that blessings will result from obedience. The book of Proverbs states this truth in hundreds of different ways. We have already noted that all God's commands are latent promises, because in them God implies that matters will turn out well for us if we do his will. These truths should never be ignored.

On the other hand, we dare not consider God's commands and promises as a deal or a contract which obligates him to keep us happy and comfortable all the time. The life of faith is not that simple. "We must go through many hardships to enter the kingdom of God" (Acts 14:22), Paul and Barnabas in all honesty told new Christians. Yes, some believers accomplish great things by faith, as Hebrews 11 chronicles; but the same chapter reports that others endured torture, floggings, imprisonment, and other mistreatment (Heb 11:35–38). If you wish to wrestle further with this topic, we recommend Edith Schaeffer's book, *Affliction*, and Philip Yancey's *Where Is God When It Hurts?* These books become most meaningful when we keep in mind the basic biblical teaching about our justification as a gift of God that now works itself out in our lives, though incompletely.

Triumphalism

Triumphalism is unfounded optimism and pride concerning success in Christian life and mission. In a way, triumphalism resembles perfectionism and health-and-wealth teaching, but applied on a group level rather than an individual level: "If we Christians all become the kind of people God wants us to be, then this will be nearly heaven on earth." A prevalent contemporary example of triumphalism appears in flag-waving civil religion: "If America would return to its religious roots and live righteously, then our nation will regain its former greatness and stature." Christians who believe in the millennium, an alleged thousand-year earthly reign of Christ, also tend to speak in triumphalistic terms.

So what is the problem with triumphalism? Well, what happens when the promised triumph does not materialize? For example, a group of missionaries taught their converts pretribulation millennialism. This is the belief that before the great tribulation of the end times, the Lord will remove believers from the world scene so that they will not be harmed. Years later, a fierce wave of persecution wracked that country, and many converts rejected the Savior. Why? Because they had been taught that they would be delivered from tribulation. Since being a Christian involved suffering after all, they concluded that the missionaries had been wrong about freedom from persecution and were probably equally mistaken about freedom from sin and death through faith in Christ. In other words, triumphalistic teaching caused them to question and reject the validity of the Gospel itself.

So you can see why triumphalism deserves not to be touched with the proverbial ten-foot pole. Don't make the pole any longer, though, or you might fall off the other side of the Christian walk into sanctiphobia. Just use the pole to balance between both extremes.

On the one hand, we should recognize that the optimism of triumphalism builds on a shaky *if*: If we would just get our act together, *if* you use these methods, then you will surely succeed. The *ifs* are like arrows that point to us rather than to God. Every Christian enterprise, be it personal holiness or national revival, will fail to some degree whenever its success depends on our limited human strength.

On the other hand, we dare not overlook that God's goal is triumph.[1] Christ is the one who revealed to John the triumph of "a great multitude that no one could count, from every nation, tribe, people and language, standing before the throne and in front of the Lamb" (Rev 7:9). This is not triumphalism but Triumph!

The Perils of Sanctiphobia

We have just reviewed several unhealthy teachings: works righteousness, legalism, perfectionism, Christo-materialism, and triumphalism. Entire volumes have been written about each of these dangerous teachings.[2] Unfortunately, the cure for one can lead to the opposite danger. We have called that other disease sanctiphobia. Now we need to place this virus under the microscope in order to gain a clearer understanding of what ills sanctiphobia can bring to God's people. As you squint through the lens, ask yourself, "Do I see problems caused by sanctiphobia in my own life or in my church?"

Treatment of Sin Rather Than Prevention

The constitution committee at Hope Chapel devoted an entire evening to the article concerning church discipline and excommunication. After wrestling for four grueling hours trying to put Mt 18:15–18 into practice in the 20th century, all committee members went home exhausted.

The next week Doctor O'Neil, one of the committee members, observed, "I've been thinking about church discipline all week. In the field of medicine we have stressed the treatment of diseases above preventing them. That is, until recent times. Now we are just starting to realize that prevention is just as necessary—perhaps more so."

"You mean something like 'An ounce of prevention is worth a pound of cure'?" offered Red Walsh, the chairman.

"Precisely," Dr. O'Neil affirmed. "And I am afraid we are making a similar mistake in our church."

"How's that?"

"We wracked our brains last week to compose two pages spelling out church discipline, which is like treating the disease of sin.

105

But think about this: Our constitution contains only a few passing statements about prevention, how to help our fellow believers from falling into sin and losing their faith."

Taking the doctor's words to heart, the committee discussed the matter further. They decided to add to the article on membership a list of biblical guidelines to maintain spiritual health.

The moral of the story is this: If a church is not teaching sanctification properly, it will wind up mostly treating extreme cases (divorce, child abuse, rebellious children, etc.). And often it fails to do even that, thus leaving Christians totally ravaged by their disobedient behavior and rejection of the Gospel. Or, to use another metaphor, rather than preventing fires by preaching the goal of the Gospel, they only put out the flames after people have been severely burned. This is one of the undesirable results of sanctiphobia. The people of God deserve better treatment than this.

Idolatry

When the goal of the Gospel is given little air time in the church, members may conclude that God is only playing around when he says, "Be holy." This results in a form of idolatry. Not that people build a physical idol, but they fabricate in their mind a god who is a twisted caricature of the Holy Trinity. Here is the god that the devil dupes sanctiphobics to trust in:

1. A Father who does not care if we ever learn the joy of obedience and who is unable to enforce his will. "Our marshmallow Father, who must let us enter heaven whether we're repentant or not."
2. A Son who died to give us a license to sin and who does not care if his disciples ever follow him to the ends of the earth. "We believe in Jesus Christ, his only Son, our servant."
3. A Holy Spirit who only comforts and coddles us in our mutinous behavior and who never exhorts us to higher ideals nor empowers us to bear his fruit. "The fruit of the Spirit is selfishness, pleasure-seeking, complacency, apathy, self-gratification, envy, pettiness, harshness, faithlessness, and lethargy—all with a well-polished veneer of hypocrisy."

This is not the Triune God of the Bible. Worshiping the Baal of sanctiphobia poisons the Christian faith as much as any idolatry.

"Those who make them [idols] will be like them, and so will all who trust in them" (Ps 115:8).

Cheap Grace

Now we turn to the most crucial danger of sanctiphobia: Souls for whom Christ died can be lost eternally. The Gospel is always a healing treasure. The Lord gives it to us to save us and to motivate and empower us to glorify him in all we do. However, we must avoid administering the Gospel improperly. Constantly preaching the Gospel isolated from the goals of obedience, of mission, and of glorifying the Lord eventually can anesthetize believers rather than assure them of salvation. People who have been lulled to sleep because they have not also heard the goal of the Gospel may become so complacent that they could lose their faith and be condemned.

We are not talking mere theory. It has happened time and again. In 1937 a young German Lutheran pastor recognized sanctiphobia in the church of his day. Dietrich Bonhoeffer, in his classic *The Cost of Discipleship*, dubbed the malady as "cheap grace." Here is the context in which this term first appeared.

> The grace he [Martin Luther] had received was costly grace. It was grace, for it was like water on parched ground, comfort in tribulation, freedom from the bondage of a self-chosen way, and forgiveness for all his sins. And it was costly, for, so far from exempting him from good works, it meant that he must take the call to discipleship more seriously than ever before. It was grace because it cost so much, and it cost so much because it was grace.

> When he spoke of grace, Luther always implied as corollary that it cost him his own life, the life which was now for the first time subjected to the absolute obedience of Christ. Only so could he speak of grace. Luther had said that grace alone can save; his followers took up his doctrine and repeated it word for word. But they left out its invariable corollary, the obligation of discipleship.... Justification of the sinner in the world degenerated into the justification of sin and the world. Costly grace was turned into cheap grace without discipleship (Bonhoeffer 1963, 52–53).

These words represent only the beginning of Bonhoeffer's attempt to remove surgically the cancer which had eaten to the very marrow of Christendom in Germany. No doubt his cutting words roused many cries of "heresy" and "false doctrine" from his critics. (Some readers of this volume may do the same.) If we read *The Cost of Discipleship*, we may find ourselves saying, "Perhaps you went too far there, Dietrich. Haven't you overstated your case?" And then we recall Nazi Germany and the tragedies that still awaited the world when Bonhoeffer penned these lines. In that setting Bonhoeffer, a Jeremiah-like prophet, attempted to arouse the sleeping giant church in Germany before sanctiphobia and cheap grace could grow to epidemic proportions. The epidemic spread in spite of his warnings, just as it had earlier destroyed the faithless and disobedient audience of Jeremiah.

Sanctiphobia leads to cheap grace, and those with a cheap-grace mentality are highly prone to drift into sin and eventually fall from being justified by Christ's costly grace. Satan is insidious. To trap people in hell he will do anything, even deceiving us to cut off the Gospel from its goal (James 1:21–22).

This is the first eternally disastrous result of sanctiphobia. There is a second.

Mission Sleeping Sickness

Churches that fail to emphasize obedience, mission, and glorifying God develop mission sleeping sickness. Jesus called us from darkness to be a light set on a hill; and when we do not project his light, many perish in the darkness. Meanwhile Satan rejoices.

German mission professor Georg F. Vicedom detected a close relationship between cheap grace and the failure to have a compassionate heart for the lost world. Speaking of the responsibility of the clergy, he observed,

> When the [pastoral] office merely endeavors to edify the congregation and to achieve the salvation of individual members, it is questionable whether the goal of mission is attained, because this does not provide the members with a chance to find joy in their faith through service and sacrifice. When opportunity for obedience and service is missing, the living stream of the Word cannot flow. This is often the reason why the individual members themselves no longer treasure the Word (Vicedom 1965, 91).

Preaching a Gospel cut off from its biblical goal turns preachers into anesthesiologists, lulling to sleep the giant that ought to be rising for war. In recent times no one has enunciated this thought more forcefully than the musician Keith Green in his song "Asleep in the Light." We regret we cannot play the recording for you to hear the compassionate and intense lyrics.

> Do you see, do you see
> All the people sinking down
> Don't you care, don't you care
> Are you going to let them drown
> How can you be so numb
> Not to care if they come
> You close your eyes
> And pretend the job's done . . . .
>
> Open up, open up
> And give yourself away
> You see the need, you hear the cries
> So how can you delay
> God's calling and you're the one
> But like Jonah you run
> He's told you to speak
> But you keep holding it in
> Oh can't you see it's such sin
>
> The world is sleeping in the dark
> That the church just can't fight
> 'Cause it's asleep in the light
> How can you be so dead
> When you've been so well fed
> Jesus rose from the grave
> And you, you can't even get out of bed . . . .
> (Green 1978)

In chapter 3 we referred to Gospel myopia, the tendency to see only Gospel verses in the Scripture and to overlook the texts regarding the goal of the Gospel. Mission sleeping sickness is simply an advanced stage of Gospel myopia. The church that cannot see beyond its own needs or feel compassion beyond its own membership truly is asleep in the light. Without intervention, that church

109

will let the rest of the world go to hell without opening an eye as it snoozes in the pew.

This all too common occurrence provides further tragic evidence of Satan's wiles. To trap the nations in hell, he will do anything, even deceiving us to cut off the Gospel from its goal. And while the church sleeps in the light, it never discovers the joys that the Almighty has waiting for it: the joy of obeying the Lord's good commands; the joy of leading all nations to Christ; and the joy of glorifying God before the troubled citizens of the world.

What God Has Joined Together

Lutheran theology emphasizes the need to separate and distinguish between justification (the Gospel) and sanctification (the goal of the Gospel). This is a crucial skill, for it helps us avert dangers such as works righteousness and perfectionism. However, in the previous four chapters we learned that the Bible not only teaches the Gospel and the goal of the Gospel but also constantly unites the two, intertwines, and associates them. And miraculously, the Scriptures do this without mingling, mixing, or confusing them. Justification and sanctification remain distinct and unique, even though they are joined together. For theological purposes, at times we need to distinguish between them; but in the final analysis, "What God has joined together let man not separate."[3]

Since God has joined the Gospel and its goal, we need not ask *whether* to join them but only *how* we can join them properly and accurately. Unfortunately, sometimes we disconnect justification and sanctification, treating them as though they were opponents rather than sisters. We attempt to store them in two hermetically sealed containers, as though they were volatile materials that will explode upon contact. We fail to see that God intends them to be volatile— his power for salvation (Rom 1:16) and the power from on high that makes us his witnesses to the ends of the earth (Lk 24:49; Acts 1:8). Rather than separating these explosive substances, God longs for us to unite them. We will begin to describe this skill in the remainder of this chapter.

110

Preaching Like the Apostles

While studying at the seminary, we authors learned to use the book of Acts as a textbook on preaching. We carefully read and studied the sermons of the apostles in Acts to discover key principles for preaching the Gospel. Looking back, we now realize this was an incomplete method. Yes, the sermons in Acts are useful examples for preaching evangelistically to non-Christians. Unfortunately, they are poor examples for Sunday-after-Sunday preaching to a predominantly Christian audience. Where do we find the apostles preaching to a Christian audience? In the epistles!

In their letters, the apostles continually make use of the Gospel to motivate and equip believers for obedience to the will of God. They lead believers to the goal of the Gospel by proclaiming clearly God's will for their lives. They exhort and encourage God's people to obedience, while at the same time clearly proclaiming the grace of God in Christ Jesus as the basis for our obedience, its motivation, and empowerment.

Law-Gospel-Law-Gospel

Often pastors are trained to believe that if they preach Law and Gospel faithfully, everything else will take care of itself. Sermons that teach first Law and then Gospel are excellent when the goal is to lead to faith or to encourage continued faith among those who already believe. However, the preacher who always stops after preaching Law and Gospel is overlooking the goal of the Gospel. His audience rarely is exposed to the Bible's teaching about obedience, mission, and glorifying God. Though Law-Gospel preaching is correct, it is incomplete. With a strict Law-Gospel diet, church members will tend to experience stunted spiritual growth. The sensitive believers among them become weary of always relearning the elementary teachings about Christ and never going on to maturity (Heb 6:1). Contrary to common belief, preaching Law and Gospel does not cause everything else to take care of itself.

Our study of obedience in chapters 1 to 4 reveals that there is a more appropriate and biblical way to preach and teach God's Word to a Christian audience. We authors call it the Law-Gospel-Law-Gospel method. Before describing it, we hasten to add that it applies not only to preachers but also to teachers, youth counselors, parents, elders, and, in short, to all Christians. Therefore, in our description of the Law-Gospel-Law-Gospel model, we will use the broad term "proclaimer."

1. The proclaimer of the Word should teach God's Law so that it functions like a mirror—revealing our sin, condemning us, and calling us to repent.
2. The proclaimer of God's Gospel should share Christ's saving work, calling us to trust in him alone and never turn from him.

   Thus far, the formula is exactly the same as Law-Gospel preaching, but it does not end here.

3. Next, the proclaimer should speak God's commands as our guide for Christian living, showing us the obedience and mission commitment which our Savior seeks from us, so that God may be glorified. Some preachers do go beyond Law-Gospel preaching to this point, but it is still not sufficient. Why? Because the final stress falls upon the Law, which points us in the right direction but cannot transmit God's energy that alone enables us to carry out his will. Thus, listeners often wind up feeling guilty, powerless, and frustrated.
4. Finally, the proclaimer must share the good news a second time, motivating and empowering Christians to strive toward the goal of the Gospel. Motivation comes from the cross and the empty tomb. All our obedience, mission activity, and glorifying of God are to be done purely out of thanks and praise for what God has already done for us in Jesus Christ. We strive to attain the goal of the Gospel, not in order to be saved, but because God already has saved us. Hallelujah! In trying to obey and please God, we constantly need to be pointed to the Holy Spirit as the source of the power to obey. By our own power, we have no hope of doing our Lord's will, but because the Spirit dwells within, we have a source of energy that will never fail us as long as we trust in him. Furthermore, the Bible teaches that in baptism God puts to death our sinful nature and brings to life a new nature which can obey the Lord. The prospect of "being transformed into his likeness with ever-increasing glory" (2 Cor 3:18) must always be held before the people of God as a *process* that is continually possible, *because* the Holy Spirit energizes us for holy living.

This is the Law-Gospel-Law-Gospel method of preaching, teaching, and counseling believers. Notice where the emphasis ends: on the Lord, who alone can lead us to holy living. On occasion the situation may dictate a different approach; but in general none of these four points should be left on the cutting room floor. Take a look at the messages of the apostles in their letters, and you will see this pattern recurring. Do you remember when we said that Paul wove together the Gospel and the goal of the Gospel? That is Law-Gospel-Law-Gospel teaching. Remember when we said that John seemed to put the Gospel and its goal through a blender? That is Law-Gospel-Law-Gospel preaching. Remember Jesus, the church consultant, speaking to the seven churches in Revelation 2–3? His words are Law-Gospel-Law-Gospel preaching. They provide a model for teaching the whole counsel of God, including both salvation and obedience. This is the way to join justification and sanctification so that the Gospel and its goal are not "put asunder."

Comfort and Challenge

The Law-Gospel-Law-Gospel method may not appeal to some readers who assume that the pastor's primary role is to comfort the flock. However, does the Christian pastor not also have a responsibility to challenge believers to courageous obedience in behalf of a dying world?

The answer to this question is found in the Greek word *parakaleō*, which has a double meaning. *Parakaleō* means both to comfort and also to challenge.[4] Using a noun form of *parakaleō*, Jesus refers to the Holy Spirit in Jn 14:16, 26; 15:26; and 16:7, as the *Paraklesis*. Both the King James Version and the Living Bible translate this title *the Comforter,* inviting generations of Christians to visualize the Holy Spirit only as one who comforts with the Gospel, but *not* also as one who challenges us to strive toward the goal of the Gospel. The Revised Standard Version and the New International Version provide us a more balanced view, translating the title *the Counselor.* This term more appropriately conveys the full sense of the Greek term, because a counselor both comforts and challenges, depending upon the needs of the one being counseled.

What does the title *Counselor* have to do with Law-Gospel-Law-Gospel preaching? Since the Holy Spirit, who calls pastors to shepherd the flock (Acts 20:28), both comforts and challenges Christians, it is logical to conclude that pastors should likewise both comfort and challenge the church. The example of the apostles affirms this conclusion. Repeatedly the apostles use the verb *parakaleō* to urge and encourage Christians to godly living: "These, then, are the things you should teach. Encourage (*parakaleō*) and rebuke with all authority" (Titus 2:15). Note that this key word is here translated as *encourage,* which dovetails well with the observation in chapter 2 that in the Scriptures courage means faith to obey God's will. (See also Acts 14:22; Rom 12:1, 8; 2 Cor 9:5; 1 Thess 2:11–12; 4:1; 5:14; 2 Thess 3:12; 1 Tim 2:1; 2 Tim 4:2, 6:2; Titus 1:9; 2:6; Heb 3:13; 10:25; 1 Pet 5:1, 12; and Jude 3).

We also find examples of the dual role of comforting and challenging in the secular world. A doctor must know when to tell a patient to rest and when to exercise. A nation's president should know when to soothe his people in times of trouble and when to spur them to confront a national crisis. Or picture Mike Ditka, the prototype football coach. When a player is injured or discouraged or meeting with defeat even though he is doing his best, Mike senses this is the time to hold that athlete's hand, to comfort him with a soft word. But when a player is unwilling to play with pain or not giving a hundred percent, Iron Mike knows what to do. It's time to kick butt with piercing words or multiple wind sprints or whatever he believes will arouse that player to compete at his full potential.

Every pastor needs to learn when to comfort with the Gospel. Every pastor needs to learn when to challenge believers to take up the cross of the goal of the Gospel. The same goes for every Christian whom God calls to exercise authority as parents, teachers, youth counselors, Bible study leaders, and so forth.

Even though we have cited a tough guy like Mike Ditka to illustrate our point, ultimately people like him are not our model. Our models are the apostles and the prophets. Our model par excellence is Jesus Christ, who took the form of a servant and humbled himself and became obedient to death (Phil 2:7–8). We can only properly teach God's people in a Law-Gospel-Law-Gospel manner when we exercise our authority with the understanding that "whoever wants to be great among you must be your servant, and whoever wants to be first must be slave of all" (Mk 10:43–44).

Tools to Build Something Beautiful

Pastor Simpson had delivered a challenging Law-Gospel-Law-Gospel sermon that morning. As he was shaking people's hands at the end of the service, a young man introduced himself as Craig Taylor, asking if he could have a word with the minister in private. When everyone had left, the pastor invited Craig into his office.

"You don't know me, Pastor; but I was confirmed in this church ten years ago."

"Well, tell me what has happened since then," Pastor Simpson asked with an inviting smile.

Craig told a long story that included taking the Gospel for granted, wandering into ungodly behavior, dropping out of church, moving away, a troubled marriage ending in divorce, and recently moving back into the area.

"Pastor, I returned here this morning because I remembered that I had heard the truth here. Even though you've never met me before, your sermon seemed to be aimed right at me. Wow, it hit me right between the eyes."

"I'm sorry if I was too harsh."

"Don't apologize. It was just the kind of preaching I could have used all these years that I have wandered from the Lord. This morning the Holy Spirit has brought me back home in more ways than one. I want to reaffirm my faith in Christ, a faith which I allowed to die."

"Praise God for that, Craig."

"Your sermon helped me see that there is more to being a Christian than simply getting confirmed."

"You aren't the only one who has misunderstood that, Craig."

"I suppose not. Still it was a big mistake. Back when I was a teenager, I trusted in Christ as my Savior. I knew and believed Jn 3:16. But I thought there was nothing more to it. Why was I so dumb?"

"Your problem was that you thought that salvation was a treasure chest to be hoarded rather than a tool box to be put to use."

"Huh? What do you mean?"

"Every Bible story you heard, every prayer learned, and Bible verse memorized wasn't just something for you to use for yourself but to share with others. They were all tools placed into your hands

115

for you to use. In Sunday school and confirmation class you were taught how to use your tools so that you could build a life of obedience that would glorify God before the nations."

"Wow! I never thought of it that way," Craig marveled.

Pastor Simpson continued, "The problem is that just when you learned how to use the tools well enough to become an apprentice, you closed the box and never put them to use."

"You're right, Pastor. How I regret my failure to serve my Savior and the world in need of his love. But isn't the Lord willing to receive me back?"

"He surely is, Craig. The blood of Jesus Christ covers all sins, even yours."

"With that certainty, I can start all over again, can't I?"

"Yes, Craig. He is the Lord of new beginnings."

"Good! Then I have a request to make of you, Pastor."

"What's that?"

"I don't want to repeat the mistake of doing nothing with my faith. Will you teach me how to use the tools of salvation to build something beautiful of my life, something that will bring glory to my Savior?"

"There is nothing I'd rather do. Let's start by looking at three verses in Ephesians 2." The minister opened his Bible and asked Craig to read Eph 2:8–9.

" 'For it is by grace you have been saved, through faith—and this not from yourselves, it is the gift of God—not by works, so that no one can boast.' Say, I remember those verses. I'm saved by God's undeserved love, not by anything I could do. What a relief!"

"That's right, Craig. Now read verse ten."

"Okay. 'For we are God's workmanship, created in Christ Jesus to do good works, which God prepared in advance for us to do.' I don't recall ever reading this verse before."

"What does it say to you?" Pastor Simpson prodded.

"Hmmm," he thought a moment. "It appears to mean that God will make a new start with me. He has created faith in my heart so that I might do lots of good things."

"That's right, Craig. He even has all those good works planned out for you to do. So, Craig, what do you suppose some of those good things might be? Or let me put it another way. What do you think the Lord might want to build out of your life?"

116

With a grin of amazement and joy, Craig began to dream out loud.

Digging Deeper

1. Thus far, does this book have you cheering or questioning the ideas which are presented?
2. The authors suggest that a balanced spiritual diet will include both the Gospel and the goal of the Gospel. How balanced is the diet offered in your church? In your home? In your personal devotions? In other settings?
3. Describe your personal understanding of the following teachings: works righteousness, legalism, perfectionism, Christo-materialism, and triumphalism.
4. Give examples how sanctiphobia might arise from an overreaction to works righteousness, legalism, perfectionism, Christo-materialism, and triumphalism.
5. Discuss the balance of doctrines that is necessary to avoid the problems mentioned in questions 3 and 4 and the problem of sanctiphobia. In your opinion, on which side are the greater dangers?
6. Dr. Eugene Bunkowske has observed, "We are the means of the means of grace." What do you understand him to be saying? Do you agree or disagree. (See note 1 of this chapter.)
7. Recall the story of the constitution committee and the doctor's comments about prevention of disease and treatment of disease. What does your congregation do to prevent disobedient behavior from getting out of hand? What does your church do to treat the problem of sin when it gets out of control?
8. Review the caricature of the Trinity that may result from a failure to teach the goal of the Gospel. Is this an overstatement by the authors? Have you ever known anyone with such a view of God?
9. Differentiate between what Dietrich Bonhoeffer means by costly grace and cheap grace.
10. C. F. W. Walther, a prominent theologian of the 19th century, authored a book called *The Proper Distinction Between Law and Gospel*. In your opinion, does the authors' Law-Gospel-Law-Gospel method properly distinguish between Law and Gospel?
11. What do you think of the proposal that pastors and other Chris-

THE GOAL OF THE GOSPEL

tians must both comfort with the Gospel and challenge with the goal of the Gospel?

12. Think back to the Christian instruction you received as a teenager. Did the materials teach the Gospel and the goal of the Gospel? Did you view the truths you learned as a treasure to be hoarded or as tools to be used for building something to glorify your Savior?

13. Read Eph 2:8–10. What do you think the Lord might want to build out of your life? What are the good works he has created you to do?

Notes

1. Some readers may feel that we are placing too great an emphasis on the human element in world evangelization. "God can accomplish his purposes for mankind without our efforts, can't he?" they ask. The answer is yes and no. Yes, he will succeed even if some of us fail to obey and to lift high the cross of Christ. God will prevail without the participation of individual people. On the other hand, God will certainly use some human beings to evangelize the earth, because in his wisdom he has decided to save others by means of our witness. The Lord has no "Plan B," no other strategy to reach the nations apart from human involvement. Lutherans use the term "means of grace" collectively for the saving Word and the sacraments of Baptism and Holy Communion. Dr. Eugene Bunkowske accurately balances the human and divine elements of the Great Commission with this observation: "God uses us as his means for getting the means of grace to the lost. Therefore, we are the means of the means of grace."

2. In recent years several Evangelical theologians have been debating an issue called "Lordship Salvation," which bears some resemblance to what we call the goal of the Gospel. Noteworthy titles in this debate are: *The Gospel According to Jesus* by John F. MacArthur, Jr.; *Absolutely Free!* by Zane C. Hodges; and *So Great Salvation* by Charles C. Ryrie. In our reading of these books, we find that all three of the authors run into problems in understanding the goal of the Gospel because they espouse eternal security (the teaching that once one believes, one cannot fall from faith). This is not the place to debate this point. We are merely warning readers who believe in eternal security that, in our opinion, only theology that steers clear of this error will be able to preach and teach the goal of the Gospel with accuracy.

3. See Koeberle 1964, 89–90.

4. Greek lexicons usually say that the second meaning of *parakaleō* is *to exhort* or *to admonish*. However, exhort and admonish are no longer part of the typical person's conversational vocabulary. Therefore, we have opted for the contemporary synonym *to challenge*. The authors recognize that other verbs, such as *noutheteō*, also illustrate that pastors and other Christian leaders must do more than comfort.

Part II

The Goal of the Gospel in Romans

6

The Gospel Chain
Romans 1:1–7

In part I we showed that obedience, outreach to the nations, and the glory of God are emphasized in Holy Scripture from Genesis to Revelation. In part II we will focus on one book of the Bible that develops these themes in great detail, Paul's letter to the Romans.

Most Bible scholars assume that the major theme of Romans is justification by grace through faith, although a few include sanctification as another major theme. However, we here propose a different view of the thematic structure of Romans. We believe that, when Paul composed Romans, he intended to develop not one or two but five topics, namely, Scripture, justification, sanctification, mission, and glory. In this chapter we will explain why we hold this unusual position.[1]

By the way, this chapter may be more difficult to follow than the others. It is like a yellow diamond-shaped sign announcing, "Slow—Construction Zone." Accordingly, you will have to tap your brakes and lower your speed. You may experience some bumps and jolts as we propose a new perspective on Romans. Sorry about the delay and the inconvenience, but that is how it is when the road is being widened to carry more traffic. By the time we finish exploring Romans, you will see that Paul intended it to be a five-lane expressway headed for the ends of the earth.

Traditional Assumptions

Most scholars hold in common certain traditional assumptions regarding the occasion, purpose, and theme of Paul's letter.

1. Occasion. Paul's words in Rom 15: 23–24 make it easy to identify the occasion that prompted him to write:

THE GOAL OF THE GOSPEL

But now that there is no more place for me to work in these regions, and since I have been longing for many years to see you, I plan to visit you when I go to Spain. I hope to visit you while passing through and to have you assist me on my journey there, after I have enjoyed your company for a little while.

For over a decade Paul had spearheaded pioneer mission work in present day Turkey (Asia Minor), Greece, and north into Albania and Yugoslavia (Illyricum). His base of operations had been the church in Antioch, Syria, the Gentile church where the believers had first been called "Christians" (Acts 11:26). Having completed his work in the northeastern quadrant of the Mediterranean Sea, the great missionary now had his Gospel sights set on the distant land of Spain. It would be nearly impossible for Antioch, two thousand miles from Spain, to remain his base congregation. His hope was that the church in Rome would assume this role. The phrase "assist me on my journey" implied multifaceted support: concern, prayer, goods, funds, guides, contacts, and even the appointment of Roman Christians to serve on Paul's missionary team. Bible scholars are united in the opinion that this is the occasion of Paul's letter. We, the authors, agree with this traditional viewpoint.

2. Purpose. Bible scholars usually state that since Paul was unknown in Rome, his purpose for writing was to present his doctrines systematically to the Romans so that they would recognize his teachings to be orthodox and thus be willing to support him and his mission endeavors. However, Paul was not an unknown quantity in Rome. A reading of the greetings in Romans 16 reveals that he was personally acquainted with at least 28 members of the church. Although this letter certainly is Paul's most developed discussion of Christian doctrine, we believe that the traditional assumption is incomplete. When he wrote, Paul had something more in mind than merely enunciating his teachings.

3. Theme. Nearly all Bible experts conclude that the theme of Romans is justification by grace through faith, citing Rom 1:16–17. As previously stated, the present authors believe the theme of Romans is much broader than this and that it includes Scripture, justification, sanctification, mission, and glory. This theory is totally consistent with the personality and vision of Paul the

missionary. William Barclay aptly describes what made Paul tick:

> He never saw a ship at anchor but he wished to board her and to carry the message of the good news to the men across the sea. He never saw a range of mountains, blue in the distance, but he wished to cross them, and to bring the story of the Cross to the men who had never heard it (Barclay 1957, xxiii–xxiv).

Here is a man who, since his conversion, had dedicated his life to carrying the good news to city after city. Now he focussed his eyes on Spain, seeking the support and participation of the Romans. In light of Paul's missionary mindset, how strange it is to assume that he would fail to link his teaching on justification to his concern for a lost world.

Paul is just like the missionaries who speak at our churches today, seeking our support and participation. What do our modern missionaries say? Do they merely recite Jn 3:16 and quote from the Creed to prove their orthodoxy? No, they also demonstrate the great need of the lost and exhort us to play an active, personal part in God's mission.

One Bible scholar used an interesting word picture to describe Paul's most highly regarded epistle:

> Romans, among the epistles of the New Testament, stands out like an imposing cathedral. Its symmetry of form, its logically developed structure, its evidence of plan and design, its wide sweep of thought, its sublimity and grandeur of revelation, all combine to make it one of the loveliest edifices of truth in existence (Coltman 1943, 8).

We wholeheartedly agree with this comparison. For centuries countless readers have entered the Romans cathedral and admired its rose window, stained with the blood of our Savior, depicting the doctrine of justification by grace through faith. We love gazing upon that window, for without Christ's justifying work, we would be lost and condemned by God. However, the rose window is not the only one in the Romans cathedral. Look around and you will see that Paul has artfully constructed other windows, other themes, that provide us with God's perspective on the Gospel and its goal.

Some Points, Not Just One

How did we reach this conclusion? Allow us to explain. In Rom 15:15–16 the apostle states, "I have written you quite boldly on some points, as if to remind you of them again, because of the grace God gave me to be a minister of Jesus Christ to the Gentiles." Paul says he had "some points" in mind, not just one. He further adds that he wrote "some points" because he was a missionary. Justification was surely one point, but what are the others?

To solve this mystery, we need to be Bible detectives. The mystery is: What are Paul's "some points"? Our opinion is that the points have something to do with Paul's being a missionary. Let's examine some additional evidence found in the beginning (1:1–7) and the close (16:25–27) of the letter. Read these sections here or look them up in your own Bible and keep an eye out for clues.

> Paul, a servant of Christ Jesus, called to be an apostle and set apart for the gospel of God—the gospel he promised beforehand through his prophets in the Holy Scriptures regarding his Son, who as to his human nature was a descendant of David, and who through the Spirit of holiness was declared with power to be the Son of God by his resurrection from the dead: Jesus Christ our Lord. Through him and for his name's sake, we received grace and apostleship to call people from among all the Gentiles to the obedience that comes from faith. And you also are among those who are called to belong to Jesus Christ. To all in Rome who are loved by God and called to be saints: Grace and peace to you from God our Father and from the Lord Jesus Christ (Rom 1:1–7).

> Now to him who is able to establish you by my gospel and the proclamation of Jesus Christ, according to the revelation of the mystery hidden for long ages past, but now revealed and made known through the prophetic writings by the command of the eternal God, so that all nations might believe and obey him—to the only wise God be glory forever through Jesus Christ! Amen (Rom 16:25–27).

Bible scholars do not see either of these passages as being central to the theme of Romans. They simply designate them as Paul's introductory and closing remarks, comment on the contents, and then move on to what they consider to be the important parts of

Romans. Like Dr. Watson overlooking significant clues, they, in our opinion, skim right over the very passages where Paul states his theme.[2]

Consider this clue, Sherlock. Paul begins his letter in a most unusual manner. In those days the normal salutation of letters followed a simple formula: from the author to the recipient. Normally Paul states this formula in a verse or two, as in 2 Tim 1:1–2:

> Paul, an apostle of Christ Jesus by the will of God, according to the promise of life that is in Christ Jesus, To Timothy, my dear son.

Now in Romans Paul does something totally different. Five entire verses (2–6) are inserted between "From Paul" and "To all in Rome." How curious.

Here is another clue: Paul also concludes this letter uniquely. In nearly all his other letters he closes with a short blessing of the readers. However, Romans alone of all the Pauline letters concludes with a doxology, that is, a statement of praise to God. I say, another curious clue.

Aha! Watson, I think I've got it! Paul varied from his normal style, because he wanted us to perk up and realize that he had something to share of highest significance. You see, it is in these often underrated verses that we find delineated the "some points" that Paul wished to discuss boldly in Romans. It's elementary. Let's take out our magnifying glasses and search for these points.

The Gospel Chain

In the original Greek text, Rom 1:1–7a is one long sentence. If ever in school you wrote a run-on sentence like it, your English teacher would have made your paper bleed red ink. In Greek, however, Paul expressed himself in a typical and grammatically correct way. His mega-sentence contains five key concepts that describe "the gospel of God" and the goal of that Gospel. Again in his conclusion, Paul makes reference to the same five concepts. These are the "some points" that Paul intends to develop in his letter. Below are the basic concepts, followed by the phrases from Romans 1 and 16 where they appear.

1. Revelation. Romans 1—"promised beforehand through his

prophets in the Holy Scriptures." Romans 16—"now made known through the prophetic writings by the command of the eternal God."

2. Justification. Romans 1—"regarding his Son Jesus Christ our Lord." Romans 16—"the proclamation of Jesus Christ."

3. Sanctification. Romans 1—"the obedience that comes from faith." Romans 16—"believe and obey." (In the Greek these phrases are exactly the same, although translated differently in the NIV.)

4. Mission. Romans 1—"through him we received grace and apostleship to call people from among all the Gentiles." Romans 16—"so that all the nations."

5. Glorification. Romans 1—"for his name's sake." Romans 16— "to the only wise God be glory forever through Jesus Christ! Amen."

These five concepts comprise the "some points" to which Paul refers in Rom 15:15–16. They form the links of Paul's Gospel chain. We call these five concepts the Gospel chain because they reveal the connection between the Gospel and the goal of the Gospel.

1. God's work of redeeming mankind was foretold in the messianic prophecies of Old Testament Scripture.

2. Then Christ actually appeared on the stage of history to save us through his life, death, and resurrection.

3. Those who are justified through faith in him are then sanctified by the Holy Spirit; their faith leads to obedience.

4. The highest form of obedience is to proclaim the saving Gospel to all nations, which is the express plan and will of God.

5. When this is done, then God's name is glorified among the peoples of the world, glorified as it deserves to be.

Why did Paul choose these five points? Remember his driving motive: he was a missionary (Rom 15:15–16). Therefore, he is not simply listing his teachings for the approval of the Romans. Rather, he is writing a treatise on world evangelization in order to motivate the Roman believers and every other Christian to strive toward the goal of the Gospel: the obedience of faith among all the nations for the glory of God. This, we believe, is the theme of Romans.

How Strong Is Your Gospel Chain?

A bell tinkled as Charlotte entered the jewelry store. The old jeweler, hearing the summons, left his workbench in back and stepped into the display room.

"Good afternoon, Mr. Wallace. Have you finished the work I gave you last week?" the woman inquired.

"Yes, Ma'am," he answered, pulling out a slim box from under the counter. Proudly he removed the cover, unwrapped the tissue, and lifted out the treasure: a beautiful gold chain, whole and intact.

"Oh, it looks as beautiful as the day my grandmother gave it to me!" Charlotte rejoiced. Merry with satisfaction, she clasped the chain about her neck and admired its appearance in a mirror. Then she meticulously studied each link. "I can't even tell which one was broken."

"I am honored to see that you are pleased with my craftsmanship. In my line of work, a broken chain is a lamentable object. Its usefulness and beauty are nothing unless that single link is restored."

"How true. What good is a broken chain?"

Paul's Gospel chain consists of revelation, justification, sanctification, mission, and glorification.

Is the Gospel chain complete and in good repair in my life and at my congregation? Are all the links in place, being actively taught and put into practice? Do we proclaim the goal of the Gospel as well as the Gospel itself? Consider the following sets of questions, and jot down the grades you think your church and your denomination deserve.

Link 1: *Revelation.* Do we confess the Bible to be the faultless source of all our doctrine and practice? Do we defend the integrity and sufficiency of the Scriptures? How well do we study the Bible and store up verses in our hearts? Grade: ____

Link 2: *Justification by Grace through Faith in Christ.* Do we understand and cherish this consoling message? Do we proclaim it as the only means by which we can be saved? How well do we rightly divide the Word of truth by properly distinguishing between the condemning Law and the freeing Gospel? Grade: ____.

Link 3: *Sanctification and the Obedience of Faith.* How much do we stress obedience and the work of the Holy Spirit in our lives? Do we regularly and specifically challenge ourselves to take God's

127

commands seriously and obey his will? Grade: ____

Link 4: *Mission Outreach to the Nations.* What percentage of sermons emphasize evangelism and world missions? Do these themes rate even a tithe (10 percent)? How concerned are we to demonstrate Christ's love or witness verbally to unbelievers? To what degree are we working to bring God's saving Word and Sacraments to the unevangelized ethnic groups in our vicinity and to the ends of the earth? Grade: ____

Link 5: *Glorification of God.* How many of us recognize that glorifying God means more than singing hymns in church? Do we think in terms of bringing him glory through our actions, vocation, words, and attitudes? Which receives more attention—glorifying our church or glorifying our Lord? Grade: ____

What kinds of grades did you give yourself? your church? Many churches rate fairly high grades for Scripture and justification, the first two links in the Gospel chain; but their grades diminish after that. Although there are some bright exceptions, many churches and Christians give little evidence of teaching obedience, mission, and the glorification of God. Theoretically, we desire with our work and witness to express our thanks for God's salvation, but often we tend to confine our thanks and praise to our sanctuaries, where we need not fear being looked at askance, rejected, or persecuted. Surely, we are called to more than this. "Live such good lives *among the pagans* that, though they accuse you of doing wrong, they may see your good deeds and glorify God on the day he visits us" (1 Pet 2:12; emphasis ours). The Gospel shows us our Savior; the goal of the Gospel is that we show the Savior to the world.

In summary, Christians often shortchange themselves by "short-chaining" God's message. We forge strong links of revelation and justification, only to stop short, assuming that these teachings alone require strong emphasis. "Just preach the Gospel and everything will take care of itself." But in Rom 1:1–7 Paul urges us and all Christians to add to the Gospel chain the missing links of obedience, mission, and glorification. Only then can the goal of the Gospel be met.

Thank God, there are exceptions to the general practice. Some churches give top priority to obedient discipleship and mission—and the results are beautiful to behold! These churches are filled with an air of expectancy that the Lord will add to their number.

People in their community come to know Christ through their loving lifestyle and tactful witness. Some of their own members go forth to share the Gospel with unreached peoples on this continent and others. News of new converts brings joy both at home and on the mission field (as well as in heaven). In all this the Triune God is glorified before the world. These churches are not perfect, but they have something every church needs: a complete Gospel chain.

Questions

No doubt, some readers will question our proposed theme of Romans. Allow us to respond to three likely concerns.

Question 1. "I think the theme of Romans is found in Rom 1:16–17." Let's take a look at these verses:

> I am not ashamed of the gospel, because it is the power of God for the salvation of everyone who believes: first for the Jew, then for the Gentile. For in the gospel a righteousness from God is revealed, a righteousness that is from faith to faith, just as it is written: "The righteous will live by faith."[3]

Surely, we wish to take nothing away from these classic verses. We believe them with all our heart, but we do not think that they state the theme of Romans for the first time. Instead, Rom 1:16–17 repeats several of the five themes that have already been presented in Rom 1:1–7. Obviously, on this point the authors' view conflicts with that of most other interpreters. The ambiguity arises because Paul does not specifically state anywhere in Romans, "Now, here is my theme." Therefore, all any Christian can do is theorize.

And what do you do with a theory? You test it. That is just what we will be doing in the coming chapters. We will demonstrate that when justification is considered the sole theme of Romans, it becomes difficult to explain why Paul treats other topics. In contrast, when the theme is the Gospel chain, Paul's progression of topics makes better sense. As you study Romans with us in the following chapters, you will be surprised how the Gospel chain brings out the depth and intensity of the text of Romans.

Question 2. "Does the phrase 'the obedience of faith' refer to sanctification? Perhaps Paul simply meant that believing the Gospel is the highest form of obedience."

This phrase has certainly befuddled Bible experts. To those who believe in salvation by grace through faith, "the obedience of faith" sounds like an oxymoron, that is, an apparent contradiction in terms. Therefore, many interpret *the obedience of faith* to mean simply an obedience of faith in the Gospel. To this we answer that Paul was too precise a theologian to speak of faith in such a convoluted manner. If he had meant to say faith, he would have said faith, not the obedience of faith. We concur with the NIV, which translates the phrase as *the obedience that comes from faith.* This clearly is a reference to sanctification, to the godly, obedient lifestyle that is the fruit of saving faith.

We believe that when Paul penned Rom 1:1–7 and 16:25–27, he had in mind Gen 49:10 and the global mission directive of the risen Savior.

> The scepter will not depart from Judah, nor the ruler's staff from between his feet, until he comes to whom it belongs and the obedience of the nations is his (Gen 49:10).

> Therefore go and make disciples of all nations . . . teaching them to obey everything I have commanded you (Mt 28:19–20).

We believe that Paul uses the phrase "the obedience of faith" as a kind of shorthand term for the truth that is found in these two key texts.

Question 3: "Where in Romans is the Scripture link of the Gospel chain?" According to our interpretation of Rom 1:1–7 and 16:25–27, the first link in Paul's Gospel chain is revelation, or Scripture. However, Paul does not devote a section of Romans to this topic. In fact, he only teaches directly about Scripture in occasional verses such as these:

> You have in the law the embodiment of knowledge and truth (Rom 2:20).

> They [the Jews] have been entrusted with the very words of God (Rom 3:2).

> For everything that was written in the past was written to teach us, so that through endurance and the encouragement of the Scriptures we might have hope (Rom 15:4).

We must admit that at first it seemed that the lack of doctrinal teaching about Scripture seemed to shoot to pieces our Gospel-chain theory. The problem called for more Bible sleuthing. After some snooping and statistical analysis, we discovered that Paul's use of the Old Testament Scriptures is distinctly different in Romans from his other writings. By studying the reference footnotes that appear in the NIV translation, we analyzed Paul's use of Old Testament texts. You can do it yourself with whatever Bible version you read. The following is a summary of our findings.

Old Testament Quotations in Paul's Writings

Letter	Quotations*	Pages†	Quotes/Page
1 Corinthians	17/21	15	1.1
2 Corinthians	10/14	15	0.7
Galatians	9/13	5	1.8
Ephesians	4	5	0.8
Philippians	0	4	0.0
Colossians	0	4	0.0
1 Thess	0	3	0.0
2 Thess	0	2	0.0
1 Timothy	2	4	0.5
2 Timothy	1	3	0.3
Titus	0	2	0.0
Philemon	0	1	0.0
Totals	43/55	63	0.7 quotes/page
Romans	57/69	16	3.6 quotes/page

* In some cases, the words that Paul cites appear in more than one location of the OT. Therefore, the first number in this column lists the number of times that Paul quotes the OT, while the latter number refers to the number of separate OT texts he is quoting.

† Page totals will vary with each edition of the Bible.

Readers who love statistics appreciate charts like this. Others may be groaning, but please bear with us. The most intriguing data appear in the last two lines of the chart. In the 63 total pages of his other letters, Paul quotes the Scripture 43 times. That is a ratio of .7 quotations per page. Romans is a different story, with 57 quotations in only 16 pages. The ratio is 3.6 quotations per page of Romans. This is five times more often than elsewhere.

What can we do with this evidence? One option is to ignore it, claiming that it is sheer coincidence. A wiser choice, however, is to admit that Paul's use of Old Testament Scripture in Romans marks a distinctive change in practice from his other letters.

We are compelled to conclude, therefore, that revelation, or Scripture, is indeed one of the five points that Paul emphasizes in Romans. He did not develop this theme by devoting a separate section to it. Instead, he chose an equally effective, though perhaps less evident, method, quoting the Old Testament constantly and artfully to support his arguments. He emphasizes Scripture, not by teaching about it but by using it.

Summary

If some readers balk at the idea that Romans has five themes rather than one, we know just how they feel. We were astounded ourselves when we first uncovered the Gospel chain. In fact, at first we regarded it as nothing more than an hypothesis. However, as we studied Romans in detail and applied the Gospel-chain hypothesis to each section of the epistle, it repeatedly proved itself valid and true. Have you ever looked at minerals under an ultraviolet light? Rocks that look rather drab in daylight suddenly radiate dazzling, bold colors. In the following chapters we want to share with you Paul's many brilliant teachings that burst into sight when we viewed Romans through the ultraviolet light of the Gospel chain of Scripture, Christ, obedience, mission, and glory.

Digging Deeper

1. How familiar are you with Romans? Have you read it? Have you studied it in any detail before?
2. Review the traditional assumptions regarding the occasion, purpose, and theme of Romans. Where do the authors agree and disagree?

3. Do some Bible sleuthing. Compare the introduction of Romans to the introductions of other letters by Paul. Then do the same with his conclusions. What did you discover?

4. Review the five pairs of phrases from Romans 1 and 16, on the basis of which the authors identify the five concepts in the Gospel chain: revelation, justification, sanctification, mission, and glorification. Do you think the Gospel chain is a reality or a figment of the authors' imaginations?

5. In the NIV the phrase "for his name's sake" is placed near the beginning of Rom 1:5. In the Greek text the phrase occurs at the end of v. 5. Thus a more literal translation would be, "Through him we received grace and apostleship to call people from among all the Gentiles to the obedience that comes from faith for his name's sake." How does this placement help reveal that there is a glory link in the Gospel chain?

6. Consider the word *apostleship* in Rom 1:5. To whom do you think it applies? If the responsibility of sharing the Gospel had been given only to the apostles, where would the Christian church be today? On a personal level, would you be a redeemed child of God or a lost and condemned person?

7. Have you ever had a broken chain? It could have been a decorative chain, a heavy duty chain, or a chain on a machine. Describe the situation when it broke and how you felt about it.

8. Compare your Gospel chain report cards. Explain the grades you assigned.

9. Does the phrase "the obedience of faith" sit well with you, or are you uneasy with it? Explain your answer.

10. Take a close look at Rom 1:16–17. What elements of the Gospel chain are referred to in these powerful verses?

Notes

1. We are well aware that our view is a minority opinion. We consulted 120 commentaries on Romans, plus *The Romans Debate* (Donfried, 1991), and not one commentator agreed with us that the five themes of Romans are Scripture, justification, sanctification, mission, and glory. Thus far in our research, only Dr. Arthur F. Glasser appears to have some grasp of what we are saying, as indicated by a brief summary of Romans, which he includes in an article entitled

"The Apostle Paul and the Missionary Task," in *Perspectives on the World Christian Movement* (Winter and Hawthorne 1981, 104–112).

2. We congratulate those scholars who have recognized a mission connection in Romans, such as Dr. Martin Franzmann, who used the theme "The Gospel That Goes Westward" (Franzmann 1968, 19 passim). However, they still do not hold that the theme of Romans is found in 1:1–7 and 16:25–27.

3. The phrase "from faith to faith" in Rom 1:17 has been interpreted various ways. Here is how four English versions have translated it:

NIV: "a righteousness that is by faith from first to last"

KJV: "the righteousness of God revealed from faith to faith"

RSV: "the righteousness of God is revealed through faith for faith"

TEV: "it is through faith from beginning to end"

To all the varied translations and interpretations, the authors propose another possibility. We believe that the first faith refers to faith in God's promises of mercy in Christ Jesus. The second faith is the courage to obey God's commands and do his will. Thus the phrase could be translated "a righteousness that progresses from faith that saves to faith that obeys." We do not insist that our interpretation is the only way to understand this difficult phrase, but we offer it as an option that would be wholly consistent with Paul's Gospel chain.

7

Fallen Short of the Glory
Romans 1:8–3:20

Paul's Letter to the Romans has already been the subject of scores of commentaries, books that comment on and explain many details of the text. We do not intend to repeat what these books have already stated. Rather, our purpose is primarily to shine a spotlight on the parts of Romans that emphasize the goal of the Gospel, namely, obedience, missions, and the glory of God.

In chapter 7 we direct our attention to Rom 1:8–3:20. Here is a preview of what we will see. (1) In Rom 1:8–17 Paul tells how he categorizes the peoples of the earth and speaks of the obligation that he has toward them. (2) Rom 1:18–32 documents the tragedy of disobedience among the nations in order to move our hearts to compassion toward the lost. (3) In Rom 2:1–3:20 Paul declares that knowledge of God's Law will not save anyone, even us. (4) Finally, the concept of glorifying God—and its opposite, profaning his name—appears repeatedly in the first three chapters of Romans.

First for the Jew—Then for the Gentile

Before Len boarded the commuter train, he bought a copy of *The Star Dispatch*. Finding an empty seat, he turned to the business section. Just before the train doors closed, Jeffrey burst into the car, out of breath, with his tie dangling from his collar as yet unknotted.

Taking the seat next to Len, Jeffrey puffed, "Boy, I sure pulled a Dagwood Bumstead this morning."

"Well, at least you didn't forget your trousers," Len observed with a chuckle. Although the two businessmen were not close friends, they had become somewhat familiar during two years of commuter rides.

"Oh, no!" Jeffrey moaned. "I was in such a rush that I forgot to grab a paper."

"No problem; we can share mine," Len offered. "Here, take the business section. I'll read the world and national news."

"Thanks."

Ten minutes and three train stops later, the men traded sections of the paper. After a while, Jeffrey sighed loudly and said, "Did you read about the guerrilla murders in South Africa?"

"I'm afraid I did. Pretty gruesome, isn't it?"

"I'll say. I'm glad I didn't have time for breakfast. Being wrapped in old tires, doused with gasoline, and set aflame is not my idea of a good way to go. How could someone do such a thing?"

"Hey, it's a sick world," Len declared. "The latest terrorist bombing didn't sound like any picnic either."

"And sometimes I wonder if we are any safer in this country. Last week in Chicago a fellow riding a train just like this one was shot by some guy who wanted his Bears jacket."

As they rode through suburb after suburb, the men continued to play the game of "Ain't It Awful," lamenting the evils of the world, discussing all the categories of people who are in conflict: rich and poor, black and white, Muslim and Christian, Arab and Jew, leftist and capitalist, and so on. The conversation concluded as "Ain't It Awful" usually does, with the mutual observation, "This world sure is headed from bad to worse." Then they both fell silent.

As Len sat musing and mourning, he gazed out the window and saw a large, old church rising out of a lower-class neighborhood. The sight caused him to reflect on the connection between his Christian faith and the depressing conversation he had just had. "I know why the world is so messed up," he thought to himself. "The people we were reading about need Jesus. Some in South Africa or Lebanon or Ireland may call themselves Christians, but their violent actions deny the claim. The labels that people wear—Arab, communist, black, white—really aren't the crucial issue. In fact, now that I think about it, everyone in the world fits into one of two categories. Either they are lost in unbelief and headed for eternal death, or they are saved by Christ and headed for eternal life. Why, it's the same for everyone on this train!"

Len glanced at his friend, now caught up in the crossword puzzle. "I wonder which category Jeffrey is in. Is he lost, or is he saved?

136

I don't even know if he goes to a church. Come to think of it, he doesn't know if I go to one. After all, what has he seen in me, to let him know that I'm a Christian? What has he ever heard from me about God's love for this lost world?"

Chin in hand, Len pondered for a moment how he might broach the subject with Jeffrey. In a minute the Holy Spirit turned on a light bulb, and Len began to speak, "Say, Jeffrey, have you ever wondered why the world is so fouled up? Have you ever thought that maybe it could be restored?"

Because Len was a Christian, he categorized the world as "saved" and "lost." The ability to categorize things is essential. Through constant observation, the toddler learns to distinguish men from women, dogs from cats, and countless other items. As we grow up our awareness of categories increases. A seamstress learns many kinds of cloth, threads, and stitches. A fisherman knows many types of fish, bait, and tackle. A biologist memorizes the Latin names for all the categories of flora and fauna. So, you see, categorizing is essential to the use of all knowledge.

The apostle Paul does some categorizing himself in Romans 1. Recognizing the variety of people living in the city of Rome, he states, "I am obligated both to Greeks and non-Greeks, both to the wise and the foolish" (Rom 1:14). The Greeks of Paul's day were the scholars, the educated, the wise. The non-Greeks, by comparison, were considered uneducated and foolish. In fact, the original word translated as "non-Greek" is *barbaros,* from which we get our word "barbarian."

Now, why is Paul categorizing people? Because, as he says, he is obligated to them. In what manner is he obligated? Look at Rom 1:15, "That is why I am so eager to preach the gospel also to you who are in Rome." Paul feels obligated to preach the Gospel to both the learned and the unlearned in the city of Rome.

Paul's attitude is amazing when we compare it to the exclusiveness found in many churches today. The people at Holy Trinity by the Grain Elevator may become so used to seeing the same old faces every Sunday that they have no desire to tell other folks in their town about God's saving Word and sacraments. The thought of opening their hearts and doors to migrant Hispanic workers never crosses their minds. They just don't feel the obligation of which

137

Paul speaks. The same can occur in urban or suburban churches, especially when their community is experiencing ethnic changes. Although blacks are now living next door to them, Caucasian Christians may sense no obligation to invite them to their church. When believers meet Muslims or Hindus at the local PTA meetings, they sense no obligation to invite them to study the Bible with them. Although there are exceptions, thank God, Paul's sense of obligation and urgency is often lacking.

Paul categorizes people once again in Rom 1:16: "I am not ashamed of the gospel, because it is the power of God for the salvation of everyone who believes; first for the Jew, then for the Gentile." How often have you heard this verse quoted? Probably quite often, but how many times have you heard Rom 1:16 quoted minus the last phrase, "first for the Jew, then for the Gentile"? Quite often we drop that phrase, with the result that we may fail to recognize the global implication of Paul's statement about the Gospel.

The first half of 1:16 says that the Gospel provides salvation for *everyone* who believes; but how broad is everyone? Sure, we all know what *everyone* means. It's a simple word we learned to spell in the second grade—but in the real world of day-to-day church life, it is so easy to act and plan as though *everyone* means just the people who are like us. Aware of this lack of vision, Paul adds a phrase to categorize *everyone* for us: "first for the Jew, then for the Gentile." Everyone on the face of the earth fits into one of these two categories.

Category one is the Jews, the people who had the Holy Scriptures and the promises of the coming Savior. Paul says "first for the Jew" because the Jews had a close relationship with God's plan of salvation.

Category two is the Gentiles, every person not in category one. Paul describes category two in Eph 2:12, "You were separate from Christ, excluded from citizenship in Israel and foreigners to the covenants of the promise, without hope and without God in the world."

Paul's reference to the Jews and the Gentiles impels us to think of our entire world that needs to hear the Gospel, which "is the power of God for the salvation of *everyone* who believes." Throughout Romans you will see Paul refer again and again to these two categories: Jews and Gentiles. In every case, he is encouraging us, his readers, to think globally, to recognize that the Gospel is intended not only for us but for *everyone*.

Geography

Some readers may react to Paul's categorizing with less than enthusiasm: "Dividing the world into saved and lost people is pretty easy, but when we take into consideration all the geographic and cultural differences in this world, my mind gets boggled. Geography and social studies were not my best subjects back in school."

We can understand this reaction. The world is so varied that we can easily feel buried. Anthropologists and mission strategists have identified about 24,000 different cultural/geographical groups of people who need to be reached with the Gospel. Thus far, we have planted strong churches in only 8,000 of those target people groups.

For those of us who have trouble thinking in terms of thousands, Dr. Morris Watkins has simplified things for us in *Seven Worlds to Win*. In this book, which would make a great high school social studies text, Watkins focuses on seven categories: the Chinese world, the Buddhist world, the Hindu world, the Muslim world, the Bibleless and illiterate world, the Communist world, and the so-called Christian world. Once you learn to deal with seven categories, you will gain the ability to think in terms of larger numbers.

Even so, those who had trouble passing old lady Baker's ninth grade geography class may think it is just too great a hardship to become informed about God's world of lost children. If that is how you feel, consider this story told to me [Phil] by Bob Roegner, a former missionary to the Kisi people of Liberia, West Africa.

> I had just finished a particularly good lay preachers' class one Sunday afternoon. A new student in the class named Falla approached me. He had confessed Christ and been baptized only two months before.
>
> "I want to study geography," Falla said.
>
> Startled, I replied, "Falla, you don't need to study geography. You have been a Christian such a short time, and there are other more important subjects for you to study first." But Falla remained firm in his conviction to study geography, so I asked, why?
>
> "I want to study geography to know the names of more places

and peoples to pray for, so God will carry the good news of Jesus Christ to those places, just as he is doing for my own Kisi people."

God bless Falla! His desire was no small challenge, because there are no geography books in the Kisi tongue, and he cannot read English. In spite of this problem, the Spirit of God would not let him be satisfied with knowing that he alone had been saved. Like Falla, our African brother in the faith, may we be moved by the Spirit to learn about the many people who are not yet reconciled to the Father by the blood of Christ. To urge us to do so, Paul speaks about categories of people.

The Tragedy of Disobedience

Now we turn our attention to Rom 1:18–32. The traditional interpretation of this section says that here Paul teaches God's Law, which shows human sin and condemns sinners. Paul certainly does this in preparation for proclaiming the Gospel in Rom 3:21ff. However, if we view Rom 1:18–32 in terms of the whole Gospel chain, what more might we see? We invite you to read this lengthy passage in your Bible while keeping in mind the concepts of revelation, obedience, missions, and the glory of God.

What do we learn here about obedience? God had intended mankind to live in holiness and purity. This was his purpose for the whole human race. Our history was to be a canvas painted with bright, delightful hues; but the scene Paul paints here is filled with mournful shadows. Man, the crown of creation, has fallen into the slimy dungeon of perversion and sin. Especially in verses 29–31, the fierce words of indictment pelt the canvas with steadily increasing intensity:

> They have become filled
> with every kind of
> wickedness,
> evil,
> greed,
> and depravity.
> They are full of
> envy,
> murder,

140

strife,
deceit,
and malice.
They are
gossips,
slanderers,
God-haters,
insolent,
arrogant,
and boastful;
they invent ways of doing evil;
they disobey their parents;
they are
senseless,
faithless,
heartless,
ruthless.

These terms for human evil strike the conscience like bullets from a firing squad, blotting out every vain dream that fallen people can ever redeem themselves. Do you see what Paul is doing here? He is not simply proving to us the catechism truth that the Law shows us our sin. He is painting a picture of the depravity of humankind so that we will weep with compassion for all who live and breathe on this earth without really living. And even though Paul's portrait is over 1900 years old, the paint glistens as though it were still wet, for it accurately depicts our world at the end of the 20th century. It is as contemporary as the newspaper that the commuters Len and Jeffrey read on their way to work.

What do we learn of the glory of God from Rom 1:18–32? The Creator was to have been glorified through the righteous dominion of Adam and Eve and their descendants. Honoring God as their king, we were to have been like princes and princesses. But "they neither glorified him as God nor gave thanks to him. Although they claimed to be wise, they became fools and exchanged the glory of the immortal God for images. . . . They exchanged the truth of God for a lie, and worshiped and served created things rather than the Creator" (1:21–23, 25). Paul shows us how far the nations have fallen from glory, as a way of motivating us to see them restored. When

men and women reject God's glory, they forfeit the glory and dominion that God intended for them. All that remains is the slavery
of idolatry. This bondage is just as tragic and binding when people
worship fame, financial security, and Ferraris as when they bow
down to idols and demons.

How about the revelation of God in Romans 1? We cannot help
but see the contrast between "a righteousness from God is revealed"
(1:16) and "the wrath of God is being revealed" (1:17). People will
receive either wrath or righteousness, judgment or mercy. How does
God reveal his wrath? The ultimate revelation of God's wrath will
come on Judgment Day when Christ comes again to judge and
condemn all those who have refused to repent. At the present time
God reveals his wrath in what may seem to be a strange way. Three
times Paul writes, "God gave them over . . . . " (1:24, 26, 28). This
means simply that he lets sin run its course and allows its poison
to infect our lives. Does this mean that God no longer cares about
sinful mankind? Not at all. He desires that people will feel sin's awful
consequences and thereby be led to repent of their wickedness.
The homosexual with AIDS who hears and believes the Good News
in his closing months knows that God desires him and all people
to be saved. The convicted, white-collar thief who is led by the Holy
Spirit to turn from his sin, seek forgiveness from Christ, and abandon
his greedy practices has learned that the blood of Jesus Christ cleans-
es us from all our sin. The evolutionary atheist who is stranded
without God and without a hope in the world finally discovers
meaning when God bursts into his awareness as Creator, Savior,
and Friend. The Lord gives his prodigal children over to sin in the
hope that they will return to their senses and come home to his
loving arms (Ezek 20:25–26).

Finally, what do we learn of mission in Rom 1:18–32? Surely
everything we have noted thus far demonstrates the world's need
to be evangelized. Men, women, and children without Christ are
indeed "without hope and without God in the world" (Eph 2:12).
Countless missionaries on furlough have confronted the congregations they visit with the huge numbers of people who are dying
without Christ every day. Rather than speak of the quantity of the
lost, however, Paul stresses the quality of the lost. Unrighteous in
God's sight, they have no hope in sight.

No hope, except one. "In the gospel a righteousness from God is revealed" (1:17). The Gospel offers the only ray of hope for this rebel world full of unrighteous people. How does God reveal his Gospel of righteousness? Only through the proclamation of his saving word. And who is to proclaim it? "Those who are called to belong to Jesus Christ" (1:6). "We received grace and apostleship to call people from among all the Gentiles to the obedience that comes from faith" (1:5). We cannot abandon the godless and unrighteous people of this world, thinking, "Since God gave them over to their sin, can't we do the same?" No, God has given us the Gospel in order to save lost and condemned people by its life-giving power.

Knowledge of God's Law Doesn't Save

To be given good advice is one thing; to live by it is another. Once this writer [Phil] had bronchitis and had to go to the hospital for chest X-rays. Waiting in the doctor's office, I chuckled at a humorous poster. A smiling skeleton, holding a cigarette in his bony hand, announced, "I died from cancer, and it didn't hurt a bit." No doubt that sarcastic message had been placed there to discourage the use of tobacco. Something was jamming the message, however; for right beside the smoking skeleton sat the doctor, analyzing my X-rays while dragging on a cigarette.

A similar reaction can occur while reading Paul's catalog of vices in Rom 1:18–32. It's easy for religious Christians to think, "Yes, those unbelievers sure are awful. No wonder God will condemn them. I guess they just don't know God's laws like I do." However, mere knowledge of what is right does not make us righteous. That is Paul's point in Romans 2. He demonstrates that even we who know the Law of God fail to keep it. Note the tone of sarcasm in 2:17–24.

> Now you, if you call yourself a Jew [or a Christian]; if you rely on the law and brag about your relationship to God; if you know his will and approve of what is superior because you are instructed by the law; if you are convinced that you are a guide for the blind, a light for those who are in the dark, an instructor of the foolish, a teacher of infants, because you have in the law the embodiment of knowledge and truth—you, then, who teach others, do you not teach yourself? You who preach against stealing, do you steal? You who say that people should not commit adultery, do you commit adultery? You who abhor idols, do you rob temples? You who

brag about the law, do you dishonor God by breaking the law? As it is written: "God's name is blasphemed among the Gentiles because of you."

As believers in the grace of Christ, we know that our salvation is not based on any good deeds that we performed before we trusted in his mercy (Eph 2:8–9; Titus 3:5). Paul's reproach in Rom 2:17–24 warns us that we are likewise not saved by the good we might do *after* our conversion. We have been declared saints by God; but, this side of heaven, we are still sinner/saints, capable of transgressions and self-delusion such as Paul portrays for us. Although God longs to see us live righteously, we are still incapable of faultless living. Awareness of this will motivate us to depend fully on God's power to produce holiness in our lives.

On the other hand, we dare not take a lackadaisical view toward obedience, rationalizing, "Since I am not capable of perfection, I don't have to strive for holiness in my daily activities." Such an attitude can lead to the cheap grace mentality of which we spoke in chapter 5—"I like to sin and God likes to forgive sin; what a convenient arrangement." This is one of the most common and dangerous heresies seeking to enter the hearts and minds of believers.

Paul is fully aware of the danger. That is why he proceeds to discuss the need to be truly a Jew and truly circumcised. A paraphrase of Rom 2:28–29 shows us how contemporary Paul's argument is: "A man is not a Christian if he is only one outwardly, nor is conversion merely outward and physical. No, a man is a Christian if he is one inwardly; and conversion is conversion of the heart, by the Spirit, not by the written code." The timing of this warning is significant. Paul closes the door on cheap grace before he has even explained salvation by grace. Any understanding of salvation that justifies or winks at intentional disobedience must be nipped in the bud, as the wise apostle does here.

Seeking God's Glory

Romans 2 also teaches us more about the glory of God. Consider these verses:

To those who by persistence in doing good seek glory, honor, and immortality, he will give eternal life. But for those who are self-seeking and who reject the truth and follow evil, there will be wrath and anger. There will be trouble and distress for every human being who does evil: first for the Jew, then for the Gentile; but glory, honor and peace for everyone who does good: first for the Jew, then for the Gentile.

For it is not those who hear the law who are righteous in God's sight, but it is those who obey the law who will be declared righteous (Rom 2:7–10, 13).

These are difficult verses, especially for the Christian who knows salvation is by grace through faith, not works. Do these verses declare that we are saved by faith *and* works, as some teach? We will avoid stumbling to this false conclusion if we keep in mind the big picture of obedience and the goal of the Gospel.

Since God created Adam and Eve, his purpose for mankind has always been that we enjoy his blessings of glory, honor, immortality, and peace. On the one hand, these benefits are lost through self-seeking, rejection of the truth, and following evil (Rom 2:8). On the other hand, they are regained by seeking glory, in particular God's glory, believing the truth, and following righteousness.

Therefore, Paul here is not contradicting other clear Gospel statements. He is simply referring to the Bible's consistent pattern of repentance and salvation leading to obedience. His conclusion in 2:13 is the same as Jesus' warnings not only to hear the saving Word but also to put it into practice. All people have been redeemed. The hearing and believing appropriates that redemption to us, but if the putting into practice does not occur, then the believing is dead, nothing more than sham.

To Profane or To Glorify God's Name

Hank, Ron, and Art had lumbered out of bed at 5 a.m. to catch some big ones at their favorite fishing hole on Robinson Lake. After a couple strikes but no catches, their bobbers floated immobile on the calm pool. With the lull in the action, the anglers took to chatting about proper bait and tackle, followed by a rundown of last night's baseball scores. Then Hank broached the subject that was really pressing on all their minds.

"I thought fishing would take my mind off the problems at church; but try as I may, I keep seeing last week's headline: 'Local Man Charged with Embezzlement.' If the changes are true, Denny has destroyed his life.

"It is true," Art said. "On the news last night they reported that he had confessed to everything."

"Oh?" Hank responded. "I hadn't heard that development."

"Yup. Pastor Rizzo has been visiting him in jail all week. His sharing of the Word led Denny to stop covering his tracks. He's confessed to the Lord and to the authorities."

"Well, that sort of wraps it up then," Hank concluded.

Ron, silent until now, was provoked by Hank's words. "Hank, it isn't wrapped up! The trouble is just beginning! Everyone knows that Denny was an elder at Calvary Church. So his sin taints the name of all of us. Why, at least ten people at work have confronted me about Denny's arrest."

"What did you tell them?" Art asked.

"I told them that Christians are not perfect, just forgiven. But they didn't seem impressed by that. In fact, two of them just snickered and walked away. I feel like the good name of all of us has been besmirched by Denny's misconduct."

Art observed, "The problem is even deeper than that, Ron."

"What do you mean?"

"The public sins of God's people reflect on the Lord. Our good names don't matter. Calvary's name doesn't matter. What matters is that God's good name is disgraced."

As they all pondered that thought, the bobbers continued their lethargic voyage. Then Art added, "And when Christians disgrace the name of God, their prospects of being effective fishers of men are about the same as ours are today."

Rom 2:24 gives us a shocking critique of the all too common failure of God's people to glorify the Lord as he deserves. The verse reads, "As it is written: 'God's name is blasphemed among the Gentiles because of you.' "

Blasphemy is a mighty strong word. In what manner is this term applicable to believers in the past and also today?

You will recall from chapter 2 that in the Old Testament era God's mission strategy was to capture the attention of the nations through the holy, loving behavior of Jewish believers, both in Israel and wherever they lived. By the time of Christ, Jews resided in numerous towns and cities from Spain to the borders of India and perhaps even farther. By their righteous lives they were to introduce all the nations to the Lord, the ruler of heaven and earth.

This responsibility belongs not only to the Jews but to all who in faith seek refuge in the God of Israel. All of us who confess Christ today have the same duty. "Live such good lives among the pagans that, though they accuse you of doing wrong, they may see your good deeds and glorify God on the day he visits us" (1 Pet 2:12). This is the divine plan for seeking and saving the nations: proclamation of the Gospel, confirmed by godly living.

However, this plan often fails to work, not because it is a poor plan but because we fail to put it into practice. This is why Paul concludes, "As it is written: 'God's name is blasphemed among the Gentiles because of you' " (Rom 2:24). Paul is referring to Ezek 36:22.[1] There are many places in the Old Testament where the disobedience of Israel is lamented. Paul selected this verse with great care because of the significance of its original context. Look at Ezek 36:22–27:

> Therefore say to the house of Israel, "This is what the Sovereign Lord says: It is not for your sake, O house of Israel, that I am going to do these things, but for the sake of my holy name, which you have profaned among the nations where you have gone. I will show the holiness of my great name, which has been profaned among the nations, the name you have profaned among them. Then the nations will know that I am the LORD, declares the Sovereign LORD, when I show myself holy through you before their eyes.
>
> "For I will take you out of the nations; I will gather you from all the countries and bring you back into your own land. I will sprinkle clean water on you, and you will be clean; I will cleanse you from all your impurities and from all your idols. I will give you a new heart and put a new spirit in you; I will remove from you your heart of stone and give you a heart of flesh. And I will put my Spirit in you and move you to follow my decrees and be careful to keep my laws" (Ezek 36:22–27).

As you read the first paragraph, vv. 22–23, do you sense the emotions the Lord is expressing? He is more than a little bit perturbed, isn't he? He expresses his annoyance in the reiteration of the word *profaned,* which means the same thing as *blaspheme.* The Lord is not speaking here of using his name in vain by cursing and swearing, as is prohibited in the Ten Commandments. He refers to hallowing his name—making it holy in the eyes of the world by leading a holy life according to his will. Tragically, his people have dragged his name through the mud, besmirched it with the filth of their sin, and caused unbelievers to snicker about "that worthless God of Israel." By quoting Ezek 36:22, Paul not only points out our sin; he also reveals the effect of our sin on God's holy name. When we disgrace God's name, the nations lose interest in knowing the God of grace.

When the godless disobey, no one is surprised or speaks negatively about God; but when those who claim to be God's people live in sin, then his name is profaned among the nations. His name is blasphemed among the unbelievers when Protestants and Catholics fight in Ireland, when apartheid is defended on supposedly biblical grounds, when believers get a divorce for unscriptural reasons, when a Christian tells the same dirty jokes that unbelievers tell or nurses a bitter grudge against a coworker.

Now look at the amazing promise in the second half of Ezek 36:23: "Then the nations will know that I am the LORD, declares the Sovereign LORD, when I show myself holy through you before their eyes." In spite of the poor track record of God's people, he promises that he is going to do something that will make all nations acknowledge that he is the Lord: he will show himself holy through us before their eyes.

Try to fathom the personal significance of this promise. God will reveal his holiness *through us,* in our day-to-day lives, in our thoughts, words, and actions. How will God accomplish this feat? Verses 25–27 foretell the miraculous method God will use:

1. He will sprinkle and cleanse us his people with clean water;
2. He will give us a new heart and an obedient spirit; and
3. He will place his Spirit in us, thus motivating us faithfully to obey his ways.

Imagine that you are in need of a heart transplant. You seek the best doctor to be found, because you want to survive the operation. If holiness is ever to issue forth from our sinful hearts, we will first have to undergo a spiritual heart transplant. We cannot perform this surgery on ourselves, so God in his mercy promises in Ezek 36 to remove from us our heart of stone and replace it with a heart of flesh.[2]

Before Their Eyes

Before we proceed to the following chapters of Romans, we should note one more dimension of Ezek 36:23: "Then the nations will know that I am the Lord, declares the Sovereign LORD, when I show myself holy through you before their eyes." Remember, Paul's theme in Romans demonstrates how God equips us for holy living and for reaching the whole world with the Gospel of Christ. In light of this theme, Ezekiel's words "before their eyes" take on added luster.

Often we compartmentalize our holy living into convenient little time slots on Sunday and perhaps also Wednesday evening. We assume that it is primarily during worship that we praise God and bring him honor. But think about it. How can we display the holiness of our Lord before the eyes of the nations while we are hidden behind the walls of a church building? Yes, we do praise God in church; but the only way we can glorify him before the eyes of the nations is to leave that building and be seen by unbelievers. If you believe that punching a worship-service time card is all that God expects of Christians, you have failed to recognize his purpose in saving you. His goal is to be glorified—through you! His goal is to be glorified through you—before the eyes of the nations! Worship is only the warm-up practice, the spring training, the time trials, boot camp, orientation, and training school to prepare us for the real-life task of serving God before the nations, so that they may know that he is the Lord.

Shepherd and author Philip Keller explains how the "before-their-eyes" principle is carried out by shepherds in the Middle East. Rather than using dogs or horses to round up stray and scattered sheep, the eastern shepherd uses his own sheep to gather others. All he does is lead the flock out into the countryside where his sheep graze alongside wild and wayward sheep. In the evening, when the shepherd gathers his flock, many of the lost sheep follow those who know the voice of the master, thus becoming part of his flock too. Keller applies this procedure to witnessing to Christ in both word and deed:

> He simply asks me to be one who will be so attached to him, so fond of him, so true to him, that in truth I shall be like his pet lamb or bellwether. No matter where he takes me; no matter where he places me; no matter whom I am alongside of in my daily living, that person will be induced to eventually follow the Shepherd because I follow him (Keller 1978, 103).

There is no greater honor than that, through us, the Lord displays his holiness before the eyes of the nations.

Summary

By speaking God's condemning Law in Romans 1–3, Paul has caused us to see both our sin and the fallen state of the whole human race. This information moves us to conclude that no one can be saved by keeping God's Law. Forgiveness and eternal life shall only be ours by means of the powerful Gospel, which we are obligated to share with everyone, whether Jew or Gentile. Also, by quoting from Ezek 36:22, the apostle has raised our hopes and our curiosity, hasn't he? We wonder, "How has God fulfilled his promise to give us a new heart and a new spirit?" Paul will answer our question in complete detail in Romans 3–8.

Digging Deeper

1. Do you know anyone like Falla, the mission-minded Liberian (see page 139)?
2. Choose the most appropriate ending to this sentence: When I consider that billions of people on this earth are lost without Christ, I feel
   ___ a. frustration.
   ___ b. ho-hum.
   ___ c. mildly perturbed.
   ___ d. upset.
   ___ e. nothing, because I never think about it.
3. Paul categorizes the world as either Jew or Gentile. Make a list

of the ways that the peoples of the world are categorized by those in your community.

4. Paul categorized people for the purpose of identifying their cultural distinctiveness and their need for the Gospel. What are the reasons for the ways that people are categorized in your community?

5. Devote a whole day to categorizing as Paul does. Every time you meet someone or hear about people in other parts of the world, ask yourself two questions: (a) How is this person or group culturally different from me? (b) Is this person or group probably headed for heaven or for hell? The purpose of this exercise is not to judge people, for only God knows each person's ultimate end. Rather, the intent is to become sensitized to the fact that "multitudes who sleep in the dust of the earth will awake: some to everlasting life, others to shame and everlasting contempt" (Dan 12:2).

6. In *Seven Worlds to Win,* Morris Watkins focuses on seven ethno-religious categories of people: the Chinese world, the Buddhist world, the Hindu world, the Muslim world, the Bibleless and illiterate world, the Communist world, and the so-called Christian world. Read Rom 1:15. What obligation do you and your church have to the seven worlds that need to be won?

7. Use your imagination. Meditate on Rom 1:18–32, picturing the lost in your mind. As the text progresses, imagine the people described there as receding farther and farther from God. Do not do this in a rushed manner. Take your time and let Paul's imagery break your heart with divine compassion for those who are in this lost condition.

8. Brainstorm for a few minutes. When you hear the word *glory,* what words or thoughts come to mind? Jot them down. When you finish, analyze your list. How many items have to do with the glory of God? How many refer to the glory of the human race?

9. That was fun. Let's brainstorm again. When you hear the phrase *glorify God,* what thoughts come to mind? Take your time compiling another list, and then look it over. How many items have to do with glorifying the Lord inside the walls of your sanctuary? How many deal with glorifying him out before the eyes of the

world? Analyze the ratio of "inside glorifying" to "outside glorifying."

10. Phillip Keller says we are like sheep who, while out in the pasture, attract wandering sheep to the Good Shepherd. Sheep cannot do this while in the fold. How can we attract people to Christ while we are sitting in church?
11. Memorize Ezek 36:23: "Then the nations will know that I am the Lord, declares the Sovereign LORD, when I show myself holy through you before their eyes." Ponder its meaning for you and your church.
12. Compare and contrast these two verses: (a) "God's name is blasphemed among the Gentiles because of you" (Rom 2:24); and (b) "God is not ashamed to be called their God" (Heb 11:16).

Notes

1. Rom 2:24 is based on both Is 52:5 and Ezek 36:22. Paul's use of Isaiah 52–53 in the book of Romans will be dealt with later, in chapter 13. Here in chapter 7, we wish to point out the amazing context of Ezekiel 36.
2. Ezek 36:24 adds that, for the Jews at that time, God's plan of sanctification included bringing them back from exile to Israel. Verses 25–27 are stressed here because of the prophecy about God's sanctifying methods for all believers.

8

Righteousness
Romans 3:20–5:21

Seeing It New

Visiting a familiar place after having been away for some time or after a life-changing experience can give you a whole new perspective on what is there. This writer [Bob] grew up in the Detroit area and as a child would frequently visit Greenfield Village and the Henry Ford Museum on family outings or school field trips. As an adult I moved to another state and did not return to these historical sites for many years. When I did, I was amazed by the things which I saw as an adult that I had missed as a child.

Such was the experience we had when we studied Rom 3:20–5:21, after we had learned what the Scriptures say about obedience. Although this familiar section of the Bible had lost none of its original meaning or beauty, we now found it to contain a wealth of truth about the meaning of righteousness that we had never grasped before. Righteousness is usually defined as "a right standing with God"; but as you read on, you will discover many different aspects of the concept of righteousness.

In this chapter we will find out what Paul means by "the righteousness that comes by faith," and why Abraham was an excellent example of it. We will also discover what Paul has in mind when he speaks of the "hope of glory." We will learn how Christ, the second Adam, causes righteousness to reign, rather than sin and death. Finally, we will see the danger of neglecting either Paul's warning against works righteousness or his emphasis on "the obedience that comes from faith."

The Righteousness That Comes by Faith

Rom 3:20–5:21 is Paul's fundamental treatise on justification by grace through faith in Jesus Christ. In Rom 3:23–25a, Paul uses three key terms that present us with three different word pictures for our salvation:

> For all have sinned and fall short of the glory of God, and are *justified* freely by his grace through the *redemption* that came by Christ Jesus. God presented him as a *sacrifice of atonement,* through faith in his blood (emphasis ours).

Use your imagination to appreciate the Gospel message conveyed by each of these pictures.

The Image of the Courtroom

The first key word, *justified* (also translated as *declared righteous* in Rom 3:20), presents us with a judicial image. Picture yourself as a defendant standing trial in a courtroom. God, seated behind the bench and robed in all his majesty, is the judge. Knowing that you are guilty, you tremble with fear. Standing beside you, however, is your advocate, your defense attorney, Jesus Christ. Jesus pleads eloquently on your behalf before his Father, and even though you are guilty, God the Father graciously declares you *righteous,* or *not guilty,* for Jesus' sake. Your entire burden of guilt is lifted, and you no longer have to stand in fear before God. In a line from his song "Jubilee," Michael Card expresses eloquently how it feels

> To be so completely guilty,
> And given over to despair.
> To look into your Judge's face
> And see a Savior there
> (Card 1989).

That's what it means to be *justified.*

The Image of Sacrifice

But why would the righteous Judge declare a guilty person *not guilty*? How can this be done? Paul uses another metaphor, "a sacrifice of atonement" (Rom 3:25), to explain. With this phrase he takes us back to the Old Testament Day of Atonement and to the sacrifices that were offered for the sins of the people. However, none of the animals sacrificed truly atoned for sin. In the same way, nothing you do could ever atone, that is, pay the penalty for your sin.

Imagine that you are condemned to die in the electric chair because you have murdered an innocent person. All your appeals and legal maneuvers have failed, and you are being led to the place of execution. At the last moment appears the brother of the innocent victim of your crime. In his hand he holds a pardon from the governor allowing you to go free—with one stipulation: the brother must take your punishment upon himself and die in your place. This he willingly agrees to do.

Unbelievable? Yes. Nonetheless, this is what Jesus Christ has done for you! By his life of perfect obedience and his death of perfect love, he made the one sacrifice to God that really and truly atones for sin. By his death on the cross, he paid the penalty in full for all your sins; and through faith in him, his perfect righteousness is credited to you. Therefore God is right in declaring you "not guilty."

The Image of Ransom from Slavery

The third key word that Paul uses in Rom 3:23–25 to picture our salvation is *redemption*. With this word he introduces the concept of slavery. Imagine yourself living in the pre-Civil War South. You are a slave, cruelly mistreated by a master who forces you with whip and club to fulfill his harsh demands. Utterly miserable, you long for a freedom that seems impossible. One day, however, a kind woman comes along and pays the ransom necessary to set you free. Would you feel gratitude toward that person? Would you offer her willing service because she showed you mercy?

Christ is the one who paid the ransom to redeem us, to buy us back from our slavery under sin. This picture shows us what God has accomplished in declaring us righteous. Not only has he removed the guilt of our sin, but he has also redeemed us from slavery to sin, freeing us to serve him.

In these three images the Gospel rings out—loud and clear. God has declared us righteous for Christ's sake through our faith in him. Works of the Law have nothing to do with it! Quite naturally, therefore, Paul asks, "Do we, then, nullify the law by this faith?" And, in answer to his own question he replies, "Not at all! Rather, we uphold the law" (Rom 3:31). The Law is not nullified by the

Gospel, because Christ himself perfectly fulfilled the righteous requirements of God's Law. We are justified because Christ our Savior was just. Christ's sacrifice of atonement is the legal basis for God to declare us righteous. He maintains his integrity as an impartial, righteous judge while still setting us free, because of Christ's sacrifice.

Abraham, the Father of All Who Believe

In Romans 4, Paul moves from speaking in general about the righteousness that comes by faith to the specific example of Abraham. We treasure this section of Romans because here Paul makes it so abundantly clear that, like Abraham's righteousness, ours also is an imputed righteousness. Imputed means that it is credited to us for Christ's sake. The word Paul uses for credited or imputed is the Greek verb *logizomai*. It means to reckon or account, to credit or charge something to someone. By faith, Christ's righteousness is credited to our account, and God reckons us as being righteous in his sight. Paul makes this so plain in Rom 4:23–25:

> The words "it was credited to him" were written not for him alone, but also for us, to whom God will credit righteousness—for us who believe in him who raised Jesus our Lord from the dead. He was delivered over to death for our sins and was raised to life for our justification.

What a tremendous Gospel promise! Yet, as we revel in it, we must guard against "Gospel myopia" by asking ourselves, to whom do these words apply? Paul makes plain that this promise of righteousness is as wide as the whole wide world. He carefully points out that when righteousness was credited to Abraham by faith, he was still uncircumcised; in other words, he was still a Gentile. Therefore, Paul stresses that Abraham is the father of *all* who believe, whether they are Jews or Gentiles.

At the beginning of Romans 4, Paul quotes Gen 15:6. In its original context, this verse follows on the heels of God's promise to Abraham that his descendants would be as numerous as the stars in the sky. This is the promise that Abraham believed, and his faith was credited to him as righteousness. On that night Abraham with the naked eye could see a few thousand stars. Today, with the aid of telescopes, we know that there are billions. Was Abraham's vision of what God would accomplish limited to what he could see? Probably not. He knew God's promise meant that there would be countless people who would be called "children of Abraham" because they shared his faith.

God wants us to have that same faith and mission vision. You may personally know only a few hundred people. Even if you go to a huge stadium, you can see no more than 100,000 people at one time; but we know that there are more than 5 billion people on this earth. God wants to save them just as much as you and me. We're worth no more to him than they are. Is our faith wide enough to believe God loves them all? Christ died for all of them, and the Holy Spirit wants to use us to lead each and every one of them to share Abraham's faith in the one true God.

In this section Paul emphasizes the global implications of God's salvation. He insists that blessedness is for both the *circumcised* and the *uncircumcised* (4:9). He calls Abraham the *father of all who believe* (4:11), *a father of many nations* (4:18), and *heir of the world* (4:13). All who presently believe are part of Abraham's inheritance, as are people all over the world whom we must claim for him by proclaiming the Gospel to every nation. Abraham will greet us at the gate to heaven, and he'll be looking for his inheritance. Let's not let him down. If we fail to believe that the Gospel is intended for everyone on the face of the earth, then, even though we ourselves are saved, the goal of the Gospel will not be fully realized in our lives.

In Romans 5, Paul repeatedly uses the terms *all men* and *the many*.

> Therefore, just as sin entered the world through one man, and death through sin, and in this way death came to *all* men, because all sinned . . . . But the gift is not like the trespass. For if *the many* died by the trespass of the one man, how much more did God's grace and the gift that came by the grace of the one man, Jesus Christ, overflow to *the many*! (Rom 5:12, 15; emphasis ours).

By these terms Paul is helping us recognize that the grace of God for eternal life is intended for all. In order for *all men* to receive this life, they must believe; and in order for them to believe, the Gospel of Jesus Christ must be proclaimed. Thus, in these phrases Paul presents the mission aspect of the goal of the Gospel one more time.

The Greek words that Paul used for *the many* are *hoi polloi.* The phrase, *hoi polloi,* has been taken over into English to refer to the common people, the masses. Writers often use the term as a put down. It brings to mind the lower classes, perhaps the sprawling crowds living in poverty on the streets of Bombay or those packed into the high rise projects in Chicago or New York. Paul warns us not to look with disdain on the *hoi polloi—the many.* These are souls Christ died to save! Their sins have been paid for by his precious blood. How can we ever turn our backs on them or divert our eyes from them? Christ died for *the many,* but how many of them will ever come to know him as their Savior from sin depends upon how strenuously we work at proclaiming the Gospel and how well we connect the Gospel with its goal of living righteously to glorify God.

The Hope of Glory

Paul begins Romans 5 by reminding us that, by grace through faith in Jesus Christ, we have peace with God. This marvelous truth gives us reason to "rejoice in the hope of the glory of God" (Rom 5:2). What a great hope that is when you consider what Paul said about mankind's lack of glory in Romans 2–3! There Paul made it very clear that every human being was in desperate need of the righteousness from God that comes through faith, "for all have sinned and fall short of the glory of God" (Rom 3:23). What does Paul mean by *the glory of God?* There are several aspects.

Aspects of Glory

1. The glory of God can mean the glory we receive from God, a *doxology,* that is, his approval or praise. When a child comes home with straight As on her report card, Mom and Dad are likely to heap praise on their daughter and commend her highly for her excellent work. If, however, this same child comes home the following quarter with a report card full of Ds and Fs, there will be no glorious words of approval but only stinging words of correction and reproof. Before God, our report card is one

big F for failure to obey his Law. Thus we have fallen far short of receiving the glory of his praise.

2. The glory of God can also refer to the glory he bestowed on us at creation, the glory he wanted Adam and Eve to share in the garden. This is the glory of reflecting his image and obeying his will. Because of our sinful rebellion, we have also fallen short of this aspect of God's glory.

3. The glory of living according to God's plan brings glory to his name. God intended for our lives to be a *living doxology* to him. When Pete Rose was playing professional baseball, he brought much glory to the game. He played baseball with more enthusiasm, drive, and determination than anyone, and racked up more hits than any other player in the history of the game. At the end of his career, however, Rose's gambling activities only heaped shame and disgrace on himself and on the game he loved. By our sin, we have brought only shame and disgrace on God and his name. We have fallen far short of his glory.

4. Finally, the glory of God means sharing his glory for all eternity in heaven. On our own, we have no hope of this glory. As sinners, we deserve only everlasting punishment and condemnation. Yes, Paul was right in saying that "all have sinned and fall short of the glory of God" (Rom 3:23). However, God wants to restore us to his glory.

When Paul talks about "rejoicing in the hope of the glory of God" (Rom 5:2), we need to consider all four aspects of glory. He means not only our future hope of sharing God's glory in heaven but also the possibility of glorifying God this side of heaven. Even though we will never perfectly display God's glory here on earth, we have the sure hope of being able to glorify God right now to a substantial degree, because in Christ we have been made righteous, that is, both declared righteous and empowered to live righteously through faith in Jesus Christ.

Transformed to Give God Glory

Plainly, "the hope of the glory of God" that Paul is talking about (5:2) is both celestial (heavenly) glory and terrestrial (here and now) glory. Both of these aspects of glory are founded entirely on the good news of what God has done for us in Christ. Therefore, after speaking of the hope of glory, Paul returns to the heart of the Gospel message to remind us of the wonderful things Christ has accomplished for us:

> You see, at just the right time, when we were still powerless, Christ died for the ungodly. Very rarely will anyone die for a righteous man, though for a good man someone might possibly dare to die. But God demonstrates his own love for us in this: While we were still sinners, Christ died for us.
>
> Since we have now been justified by his blood, how much more shall we be saved from God's wrath through him! For if, when we were God's enemies, we were reconciled to him through the death of his Son, how much more, having been reconciled, shall we be saved through his life! Not only is this so, but we also rejoice in God through our Lord Jesus Christ, through whom we have now received reconciliation (Rom 5:6–11).

This is one of the most beautiful sections in the Bible because it displays the absolute grace of God. Look at the way in which Paul describes us at the time when God sent his Son into the world to save us. We were *powerless.* We were *ungodly.* We were *sinners* and *God's enemies.* Could there ever be any question about our unworthiness to receive God's amazing grace?

At the same time, Paul's repetition of the phrase "when we were" implies that there has been a subsequent transformation and that we no longer are what we used to be. There is an implicit contrast between the past and the present, because "God has poured out his love into our hearts by the Holy Spirit" (5:5).

Let's look at this contrast by placing our former and present states side by side.

We were powerless.	Now we have the Spirit's power.
We were ungodly.	Now we have been declared righteous in Christ.
We were sinners.	Now we have been equipped to live righteously.
We were God's enemies.	Now we have been reconciled to him through the death of his Son.

What a contrast! True, we are still sinners—even after we have

160

been saved. But God has already promoted us to the rank of sinner/ saint while we await our final promotion to the rank of sin-free saint in heaven.

Our sin and rebellion make us totally worthless to God (Rom 3:12). How wonderful it is to realize that Christ died for the worthless in order to make us people worth dying for, worthy of bearing his name! We have every reason to rejoice, for Jesus has reconciled us to God, and his Spirit is at work in our lives. What a transformation he causes in our attitudes! Now we see sin not so much as breaking God's Law but rather as breaking God's heart. How could we ever desire to break the heart of him who loved us so much that he gave his own Son to die for us? God's love in Christ Jesus motivates us to obey God's will to the glory of his name!

Adam One and Adam Two

In order to help us understand even more completely what God has done for us in Jesus, Paul concludes this fabulous Gospel section by comparing Adam and Christ. Once again, by means of this comparison, he paints the big picture, reminding us of everything God intended for us when he first created us and of everything he wants to accomplish in us by sending his Son.

In Rom. 5:12–21, *reign* is a key word that Paul uses four times to highlight what God has done for us in Christ, the second Adam. Paul begins by telling us that death reigned by the trespass of the first Adam, making all of us sinners and condemning us to die. Paul points out that the first Adam's sin caused death even before the law of Moses was given. When God gave Moses the law, it did not have the power to restore humankind to the first Adam's state. This had to wait until God's own Son became the second Adam.

In Eastern Europe, Romanians lived under the reign of Marxist dictator, Nicolae Ceausescu, for 42 years. His was Europe's most repressive communist regime; and Ceausescu's hated policies left a bitter legacy of oppression, impoverishment, and mistrust in the lives of the Romanian people. In Panama, military strongman Manuel Noriega made that country his own personal drug capital where he freely engaged in smuggling, money laundering, and protection rackets for other drug traffickers. He held the narrow isthmus in his stranglehold. Truly, death reigned under both these tyrants through the Securitate forces in Romania and the drug dealers in Panama. Then, in December of 1989, death's reign was overthrown as both their kingdoms toppled. The communist government in Romania collapsed under the onslaught of its own people, who could no longer bear the burden of its evil. And Noriega's reign in Panama was cut short by an invasion of thousands of American troops. Finally, there was hope for freedom in both these lands.

In a similar but, in fact, much greater way, Christ came to rescue us from death's reign. Adam was his pattern (Rom 5:14). He was everything God wanted the first Adam to be: perfect, the very image of God, and completely obedient to God. His total obedience and perfect sacrifice brought salvation to all, just as Adam, by his sin, brought death to all. Christ accomplished what God had intended for Adam to do. He has produced a race of people who can be God-loving, obedient, and live in fellowship with him forever, giving glory to his name. God has declared this new race righteous through faith in Christ, the second Adam, equipped them for righteous living by the power of the Holy Spirit, and prepared for them perfect righteousness in heaven.

The Reign of Righteousness

Note carefully what Paul says reigns under the second Adam:

> For if, by the trespass of the one man, death reigned through that one man, how much more will those who receive God's abundant provision of grace and of the gift of righteousness reign in life through the one man, Jesus Christ (Rom 5:17).

Since death reigned under the first Adam, we might have expected Paul to say that under Christ, life reigns. Instead, Paul says that "righteousness reigns in life" (Rom 5:17). Certainly, this means that we have eternal life because we have been declared righteous on account of Christ through faith in him. But is there more? Could Paul also be reminding us that this side of heaven we ought to live righteous lives to the glory of God because of what Christ has done for us? In Romans 6, Paul uses the word *reign* to tell us that we must not let sin reign in our bodies (Rom 6:12). That same word used here (5:17) indicates that Paul is already connecting the Gospel itself with the goal of the Gospel. He is tying justification to sanctification, something we must always do, because it is impossible to have one without the other.

Notice Paul's careful distinctions. In Rom 5:15 he distinguishes between (1) grace, and (2) the gift that came by grace. Again in Rom 5:17, he distinguishes between (1) God's abundant provision of grace, and (2) the gift of righteousness. In so doing, Paul is deliberately making a distinction between justification (grace) and sanctification (the gift of righteousness).

At this point, it may seem as though the authors are splitting hairs (something theologians love to do). Nevertheless, there are times when even a hair's breadth can make a crucial difference. A machinist understands that a single micron (one millionth of a meter) can be critical in determining whether or not a part will function properly. Electrical engineers measure the speed of computer chips in nanoseconds, each of which is one billionth of a second. Fine distinctions are sometimes important; and on this occasion we need to make a fine distinction between God's grace, which is justification, and the gift of righteousness that comes by grace, which is sanctification.

Through faith in Jesus Christ we have received two treasures. We are justified, that is, God has once-for-all declared us righteous. In addition, we are sanctified. This means God has equipped us for righteous living, a process through which we daily become more like Christ. This double blessing that God has given us in Christ is something law enforcers wish they could give to law breakers.

Judge Louis Morgan sat behind the bench trying desperately to conceal the disgust he felt inside. The case against the defendant had been clear cut. He was guilty. The evidence was irrefutable. The witnesses unimpeachable. "Why did that legal technicality have to get in the way of what should have been an easy conviction?" he asked himself. "I know he's just going to go back out on the street and commit the same crime again! It's so easy for me to set him free. Why can't it be just as easy for me to change him so he won't continue to hurt people?"

God's goal is not only to justify us. As the just judge, he does not let the guilty go free to continue in sin. For the sake of his Son's self-sacrifice, he declares us not guilty so that we may be restored to the righteousness which we had at creation. His goal and purpose in declaring us righteous is to rehabilitate us.

To rehabilitate means "to restore to a condition of good health, ability to work, or the like." It also means, "to restore to former capacity." A human judge might wish that he could rehabilitate the criminals who come before him, but that is not within his power. He might be able to declare them "not guilty," but he cannot equip them to live as law-abiding citizens. Yet this is exactly what our righteous Judge can do. He has the power to rehabilitate us through his Word (2 Tim 3:16–17) and his Spirit (Gal 5:25).

The fact that God is able to rehabilitate sinners is also the reason Paul could say that the Gospel does not nullify the Law (Rom 3:31). As we spread the Gospel of Jesus Christ with it, we are spreading the obedience of faith to the ends of the earth. Through the Gospel God is making it possible for Jew and Gentile alike to attempt to follow the Law, using it to guide their lives.

This is illustrated by a story I [Bob] remember about Ludwig Nommensen, pioneer missionary to the Batak tribe of Sumatra, Indonesia. At the end of two years, when Nommensen was supposed to leave, the chief asked him what made Christianity unique. After all, his people's religion also spoke against stealing, adultery, and bearing false witness. Nommensen answered, "My Master gives me the power to keep his laws." As a result, the chief allowed Nommensen to stay six more months in order to teach the people the power of the Gospel to transform lives.

When the six months were up, the chief said, "Stay. Our religion tells us what to do. Your God says, 'Come; I will walk with you and give you the strength to do good.'" Today, God walks with nearly half-a-million Batak Christians. As they live according to his plan, their lives testify that the Gospel does not nullify the Law but rather upholds it by equipping the ones he has justified for righteous living.

Because God's Gospel does not nullify his Law, Paul does not want to separate the Gospel from its goal. He uses the word *credit* in Romans 4 and *reign* in Romans 5 (repeating both in Romans 6 where he speaks of sanctification), implying that in Romans 3–5 he is already connecting justification with its results. His painstaking distinction between the grace of God and the gift of righteousness in Romans 5 demonstrates the same thing. In Paul's thinking, therefore, righteousness means both the righteousness that declares us not guilty and the power that destroys sin's domination of our lives.

The thought of a lived-out righteousness cannot be separated from declared righteousness.[1]

Every Church Has Its Weakness

The apostle summarizes Rom. 3:20–5:21 in the following words:

The law was added so that the trespass might increase. But where sin increased, grace increased all the more, so that, just as sin reigned in death, so also *grace might reign through righteousness to bring eternal life* through Jesus Christ our Lord (Rom 5:20–21; emphasis ours).

Clearly, Paul's summary reminds his readers of the "righteousness that comes through faith." This message of justification by grace through faith is the heart and core of the Gospel, to be treasured above all else. But there is another reminder to be found in Paul's summary.

To understand properly Paul's closing statement in Rom. 5:20–21, we need to remember his theme in Rom 1:5, "the obedience that comes from faith." The obedience of faith is the goal and result of the righteousness that comes through faith in Jesus Christ. In 5:21, Paul indeed says that God's grace alone causes our salvation. At the same time, however, he is reminding us that by God's grace we are *equipped* for righteousness, for the obedience of faith, so that the witness of our righteous living and speaking may bring others to eternal life, leading them to faith in Jesus Christ. When this happens, God's grace will overflow to the many. Clearly, the goal of the Gospel, the reason we have received God's grace, is to call people from among all nations to the obedience that comes from faith, to the praise of his name (1:5).

We dare not forget the three key concepts Paul includes in Rom 5:20–21: (1) His warning against righteousness by keeping the Law is crucial. (2) The Gospel of justification by grace through faith is central. (3) The obedience of faith is the goal of the Gospel and must never be forgotten. Unfortunately, numerous churches have forgotten one or the other of these concepts at various times. The following story illustrates this danger. The author did not arbitrarily decide to pick on the three church bodies described below. The story is true. However, the same dangers could just as easily be exposed in other Christian denominations or in specific congregations within denominations.

John and Sue met while they were in college and decided to get married right after graduation. This raised the question of where, since John had a solid background in one denomination while Sue had been raised in a very different Christian tradition. They agreed to try to find some common ground, since neither of them was entirely happy with their own religious upbringing.

John valued certain things about his early religious training. Ever since his days as an altar boy, he had appreciated the sense of awe and reverence for God which the liturgies and ceremonies of worship in his church conveyed. However, he was frequently troubled because he had no real assurance of salvation. He was never certain that he had done enough good with the grace he had received through the sacraments to merit God's favor for eternity. Therefore, heaven was always a big question mark.

What John felt was the effects of being part of a church that had forgotten Paul's warning to those who try to be righteous by keeping the Law (3:20). When that happens, the "obedience of faith" may become nothing more than another term for works righteousness.

Sue, on the other hand, heard the Gospel many times in the small Protestant church where she grew up. She understood and believed that Jesus died on the cross to pay for all of her sins. At the same time, however, she had also heard much about Law; and there didn't seem to be much connection between the two. In practical terms, Sue's religious training seemed to consist of a long list of don'ts which were regularly reinforced with warnings about hellfire and damnation. Fears of condemnation seemed to be the major motivation for doing the right thing.

Sue was sensing that her church had failed to make the connection between being justified by faith and the obedience that comes from faith. Forgetting that true obedience flows from faith, churches may fall into the trap of legalism. When this happens, obedience becomes simply a matter of morality urged on people with threats and warnings rather than a way of life motivated by the Gospel and enabled by the Holy Spirit.

John and Sue visited many different denominations as they looked for a church in which to be married. They finally decided that they both felt most comfortable in a church near the college campus. It seemed to offer them the best of both worlds. John appreciated the liturgies that regularly formed the heart of the worship services. Sue liked hearing the Gospel clearly proclaimed each Sunday. This church gave John the assurance of salvation he had been lacking in the past, while Sue enjoyed some relief from the often legalistic tone of the preaching in her home church.

This new church really did become "home" for John and Sue, yet sometimes they still felt something was missing. In his old church, John had heard a steady emphasis on good works; and even though he now understood that good works could never save him, he almost wondered now if there was something wrong with good works. Sue hadn't liked the "don't do this, don't do that" attitude in the church of her youth, yet she couldn't understand why she heard so little about obedience to God's Law in their new congregation.

What John and Sue were experiencing in the denomination they had chosen was a tendency to emphasize the righteousness that is by faith and to ignore the obedience of faith. When this happens, one can easily lose sight of the goal of the Gospel. Then God's purpose in redeeming us suffers from neglect. Sanctification, mission, and the glory of God are not given their proper place in the Christian life. Although their church properly proclaimed repentance and faith, it overlooked the fruit of faith.

Christians must be on guard against all the dangers found in these three churches. The pure and precious Gospel of God's grace must ever be proclaimed in all its power. Isaiah said, "How beautiful on the mountains are the feet of those who bring good news, who proclaim peace, who bring good tidings, who proclaim salvation, who say to Zion, 'Your God reigns!' " (Is 52:7). But it is only when the grace of God produces righteous living that attracts other people to Christ that our God truly reigns!

Digging Deeper

1. Imagine yourself in each of the three pictures Paul drew in Rom 3:24–25 to describe salvation: the courtroom, where you are declared righteous; the atonement, where your sin is paid for by the sacrifice of another; and slavery, where the ransom is

paid to set you free. Talk about the feelings you experience as you picture yourself in each situation.

2. Write a thank you note to God for the free gift of justification by grace through faith. Share it with someone you know.

3. The next time you are in a crowded place, look around and notice the people. Estimate how many there are. Notice their different ethnic or social backgrounds, and think of the millions of others they represent. Ask yourself, how many of them know Christ? Remind yourself that the promise of salvation is for them also. What is your role in sharing the Gospel with the many?

4. Read ahead to Romans 6, especially verses 11–14. There Paul tells us that we should reckon, or account (*logizomai*), ourselves as being "dead to sin and alive to God in Christ Jesus" (6:11). He also says not to let "sin reign in your mortal body" (6:12).

5. After reading Romans 6, state the reasons why you agree or disagree with the following: Paul uses the same words, *reign* and *reckon,* in both Romans 4 and 6. He is implying that the declared righteousness that is ours and appropriated by faith in Jesus Christ should result in a lived righteousness by which we serve God and glorify him. God first reckons us righteous so that we can then reckon ourselves as new creations.

6. Think about the four aspects of glory and see if you can match these Bible passages with them.

   ___ Heb 2:10   a. Receiving God's praise
   ___ Rom 2:24   b. Living according to God's image
   ___ Mat 25:23   c. Bringing glory to God's name
   ___ Col 3:10   d. Sharing God's glory eternally

7. Consider how Paul in Rom 5:6–11 describes what we were like before Christ came to save us. In your own words, describe the changes that Christ's salvation has made in you. What kind of transformation have you experienced?

8. Make a list of comparisons between the first Adam and Jesus Christ, the second Adam (see Rom 5:12–21). In what ways were they similar? In what ways different?

9. In your mind, picture sin and death as dictators. Describe what it would be like to live under their reign.

10. Explain the difference between the two gifts that Paul, in Rom 5:15 and 5:17, says we have received from God.

11. Think about the dangers found in the three churches John and Sue belonged to. Do you see similar dangers in your church? What can you do to help your church overcome such danger?

Note

1. Gottlob Schrenk emphasizes this same idea in his article on *dikaiosune* (*righteousness*) in the *Theological Dictionary of the New Testament*: "Without any sense of difficulty or contradiction, the thought of pardoning and forensic righteousness passes over into that of righteousness as the living power which overcomes sin. The righteousness which is given commits the believer to the living power of that righteousness which breaks the bondage of sin" (Schrenk 1971, 209).

9

Sanctification
Romans 6:1–8:27

In Romans 6–8, Paul enters new territory. Having explained how God declares us righteous, now he reveals how the Lord equips and empowers us for righteous, obedient living that glorifies our Creator. Churches are filled with people who, although desiring to do good, constantly wrestle with temptation, sin, guilt, and feelings of wretchedness. Here Paul honestly addresses this common struggle and realistically portrays how the Gospel daily lifts us up both with its promise of pardon from sin and with its promise of power over sin.

Theologians call the process by which God makes us holy *sanctification*. Unique among all Paul's writings, these chapters meticulously develop sanctification concepts, which he deals with only briefly in his other letters (2 Cor 5:17; Gal 2:20; Eph 4:22–24; Col 3:1–10). But why is it in Romans that Paul devotes three full chapters to explaining the intricate details of sanctification? Why is it here that he so honestly examines the frustrations of being simultaneously saint and sinner? Those who hold that Romans has only one major theme, justification, are unable to answer these questions convincingly.

Paul wrote, not with one theme in mind, but with a chain of themes that we have identified as Scripture, salvation in Christ, obedience, worldwide mission, and the glorification of God. In view of this five-link Gospel chain, the appearance of three lengthy chapters on sanctification is not at all surprising but wholly expected and logical.

Is Sanctification Good News or Bad News?

In Romans 1–3:20, Paul described the unrighteousness of the human race. Created to be joyful doers of God's holy will, we be-

170

came miserable pursuers of our own selfish desires. Unable to reform our sinful nature, we are objects of God's wrath and punishment. This teaching is called the Law of God.

In Rom 3:21–5:21, Paul portrayed how Christ liberates us from the Law's accusation. Trusting in God's promise of pardon through the valid and acceptable sacrifice of Jesus Christ on the cross, we are declared righteous and set free from the sentence we deserve. This teaching is called the Gospel, the good news of Jesus Christ, or justification.

In Romans 6—8, Paul reveals how God helps us to defeat sin in our daily lives. Here is a question for you to ponder as you read this chapter: Is the Bible's message of sanctification *Law* or *Gospel*? Is it bad news or good news? Opinions certainly vary. Your response to items below are likely to indicate whether you view this area of biblical teaching as Law or Gospel. Take a moment to investigate your attitude.

Sanctification Attitude Check

	Agree	Sometimes	Disagree
1. I prefer to read only the parts of the Bible that comfort me rather than the sections that challenge me to live for Christ.	1	2	3
2. The Bible's teaching about obedience leaves me feeling guilty rather than hungering and thirsting for righteousness.	1	2	3
3. When the Scriptures tell me to put on the new self or to put on Christ, this only sounds like another rule that I am incapable of keeping.	1	2	3
4. The Law only accuses and condemns people, even Christians. It is ineffectual as a rule or guide for life.	1	2	3

5. I find little practical comfort in the promise that the Holy Spirit will help me in times of temptation.	1	2	3

Add up your figures. If you scored 10 or higher, you tend to view sanctification as good news. If you scored under 10 points, you probably view sanctification as bad news. Now you have an idea of where you stand regarding this issue.

We authors wish to be candid with you. If your score was low, our goal in this chapter is to adjust your attitude. This is our goal because we believe it was Paul's goal when he penned Romans 6–8. Although our obedience in no way contributes to our salvation, nevertheless, Paul wants us to recognize and rejoice in the good news that God provides strength to oppose sin. Indeed, God's provision of such strength is part of the salvation that Christ has procured for us. As Milton Rudnick affirms:

> The Gospel in its fullness says not only, "Your sins are forgiven for Jesus' sake," but also, "With His love and Spirit he will enable you to struggle against sin and grow into his own likeness."

> In this connection it is important to note that justification and sanctification, although they must be distinguished, must never be separated. Both are gifts of God and essential components of the Gospel. It is an error to identify only justification with the Gospel and associate sanctification with the Law. "Through God's grace you can change (and, therefore should)" is as much a part of the Good News as "God does not hold your sins against you."

> In the witness of the Gospel, justification does have a primacy. God's forgiveness in Christ is the basis of his transforming work in the believer. Because he pardons us he also changes us, but not *vice versa*. Sanctification is a result of justification. That does not mean, however, that sanctification is optional or dispensable. It is a necessary result of justification and an integral part of the Gospel (Rudnick 1977, 17–18).

In what sense is sanctification a necessary result of justification? There is a necessity of *order* (no sanctification without justification); a necessity of *presence* of the indwelling grace so faith may be known; a necessity of *duty* in gratitude for Christ's benefits and obedience to the divine commandment; a necessity of *consequence* in the obedience of faith. And yet, those who by faith receive justification do not *always* lead sanctified lives. So it is all the more important that we understand the interrelationship between justification and sanctification.

Perhaps you have tended to view obedience exclusively as a matter of the Law, which accuses us. However, Paul reveals that God gives us gifts—a new heart and his Holy Spirit—to *empower* us to reach the goal of the Gospel: holiness, sharing Christ with all the world, and glorifying the name of God our Savior.

In Need of a Heart Transplant

Walt: I got bad news from the doctor last week. He says I need to have a heart transplant.

Stan: I'm sorry to hear that, Walt. With your financial liabilities, how are you ever going to swing it?

Walt: No problem, I saw an ad in a magazine for a do-it-yourself heart surgery kit.

Stan: Ha, ha. Walt, you're such a card. How can you joke about something so serious?

Walt: Who's joking? They are sending me all the equipment I need, plus an intuitive instruction manual. For only $299, it sounded like a steal. So I ordered one.

Stan: You aren't kidding, are you?

Walt: No, Stan; I'm dead serious.

If you needed heart transplant surgery, would you operate on yourself? No way! How about if you had a nurse, the instruments, and a hospital operating room at your disposal? Still no! What if you were a skilled surgeon? Would you transplant your own heart? Of course not, because you could never perform a successful operation. If you were dead set on doing it, you would only wind up dead. So if you need a new heart, you better find the right surgeon for the job.

Spiritual heart transplants prove just as difficult to perform. Try as we may, we cannot transform our sinful hearts into obedient ones. The only surgeon who can is the Lord, who promised, "I will remove from you your heart of stone and give you a heart of flesh. And I will put my Spirit in you" (Ezek 36:26–27). In the time of the prophet Ezekiel, over five hundred years before Christ, God prom-

173

ised us a heart transplant, an internal change in the depths of our being. His Spirit can move us from chronic disobedience to a desire to follow his decrees and to be careful to keep his laws (Ezek 36:27).

Thanks be to God, his grace does not stop at the point of declaring us righteous. He goes on to rehabilitate us sinners, to equip us for obedience by means of a heart transplant. In 2 Cor 1:20, Paul declares that "no matter how many promises God has made, they are 'Yes' in Christ," meaning that Jesus fulfills them. Through Ezekiel, God promised us a new heart. How did Christ fulfill this promise? This is the miracle that Paul explains in Romans 6–8. If you are not aware of this biblical doctrine, you are in for a wonderful surprise.

The Miracle of the New Self

Paul describes the believer's spiritual heart transplant in Romans 6:

> What shall we say, then? Shall we go on sinning so that grace may increase? By no means! We died to sin; how can we live in it any longer? Or don't you know that all of us who were baptized into Christ Jesus were baptized into his death? We were therefore buried with him through baptism into death in order that, just as Christ was raised from the dead through the glory of the Father, we too may live a new life.

> If we have been united with him in his death, we will certainly also be united with him in his resurrection. For we know that our old self was crucified with him so that the body of sin might be rendered powerless, that we should no longer be slaves to sin— because anyone who has died has been freed from sin (Rom 6:1–7).

Many a Christian slave has faced death with the triumphant cry, "Free at last! Thank God, I'm free at last!" Although we will never be morally perfect this side of heaven, Paul assures us that we need not remain slaves of sin, because, even though we may not be aware of it, a death has occurred in our lives that liberates us from the power and dominion of sin.

In mysterious words Paul informs us that this death occurred by means of baptism. We were united with Christ in his death, "baptized into his death." Similarly, "just as Christ was raised from the dead ... we too may live a new life." What does this mean?

As believers in Christ, we are aware that a transaction took place when Christ died. He identified with us sinners bearing our guilt and punishment as he gave himself up for us on the cross. To that transaction Paul adds a second. Not only did Christ identify *with us*, but through baptism we are identified *with Christ*, by being "baptized into Christ Jesus" and "baptized into his death." Theologians call this concept the mystical union of Christ and the believer. The mystical union means that, when Christ died, our sinful nature was dethroned, deposed, ousted. The mystical union also entails a resurrection. Just as Christ rose from the dead, so there arises in our inner being a new nature, a holy and obedient nature.

Prior to confessing Christ and being baptized, who is it who rules a person's will, emotions, thoughts, and actions? The despot is our sinful nature, also referred to in Scripture as the flesh, the old self, the old man, the heart, and so on. However, the sinful nature usually is nothing more than a puppet ruler, bending to the evil influences of Satan and the unbelieving world.

With our baptism a revolution occurs. The Holy Spirit invades the heart, throwing the sinful nature out of office; and in its place creates a new nature that is capable and even desirous of obeying God. This change in ruler is more than a *coup d'etat*, however. It is a *coup de cour*, a revolution of the heart. Other biblical terms for the new nature include the spirit, the new self, the new man, the new life, the new creation, the mind, the image of God, Christ in you, to be in Christ, and to put on Christ.

How does this transformation occur? Well, it is as easy to explain as any other miracle. It happens purely by the grace and power of our loving God who wishes not only to redeem us but also to rehabilitate us. Having united us with Christ through baptism, the Lord shares all his experiences with us. He has died; we died to sin. He rose again; we have new life.

Grafted into Christ

Paul is not the only New Testament teacher to describe this miraculous transformation. Jesus himself taught about the new spirit within us, using the language of plant husbandry:

> I am the vine; you are the branches. If a man remains in me and
> I in him, he will bear much fruit; apart from me you can do
> nothing. . . . This is to my Father's glory, that you bear much fruit,
> showing yourselves to be my disciples (Jn 15:5, 8).

The fruit that Jesus says we are to bear includes both good works, which demonstrate Christ's love in action, and good confession of faith, which the Holy Spirit uses to lead others to Christ. These are the acts of righteousness for which we were created and redeemed (Eph 2:10). How will we ever bear such fruit? Can we produce a harvest on our own power? Not at all, for Jesus warns, "apart from me you can do nothing." The power to live for God must come from God himself. As singer Keith Green quipped, "He is divine and we are dee branch."

Jesus' words make perfect sense when we consider how plant husbandry functions. When a particular plant, vine, or tree fails to bear good fruit, the caretaker has two options. He may tear out or cut down the unproductive plant so that the space can be used for another, or he may graft its branches into a productive plant. This plant surgery brings dramatic effects.

Like a vinekeeper seeking choice grapes, God continually looked for righteousness in us, his creatures (Isaiah 5). However, generation after generation, century after century, in his search for human holiness, he came up empty-handed—until there arose one Man who indeed met all of his righteous requirements. Jesus Christ was the only fruitful vine in all of human history. Praise God, in his mercy he has not torn us out nor cut us down as we deserve. Instead, he has opted to graft us and millions of others into the one fruitful vine, into Jesus, putting to death what is weak and diseased in us. As long as we remain in him by faith, his power to produce acts of righteousness flows into us. This is the obedience that comes through faith in Christ.

John 15 speaks of us as branches that bear fruit because we remain in Christ the vine. Romans 6 speaks of our union with Christ's death and resurrection through baptism, so that the old sinful self is crucified. Are Jesus and Paul speaking of the same reality? We may conclude that they are because of the Greek verb Paul uses in Rom 6:5, which we have italicized for emphasis: "If we have *been united* with him in his death, we will certainly also be united with him in his resurrection." The Greek word translated *united with* is *symphytoi*, which means *to be grown together with,* or *to be grafted into.* Having been grafted into Christ's death and resurrection, we have been granted his power to live a new life of obedience rather than rebellion.

The New Math of the New Self

What shall we do with this information? Is the new self only an abstract concept, or is it a reality that can have a real impact on the way we live? The impact will be significant if we do three things that Paul urges in Romans 6: know, count, and offer.

1. Know

For our new self to change the way we live, first we must know about it. This explains why Paul uses the verb *know* repeatedly in Rom 6:3, 6, and 9. He wants the Romans to be fully aware that God has equipped them for obedience. The Christian who does not know about the new self prays like this: "Lord, I have failed you so many times. Make me willing to serve you. If it is your will, change me so that I can obey you faithfully." Such praying longs and pleads for God to work a miracle which he has already performed. In contrast, the disciple who knows about the new self can pray, "Thank you, Lord, for changing me, for dethroning my sinful nature so that it need no longer dominate me. I thank you that when my new self and the Holy Spirit work in tandem, you are working in me to will and to act according to your good pleasure" (see Phil 2:13).

Songwriter Paul Thorson states the issue in sharp terms. Beginning with a reference to some mistaken New Age views of personality, Thorson proceeds to define how Christians may legitimately look at themselves:

I AM
A lot of folks are trying hard to find out who they are.
The mirrors can't be trusted, so they study silent stars.
And even true believers look within to see,
But the answer to "Who am I?" is seen in "Who is He?"

He is love. He's the Son.

He's righteous. He's the faithful one.
He's strong. He's true.
He's just and He's gentle too.

As He is so am I in His death and in His life,
Dead to sin, alive in Christ, precious in His sight.
I will ever see myself that way
When I humbly look, boldly look at Him and say,
"I am love. I'm a son.
I'm righteous. I'm a faithful one.
I'm strong. I'm true.
I'm just and I'm gentle too.
He's just and He's gentle too"
(Thorson 1978).

At first glance, these lyrics may strike us as presumptuous. How dare we refer to ourselves as righteous, faithful, or true, when we are poor miserable sinners? We can only dare to do so because God, who sees us as righteous, faithful, and true in Christ, supplies us His power and presence. Notice how carefully Thorson states the proper use of this doctrine: "When I humbly look, boldly look at Him and say...." Here is our reassurance and our hope for renewal! Based upon the knowledge of the new self within, we must think both humbly—as sinners—and boldly—as transformed saints.

Aware of how difficult it is for us to see ourselves in this new light, Paul adds a second step we can take to grasp the teaching of the new self so it can affect our lives. "In the same way, count yourselves dead to sin but alive to God in Christ Jesus" (Rom 6:11).

2. Count

To understand what Paul means by *count,* consider the following mini-drama at the Blake household:

"Dad, can you help me with my homework?" Jason pleaded. "I've got a ton to do."

"All right, Son," Dad agreed. "What should we tackle first?"

"How about math? I didn't exactly understand what Mr. Mc-Mahon was driving at today."

"No problem. I was pretty good at math when I was in the seventh grade."

Ten minutes later, however, Jason was even more confused, and Dad was frustrated.

"I can't quite follow the way your book says to calculate these problems, but this is the way we did them when I was in school."

"Sorry, Dad, but that's not the way Mr. McMahon told us to do it."

"What ever happened to the good old math?" Dad lamented.

Math educators have developed more efficient ways to teach the art of number crunching. The new math requires new ways of visualizing numbers and calculating them. So that we will visualize ourselves in a new manner, Paul teaches us the new math of the new self.

> The death he [Christ] died, he died to sin once for all; but the life he lives, he lives to God.

> In the same way, count yourselves dead to sin, but alive to God in Christ Jesus. Therefore, do not let sin reign in your mortal body so that you obey its evil desires (Rom 6:10–12).

The Greek verb for *count* that Paul chose is highly significant. *Logizomai* is a bookkeeping term. It does not imply "fudging with the figures" but "perfectly accurate accounting." Amazingly, it is exactly the same verb used earlier in Romans to describe how God counts us righteous and forgiven.

> Abraham believed God, and it was credited (*logizomai*) to him as righteousness.

> Now when a man works, his wages are not credited (*logizomai*) to him as a gift, but as an obligation. However, to the man who does not work but trusts God who justifies the wicked, his faith is credited (*logizomai*) as righteousness.... Blessed is the man whose sin the Lord will never count (*logizomai*) against him (Rom 4:3–5, 8).

God counts us as righteous and forgiven in his sight. We are to accept that verdict as being as trustworthy a statement as $2 + 2 = 4$. Likewise, he unites us with Christ in his death and resurrection, thus creating a new self within us. We are to count on this fact of sanctification as firmly as we count on the fact of our justification.

Paul's command, "count yourselves dead to sin but alive to God in Christ Jesus," is a call to faith that results in action. Suppose you

179

have just received in the mail the statements of your bank accounts. They say you have $992.50 in checking, $2,650 in savings, and your credit card accounts are all paid up. Double checking with your own tabulations, you find this information to be wholly correct. You now know you are solvent. What do you do with that information? You count (*logizomai*) on it. You can bank (*logizomai*) on it, confidently able to spend money within the set amounts.

We should do no less in regard to counting ourselves dead to sin and alive to God in Christ Jesus. Picture yourself in an exasperating situation at work. Perhaps someone has stabbed you in the back for the umpteenth time. You could deal with that person in pity and love, or you could rant and rave at him while all your coworkers look on. Normally in such a situation you might try counting to ten, but why not try counting yourself dead to sin but alive to God in Christ Jesus? Silently remind yourself, "In Christ I am dead to sin, it doesn't have to rule over me. Help me, Lord, to act according to the change you have worked in me." In such counting (*logizomai*), you will find great power, God's power, to love your enemy.

Let's consider one more setting. The Jehovah's Witnesses are ringing your doorbell again. As you stomp to the door to shoo them away, you mutter, "I'm too busy for these pests, and besides I don't know what to say to them. I'll just tell them to get lost." The devil loves this game. You give the JW's a piece of your mind, and they leave your stoop feeling persecuted and self-righteous. Isn't there another way? Sure. Counting yourself dead to sin and alive to God, your new, God-created self will see these people as a new opportunity to witness rather than a nuisance. Paul assured Timothy that the new self equips us for faithful witness to Christ: "For God did not give us a spirit of timidity, but a spirit of power, of love, and of self-discipline. So do not be ashamed to testify about our Lord" (2 Tim. 1:7–8). By means of the new self you can give the lost people around you a piece of your heart rather than a piece of your mind.

The doctrine of our union with Christ and the presence of the new nature must be taught and stressed so that Christians may live above sin, as much as that is possible this side of heaven. One church teacher who saw this need was Martin Luther. He stated that baptism "indicates that the Old Adam (the sinful nature) in us should by daily contrition and repentance be drowned and die with all sins and evil desires, and that a new self should daily emerge and arise to live before God in righteousness and purity forever" (*The Small Catechism*, 1986 translation).

The lyrics from the Petra song "Dead Reckoning" speak in similar tones:

It's a dead reckoning
Trade the old for the new
It's a dead reckoning
Learn to die daily till the new life comes through
It's a dead reckoning . . .
And the battle is already through
And its hard to believe it's true
On a hill long ago where the blood runs below
Died a King, two thieves and you.

"Dead Reckoning." Written by Bob Hartman. Copyright © 1987 by Dawn Treader Music and Petsong Publishing. All rights reserved. Used by permission.

These observations from the 16th and 20th centuries lead us to the third and final step in applying the new math of the new self to ourselves.

3. Offer

In addition to knowing about the new nature and counting on being dead to sin, Paul, repeatedly using the word *offer,* advises us to act on these facts:

Do not *offer* the parts of your body to sin, as instruments of wickedness, but rather *offer* yourselves to God, as those who have been brought from death to life; and *offer* the parts of your body to him as instruments of righteousness. . . . Don't you know that when you *offer* yourselves to someone to obey him as slaves, you are slaves to the one whom you obey—whether you are slaves to sin, which leads to death, or to obedience, which leads to righteousness? . . . Just as you used to *offer* the parts of your body in slavery to impurity and to ever-increasing wickedness, so now *offer* them in slavery to righteousness leading to holiness (Rom 6:13, 16, 19; emphasis ours).

Before knowing Christ, we were indeed slaves to sin. It reigned in our bodies. Some of the Greek terms that Paul uses here add a military slant to the slavery image. Generalissimo Sin is regarded as a ruler who demands military service of his slaves. Sin levies a quota of arms, ordering us to use the parts of our body for evil. Sin even pays his soldiers a wage—death (Rom 6:23). This is the way it was when we were under the sway of Generalissimo Sin. He need not rule over us anymore, however. Because we are "dead to sin and alive to God in Christ Jesus," we can now offer the parts of our body to God as instruments of righteousness. The Greek word for instruments literally means tools or weapons. Tools are used to build things. Under the rule of sin, we employed the parts of our bodies to construct evil. Under the rule of the new nature, led by the Holy Spirit, we can build righteousness. Viewing the parts of our body as weapons, we formerly fought on the side of wickedness, but we now take up arms for holy causes. Exactly how might this occur in real life? Here is an example.

The sandwiches were good. The coffee smelled great. And the conversation flowed as the three construction workers enjoyed their lunch. After discussing the Monday night football game, the group turned its attention and conversation to a man seated nearby.

"I wonder what kind of slime that Gook brought for lunch today," Cal sniped.

"That meat looks mighty disgusting," chimed in Leo. "I wonder how many legs it had before they killed it—six or eight."

After more jabs and cuts at their Vietnamese coworker, Cal and Leo noticed that Pete wasn't saying a word.

"What's the matter, Pete?" Cal asked. "Cat got your tongue?"

"No," Pete answered, "God has it."

"Huh? What the hell does that mean?"

"It means I can't go along with your cruel treatment of Okhan any more. When he started working here yesterday and you guys were cutting him down, I snickered along with your cracks. I thought about my cowardice all night long. Now I realize that I can't speak against Okhan, because my tongue doesn't belong to me. It belongs to Christ."

"You're trying' to pull a holier-than-thou on us!" Cal groused.

"No, Cal. I'm not saying I'm better than you and Leo. I just think it's time we stopped criticizing Okhan and started using our tongues to befriend him."

Similar decisions should occur in our lives day by day, event by event, tool by tool, weapon by weapon. The new spirit takes orders from the Holy Spirit, so let us volunteer ourselves and our bodies to serve God, who has rehabilitated us for holy living. Is this asking too much? Not at all. We have been brought from death to life. Therefore, no part of our bodies would be alive without his saving work.

In response to the Bible's clear teaching in Romans 6, you can face the temptations and challenges of each day with a prayer like this:

> Thank you, Father, that my salvation is accomplished totally by grace through faith. Thank you that my life of sanctification is also accomplished totally by your grace through faith. Trusting in your work in Christ to rehabilitate me, I count myself as having a new spirit of obedience. Therefore, I offer the parts of my body as instruments of righteousness. My eyes belong to you, Lord; what do you want me to see today? My hands belong to you; whom do you want me to touch with your love? You, my Savior, are the owner of these lips; what do you wish me to say? Amen.

With this knowledge, does living the Christian life become a piece of cake? Isn't there still a struggle involved? Yes—and Paul deals with it honestly in Romans 7 and 8.

The War with the Old

Sssssssssssssssssss-BLAM!
Christians live in a state of constant warfare.
Sssssssssssssssssss-BANG!
The war is not simply going on *around* us, it is going on
    within us.
Sssssssssssssssssss-BOOM!

The war is between our sinful nature and the new self or new spirit that God has placed in us.

No doubt, you have seen cartoons that picture a little devil whispering temptations into someone's ear. Meanwhile a little angel sits on the opposite shoulder urging correct behavior. This comic device is not far from the truth. The little devil represents the deposed sinful nature that strives to regain its control over us. The little angel stands for the new self that God has placed within so that we can

183

now do his will. Just as an exiled dictator schemes to regain power and once again milk the land for his own purposes, so the sinful nature strives to regain its control over us.

To illustrate our spiritual conflict, Paul used the example with which he was most familiar: himself. Often his letters speak of personal experiences, but nowhere in the Bible does Paul reveal his flaws and weaknesses more candidly than in Romans 7. This is true confessions time, folks:

> I am ... sold as a slave to sin. I do not understand what I do. For what I want to do I do not do, but what I hate I do. And if I do what I do not want to do, I agree that the law is good. As it is, it is no longer I myself who do it, but it is sin living in me. I know that nothing good lives in me, that is, in my sinful nature. For I have the desire to do what is good, but I cannot carry it out. For what I do is not the good I want to do; no, the evil I do not want to do—this I keep on doing (Rom 7:14–19).

This doesn't sound like the Paul we usually hear in the Bible. Paul sounds flustered. He sounds frustrated with the resurgent power of his sinful nature. He sounds ... he sounds just like us! We share the same frustrations Paul confessed, because there is a war going on inside every Christian. The war can become so fierce that we may feel as if we are incapable of resisting our enemy, our own sinful nature. Paul describes this feeling in military terms:

> I see another law at work in the members of my body, waging war against the law of my mind [the new self] and making me a prisoner of the law of sin at work within my members. What a wretched man I am! Who will rescue me from this body of death?" (Rom 7:23–24).

You know the feeling. Sin can become so strong that you feel like a prisoner of war, marching with your hands behind your head as sin nudges you along with the sharp bayonet end of his rifle. (The military application here is warranted by Paul's use of several Greek words with military connotations in Rom 7:23, 24 and 8:2.)

"Who will rescue me?" you panic. "If I screamed for help, would anyone answer my call?" In desperation Paul does cry out for help: "What a wretched man I am! Who will rescue me from this body of death?" And what is the answer? "Thanks be to God—through

Jesus Christ our Lord!" See? That settles it. Jesus rescues us. There, the issue is settled.

But wait a minute! This just doesn't sound like enough. It seems to be only a pat answer, a simplistic solution, applying a Band-Aid to a mortal wound. Do you know why we are left with a feeling of disappointment? It is because Paul's words, "Thanks be to God through Jesus Christ," occur at the end of Romans 7, and then there comes a space and a big number 8 for the next chapter. This causes us to assume that Paul has wrapped up his discussion of the war against the sinful nature and is now proceeding to some other topic.

Don't let the chapter division mislead you, though. When Paul says at the end of Romans 7, "Thanks be to God—through Jesus Christ our Lord," that is not the end of the discussion. He is just getting started. In fact, Paul devotes the first 27 verses of Romans 8 to show how Jesus Christ rescues him and us from the body of death.

How Christ Sets Us Free

Let's return to the illustration where sin was holding us hostage, his bayonet jammed into our back. Jesus rescued us from this predicament by staging a double invasion. First, he entered this world as a human being, just like us except without sin; and he sacrificed his life on the cross for all our sins. By that act, Paul says in Rom 8:3, Christ "condemned sin in sinful man."

Notice that the Redeemer "condemned sin," the criminal, rather than condemning you or me. Because of that condemnation, sin lost its right to rule over us. In earthy yet very accurate terms, we could say that because Christ went to hell for us, God damned sin in us. Sin was told to get the hell out of my life so that God could rule over me. Instead of our sin condemning us to death, God condemned sin to death. As a result of Christ's first invasion, sin can't rule over us.

The Lord staged the second invasion when he put the Holy Spirit in us at our baptisms to guide us personally away from wrong and to direct and empower us toward what pleases God. Paul explains this second invasion in Rom 8:2: "Through Christ Jesus the law of the Spirit of life set me free from the law of sin and death." In Romans 6 Paul gave us the good news that we now have a new self

185

that is capable of pleasing God. However, by itself our new self is not that strong, for the sinful nature can deceive it, taking it prisoner.

Therefore, when we face temptations, we need reinforcements, which we receive in the person of the Holy Spirit. He does battle with sin in our hearts so that we can win. Look at Rom 8:13, "For if you live according to the sinful nature [if you let it be the boss], you will die; but if by the Spirit you put to death the misdeeds of the body, you will live." Victory depends on "if you put to death the misdeeds of the body." This is an interesting phrase. We often speak of confessing sins, but not of putting them to death. We saw in Rom 8:3 that Christ condemned sin. Now we are to carry out the sentence of execution. How? Paul says it must be done by the Spirit. We call on the Holy Spirit to execute the sins in us that still rule us. No pardons will be handed down by the Governor. So don't let the sin go free!

Regarding sin's execution, Paul issues a stern warning and a beautiful promise in Rom 8:13: "For if you live according to the sinful nature, you will die; but if by the Spirit you put to death the misdeeds of the body, you will live." Sin is suicidal, but obedience to God is really living. If you allow the evil doings of the body to continue living, you will be killing your own self. However, if by the Spirit's power you put sin to death, you will live. Keep up the killing and you will keep on living.

Paul's repeated references to life and death in Romans 8 remind us of the closing chapters of Deuteronomy, especially Deut 30:19, "I have set before you life and death, blessings and curses. Now choose life." Thank God! We are able to choose life every day, by the power of the Holy Spirit who dwells within us.

Good News

Because of Jesus' first invasion, sin lost its power to control and condemn us. Because of his second invasion—the coming of the Holy Spirit—we can defeat sin in our lives. The Holy Spirit of God will always support our new self so that we can overcome sin and meet the righteous requirements of God's Law. We are empowered people, and we are forgiven people, saved by faith in the Savior. This is good news of which many Christians are not aware.

This writer [Phil] was one of them, until I was about twenty-two years old. Although I believed I was saved by faith, I thought that living the Christian life was entirely up to me. Then I came to learn that obedience is also accomplished by faith in God. Hallelujah! Sanctification is allowing the Holy Spirit to do good in us rather than our striving to do it ourselves. Living in the Spirit means trusting the Holy Spirit to do in me what I cannot do myself.

Each time I am faced with a command from the Lord, I look to him to do in me what he requires of me. It is not a case of my trying, but of trusting; not of my struggling, but of resting in him.

Paul's key words repeated in Romans 7 and 8 prove this to be true. In Romans 7, where he describes his weakness before temptation, Paul uses the word *I* 28 times (according to the NIV). Thus he is showing us that depending on our own strength will never lead us to holiness. Then in Romans 8, Paul drops the word *I* and switches to the word *Spirit,* using it 18 times. Only by the Holy Spirit's working together with our new sinless spirit, under God's grace and not under God's law, can we do God's will.

We Are Obligated People

Paul concludes his discussion by saying in Rom 8:12, "We have an obligation—but it is not to the sinful nature, to live according to it." Literally, to have an obligation means *to stand indebted to someone.* To whom do we owe something, to the sinful nature or to God? Why, surely to the One who set us free!

During the American Civil War, as the Union armies captured town after town and plantation after plantation, they freed the slaves. Once liberated, the former slaves could do whatever they wanted with their lives. Some, realizing that they owed a debt to their liberators, enlisted in the Union army and fought valiantly in many battles. In the same way, we who have been freed by Christ and the Holy Spirit ought to be eager to fulfill our obligation to fight the war against sin in our lives—and win!

This illustration offers another parallel. The freed slaves not only were obligated to the army that freed them. They also owed something to the millions of slaves who were still in bondage. In the same way, we are obligated not only to live for God but also to strive for the liberation of the billions throughout the world who

187

have not yet heard the good news that can emancipate them from sin, just as it has us. "The Battle Hymn of the Republic" is just as appropriate for us in our war as it was in the war between the states: "As he [Christ] died to make men holy, let us die to make men free."

So the war goes on, not only inside of us but also outside of us as we fight to win souls for Christ who are now held in bondage to sin and Satan. Thank God, neither war depends on us for the victory. The Holy Spirit dwells in us to give us the victory over the old sinful nature, and he works through the witness of our words and our deeds to bring others to faith in Christ so that they too may be set free—set free for life!

Living with Not-Yetness

Paul is forever the realist. In Romans 6 he rejoiced in the creation of the new spirit within. Then he balances that optimism with his true confessions of Romans 7. In Rom 8:1–18, he encourages us to walk in the Spirit and find life through his power working in tandem with our spirit. Now, in Rom 8:19–27, he honestly confronts the not-yetness of being a sinner/saint. Like children longing to be all grown up, so we long for the day when we will no longer be troubled by the sinful nature's constant jockeying to regain its former position.

We will study this portion of Romans in a different manner: through the first person report of someone in our parish. Here is her story of how the Lord touched her while meditating on this text.

Something woke me up on the first morning of my vacation. It could have been a slamming door in the hotel. It could have been the birds cheering the dawn. However, since I awoke with a joyful desire to commune with God, I knew it was the Holy Spirit who had summoned me.

Silently I dressed, jotted a note for my husband, grabbed my Bible, and left the room. The lobby of the hotel was already beginning to bustle with action, from which I fled to reach the solitude outside. Through the oaks of early autumn I strode, seeking a place of utmost solitude to commune with the Lord. Attaining the beach, I spied the place. A long pier stretched out across the water, and at the end of the dock stood a white bench. My steps on the planks echoed out over the solitude of the lake, but when I sat down there was only the sound of my God and me together.

I just happened to open the Word to Romans 8, but with God there is no "just happening." In the same way that he guided me to this perch above the waters, so he led me to these teachings of the apostle Paul. As I read Rom 8:1–18, I saw the life-or-death struggle of sin and the old nature against the Holy Spirit and my new nature. How those words hit home as I mused on my own life: "So often I play at being a Christian. Yes, I believe in Jesus as my only Savior, but when it comes to having my mind set on what the Spirit desires, this is an ongoing struggle for me. Could this mean I am spiritually dead? No, because the dead don't battle against sin. They just surrender to it. Praise God, my wrestling against the flesh is a clear sign that I am alive in Christ."

With this realization, I proceeded to seize by faith every promise of life found in Rom 8:1–18, finding each one more refreshing than the last. "The mind controlled by the Spirit is life and peace" (v. 6). "If Christ is in you, your body is dead because of sin, yet your spirit is alive because of righteousness" (v. 10). "He who raised Christ from the dead will also give life to your mortal bodies through his Spirit, who lives in you" (v. 11). "The Spirit himself testifies with our spirit that we are God's children" (v. 16).

To me, the most precious of them all was Rom 8:18. I read out loud to myself, "I consider that our present sufferings are not worth comparing with the glory that will be revealed in us." As I meditated on this verse, I envisioned a scale, with God's glory far outweighing my struggles and sufferings. Then the little word *in* caught my attention. God's glory will be revealed, not just *to* us, but *in* us! Exactly what that means I don't know, but it was reassuring to know that in eternity God's glory will be revealed in my very being and in every redeemed citizen of heaven.

Strengthened by these promises, I ventured forth into the next paragraphs:

> The creation waits in eager expectation for the sons of God to be revealed. For the creation was subjected to frustration, not by its own choice, but by the will of the one who subjected it, in hope that the creation itself will be liberated from its bondage to decay and brought into the glorious freedom of the children of God.

We know that the whole creation has been groaning as in the pains of childbirth right up to the present time. Not only so, but we ourselves, who have the firstfruits of the Spirit, groan inwardly as we wait eagerly for our adoption as sons, the redemption of our bodies. For in this hope we were saved. But hope that is seen is no hope at all. Who hopes for what he already has? But if we hope for what we do not yet have, we wait for it patiently.

In the same way, the Spirit helps us in our weakness. We do not know what we ought to pray for, but the Spirit himself intercedes for us with groans that words cannot express. And he who searches our hearts knows the mind of the Spirit, because the Spirit intercedes for the saints in accordance with God's will (Rom 8:19–27).

After I read those words, I gazed across the lake; and then a totally unpredictable thing occurred. I began to groan, exuding a mournful wail from the depths of my spirit. At first I was shocked, because I'm a hard-boiled Christian not prone to exhibit emotions; and there I was, overwhelmed by profound groans. "Lord, don't do this to me here," I protested. But looking around to see who might chance to be walking by, I saw that I was still alone—alone with the Spirit who himself intercedes for me with groans that words cannot express.

So what did I do? Rather than try to compose myself, as I would have done in public worship, I simply allowed the Spirit to compose the hymn of groans that issued from my spirit. I groaned for the lake beneath me, polluted by sinful people and frothed by detergent suds. I moaned for all creation that is longing for the blessed state to which it will return when the full redemption of humankind is accomplished. I ached for believers everywhere who long for the return of Christ and the completion of their redemption. I groaned, hungering and thirsting for righteousness in my own daily life.

How long this attack of anguish lasted I cannot say. Finally the tremors ceased, I dried my eyes and pondered what had happened. Surely, the Spirit had interceded for me with groans that words could never express. In Rom 8:15 it says the Holy Spirit grants us the ability to call God "*Abba*, Father." Then in verse 26 it says that the Spirit helps us in our weakness by groaning for us. "How can the Spirit's groaning for us be a help?" I asked myself. Then an answer seemed to come:

The Spirit helps us survive the trauma of being incomplete children of God, of not yet having the glorious freedom which the children of God someday will enjoy. The Spirit knows what it is like to be a sinner/saint, because he has taken up residence in the very neighborhood where evil lives: within us. Indeed, his indwelling must be at least as humbling as Christ's incarnation. Thus the Spirit bears the burden of the sinful nature with us and groans for us as he intercedes for us to live holy lives, assured of Christ's love.

Conclusion

Scripture, Christ, obedience, mission, and the glory of God are the topics to which Paul refers in his opening salutation (Rom 1:1–7) and closing doxology (Rom 16:25–27). Romans 6–8 proves beyond a shadow of a doubt that obedience, sanctification, is not an accidental tangent, but one of the five themes that Paul had in mind when he composed this magnificent missionary letter.

When we authors studied Romans 6–8, we took pages of extensive notes; but in this book we have only skimmed their surface. As the key section in Scripture on the subject of sanctification, Romans 6–8 deserves to be mined to the depths in order to discover all its precious store (Job 28). Therefore, we urge you to read this section of Romans again and again to learn what Bible scholars have discovered here and to discuss with other believers the practical, day-by-day meaning of being in Christ, of having a new self, and of walking in the Spirit. By means of such concentrated attention, may the Holy Spirit lead you to know and experience what it means to walk in the Spirit.

Digging Deeper

1. Which concepts in this chapter were new to you? Which were a review?
2. Read 2 Cor 5:17; Gal 2:20; Eph 4:22–24; Col 3:10. Identify similarities between these verses and Romans 6–8.
3. Compare the concept of heart surgery in Ezek 36:26–27 to the concept of grafting in Jn 15:5. In what ways do these help explain what Paul teaches in Romans 6–8?
4. How did you score on the Sanctification Attitude Check on page

171? Take it again now. Has your score changed at all after reading this chapter? Why or why not?

5. To what degree have you experienced the war against sin that Paul describes so honestly in Rom 7:7–25?

6. How can the three steps *Know, Count,* and *Offer* help a person wage this spiritual war successfully?

7. What sins have you confessed recently? What sins have you had difficulty putting to death (Rom 8:13)? Some translations of Rom 8:13 have the word *spirit*; others have *Spirit.* This occurs because Bible scholars are unsure whether Paul is referring to the Spirit of God or to our new spirit. Regardless of the translation, what does Paul promise in 8:13, and how can the blessing of the promise be realized?

8. In Romans 8, Paul encourages us to trust in the Holy Spirit for daily victory over sin. Respond to the following observation made by a pastor: "How often do we talk seriously about believing in the Holy Spirit? It seems that we mostly believe facts *about* him: He inspired the Scriptures, works faith in our hearts, and so on. If we can get beyond simply believing *about* him and also believe *in* him, that is, trust in him to act in our lives, what power for daily living will be at our disposal!"

9. Read Rom 7:1–6. Imagine being married to a demanding, despotic husband. This is how the Law treats us when we are ruled by sin. According to Rom 7:3, what is the only honorable way to be freed from such a marriage? Look at Rom 7:4 to see how this has been accomplished for us. Here are a couple more questions. What is the event by which we are married to a new husband? What is the fruit that will be born through our union with him? You will find hints in Hos 1:2, 2:14, 19–20; Eph 5:25–27; and Rev 19:6–9.

10. Considering your present situation, what parts of your body should you be offering to God as tools or weapons of righteousness?

11. Do you agree or disagree with the authors' contention that the sanctification content of Romans 6–8 substantiates their theory that the Gospel chain is the theme of Romans?

12. Use the prayer found on page 183 in your private devotions or in a group setting.

10

The Mission Link
Romans 8:28–11:36

Mission, Not Just Election

John Wesley once said, "If I had three hundred men who feared nothing but God, hated nothing but sin, and were determined to know nothing among men but Jesus Christ and him crucified, I would set the world on fire. I need men with hot hearts!" (Tan 1979, 1669). Paul was such a man. His heart was burning with desire for the salvation of men and women trapped in sin.

Paul had a burning passion especially for the lost sheep of Israel. Listen to his heartfelt cry:

> I have great sorrow and unceasing anguish in my heart. For I could wish that I myself were cursed and cut off from Christ for the sake of my brothers, those of my own race, the people of Israel (Rom 9:2–4).

> Brothers, my heart's desire and prayer to God for the Israelites is that they may be saved (Rom 10:1).

These words represent the agonizing groans of a man whose heart is being pierced by great sorrow and unceasing anguish for the lost. Paul longed desperately for the salvation of his fellow Jews. He would have carried them into heaven on his own back, if that were possible. In fact, Paul was willing to go to hell himself, if somehow that could save his fellow Jews who were God's elect.

Those who believe that justification by grace through faith is the sole theme of Romans are hard pressed to explain why Paul deals with the doctrine of election (predestination) at this point in his letter. But Paul is not merely discussing the question "who may or may not be elect?" His words in Rom 9:2 reveal a different emphasis. Paul's heart is broken because most of Israel remained in unbelief and disobedience. Throughout Romans he has been talking about "the obedience that comes from faith." Now he must answer a troubling question, "Why did this one nation, the Jews, who had so many advantages, lose them and miss out on the obedience of faith?"

Paul's principal concern is that all who do not know Christ, whether Jews or Gentiles, have been cut off from the mercy of God. To Paul this is a heart-rending fact, and it leads him to devote more than three chapters to the mission link in the Gospel chain. This mission link remains the "missing link," however, if we see in Romans 9–11 only a systematic treatment of election.

Do we groan with the same anguish which Paul felt? Will we join his ranks and become one of those men and women with "hot hearts" who will set the world on fire? The answer to that question depends largely on whether we are convinced that some will be lost, and how deeply we care about them. This is Paul's concern in Romans 9–11. We need the same zeal and anguished desire for the spread of Christ's kingdom that Paul had.

More Mission Groans

Before we examine Romans 9–11, let us turn back to a section of Paul's letter that we previously overlooked, namely Rom 8:28–39. As stated above, traditionally, people have found in these verses the doctrine of election, and they should. But another look reveals that Paul is talking about election and much more. You can't fully appreciate these verses unless you understand that the primary topic of Romans 9–11 is world evangelization; and you can't truly understand Paul's groans expressed in Rom 8:28–39 until you recognize that he is groaning about his fellow Jews.

You see, traditionally, Rom 8:28–30 has been applied to all of the general hardship and tribulation experienced by believers. It's a classic section of Scripture for a Christian funeral service, especially when the person's death seemed exceptionally tragic. This is not, however, the sort of hardship that Paul had in mind when he listed innumerable trials in vv. 35–39. The key to understanding this section is in the first three verses. There Paul says,

> And we know that in all things God works for the good of those
> who love him, who have been called according to his purpose.

For those God foreknew he also predestined to be conformed to the likeness of his Son: that he might be the firstborn among many brothers. And those he predestined, he also called; those he called, he also justified; those he justified, he also glorified (Rom 8:28–30).

In these verses we see both the Gospel and its ultimate goal. God has called us by the Gospel and justified us by faith in Jesus Christ. For what purpose? Paul says God wants us to be "conformed to the image of his Son"; that is, he wants us to be sanctified by learning obedience just as Christ was obedient. This is the third link in the mission chain. Paul then mentions yet another purpose for which God has called us: "That he [Christ] might be the firstborn among many brothers." In other words, God wants not only us but many others to believe in Jesus Christ and obey him. These words highlight the mission link in the Gospel chain.

Three Groans

It's very appropriate for Paul to mention these two aspects of the goal of the Gospel right here. He has just concluded a lengthy section on sanctification, in which he groaned because he was not completely Christ-like. "I do not understand what I do," he cried. "For what I want to do I do not do, but what I hate I do" (Rom. 7:15). This is the first of Paul's three groans.

In chapters 9–11 we hear him groan because some are lost. "I have great sorrow and unceasing anguish in my heart," he agonizes (Rom 9:2). This is his third groan.

In between, Rom 8:28–39 tells us how the mission task causes us to groan as we bear the cross for Christ. This is his second groan.

A Mission Promise

In the midst of all his groaning, Paul also gives us a tremendous promise.

If God is for us, who can be against us? He who did not spare his own Son, but gave him up for us all—how will he not also, along with him, graciously give us all things? . . . Who shall separate us from the love of Christ? . . . No, in all these things we are more than conquerors through him who loved us. For I am convinced that neither death nor life,... nor anything else in all creation, will be able to separate us from the love of God that is in Christ Jesus our Lord (Rom 8:31b–32, 35a, 37–38a, 39b).

Do these verses remind you of the fantastic promise that Jesus made when he assigned us the task of making disciples of all nations? They should, because they are Paul's commentary on Jesus' words in Mt 28:20, "I will be with you always, to the very end of the age." Rom 8:28–39 is really a promise that is especially intended to encourage us in our missionary efforts. Paul is promising God's presence and love to all who endure hardship for Christ and the Gospel. All who love God and are trying to answer his call can be assured that God will work all things for their good.

Believers' efforts to spread the Gospel always result in suffering and anguish. The harder you work for the salvation of others, the more you are saddened by the failure of some to receive the Gospel, just as Paul cried out in anguish over his fellow Jews.

Preaching the Gospel also brings all kinds of trouble and difficulty, as Paul knew from personal experience. He names every hardship imaginable. He was unjustly charged with all kinds of wrongdoing. He was persecuted, imprisoned, and threatened with death. He was stoned, shipwrecked, and put on trial. Yet, he knew that "nothing can separate us from the love of God in Christ Jesus our Lord."

What a tremendous promise that is for those who are striving for the goal of the Gospel, who are carrying out God's purpose in their lives! Before you were born, God chose you in Christ to be his own, called you by the Gospel, justified you by faith in Christ Jesus, and gave you a new self so that you could glorify him. How could you ever think he would desert you? No, in all trials "we are more than conquerors." We will go from victory to victory in bringing the nations to Christ and causing the obedience of the nations to be his (Gen 49:10).

Nevertheless, some wonder why we must endure hardship for the cause of Christ. In 1986, the American people were shocked by the explosion of the space shuttle Challenger. That such a thing could happen astounded many, but they had simply forgotten that crossing frontiers such as outer space always is dangerous business. That was true in Paul's day, and it is still true today, whether we are crossing frontiers to explore outer space or to preach Christ to the nations. Yes, we may groan, knowing like Paul that for Christ's sake "we face death all day long; we are considered sheep to be slaughtered" (Rom 8:36). But Christ's promise accompanies us when we are on his mission. He will be with us. Nothing can separate us from him. We are more than conquerors.

Elizabeth Elliott, missionary and writer, experienced firsthand the sustaining love of God. On January 6, 1956, her husband, Jim, with pilot Nate Saint and three other missionaries, flew into the jungle of Ecuador to make contact with a small tribe called the Aucas. They set up camp on a beach by the river and waited for an opportunity to meet these primitive people and share the Gospel with them. They established contact and seemed to gain the trust of the Aucas, but two days later the natives speared all five men to death.

How did the families of these missionaries react? Were they filled with hatred and revenge? Did they lose faith in God as their shield and defender? No! They continued to look for opportunities to reach out to the Aucas. Two years later, Elizabeth Elliott and her young daughter Valerie, along with Rachel Saint, the sister of Nate Saint, went into the jungles of Ecuador to begin the work of evangelizing the Aucas. Two of the Aucas who participated in the killing of the missionaries later became leaders in the Auca Christian Church. A few years later, during a visit with their Aunt Rachel, Kathy and Steven, the children of Nate and Marjorie Saint, were baptized by Auca Christians at the same spot in the river where their father had been speared to death! (*Guideposts* 1991, 45).

Elizabeth and Rachel knew that nothing, not even the death of their loved ones or the possible danger to themselves, could separate them from the love of God in Christ Jesus our Lord. Therefore, they could courageously carry on the mission work that Jim and Nate began and for which they gave their lives. He who loves them made them "more than conquerors" (Rom 8:37). Like them, countless other mission-minded Christians have been comforted and strengthened by Rom 8:28–39, where Paul reaffirms that Christ will always be with us when we are obeying his Great Commission.

Mission Questions and Answers

Now let us move on to consider Romans 9–11. The reader would benefit from looking at these chapters before proceeding. Theologians have painstakingly analyzed how Paul in these chapters answers the question, "Why are only some saved?" Most have failed to note that Paul is also providing answers to some important mission questions.

1. Is salvation only for people like us?
2. Is salvation necessary for good people?
3. Is salvation needed by all?

In the next three sections, we will learn how the apostle Paul responded to each of these questions.

Is Salvation Only for People Like Us?

Paul was convinced that many of his fellow Israelites would be lost, even though they possessed every spiritual advantage one could imagine. God had chosen them for his own. He had manifested his glory among them and made a covenant with them. He had communicated with them as with no one else, giving them his Law and promises in the Scriptures. They had the temple in which to worship God according to his direction. Even the Savior came from the Jews. Yet, in spite of all these advantages, each one a reason why they should not be lost, Paul knew that many Jews would be lost.

Why? Paul says they stumbled over Christ, the stone laid in Zion, and would not believe in him. Rather than accepting Christ's righteousness, God's gift to them, they tried to establish a righteousness of their own based on works of the Law (Rom 10:1–5).

Romans 9–11 points out the ultimate importance of faith as opposed to works. The Jews missed out on the obedience of faith because they sought a righteousness that was by works. All who obtain salvation do so by faith, whether they be Jew or Gentile. Additionally, however, Paul is trying to show the importance of proclaiming the saving Gospel so that faith might arise. Thus, not only is justification important in this section (the second link in the Gospel chain) but also the proclamation of the Gospel (the fourth or mission link).

But was Paul concerned only for his own people? Not at all! In fact, using strong evidence from the Old Testament, he demonstrates that the Gentiles have always been included in God's promises of mercy to the Jews. Paul realized that "not all who are descended

198

from Israel are Israel. Nor because they are his descendants are they all Abraham's children" (Rom 9:6–7). He quotes Isaiah, showing that God will take those who were not his people and make them his own, just as he restored Israel after they had forsaken God and been exiled for their idolatry. Paul knew God as one who would save "all Israel," that is, all who are true children of Abraham by faith. For a former Pharisee this was a monumental conclusion— all who believe are children of Abraham.

How long will it take us to come to a similar conclusion, to realize that our mission goes far beyond reaching more people like ourselves? Far too often this has been the case in the Christian church. True, we have supported mission work around the world to reach people who are different from us, but those people are a safe distance away. All too often, the only people nearby whom we have the will to win are those who look and talk and think very much like us. For this reason many North American churches have been ethnic enclaves that one could enter only by birth or marriage. We have been blind to countless people around us who are desperately in need of the Gospel, simply because they are different from us. Only recently, for instance, have North American churches begun to realize the great potential for Gospel expansion in evangelizing foreign students who are attending North American colleges and universities.

Church members in communities experiencing racial integration frequently flee to new neighborhoods, wanting to be surrounded by people like themselves. Consequently, they never get to know the new residents moving into their old neighborhoods and are unwilling to accept them into their church. As a result, churches have often been among the last organizations to see blacks and whites work side by side.

When establishing new churches, denominations have repeatedly sought sites where people are settling who are similar to the present constituency of the church body, rather than looking for the neighborhood or people group most urgently in need of the Gospel. This certainly makes church planting easier and more effective, but it is doubtful if Paul would take a similar approach were he a mission developer in North America today.

In Detroit, Michigan, one church has developed a ministry called SALAM (the Arabic word for peace) or "Sincere and Active Love for

Arabs and Muslims." In a city where the Muslim population is expected to reach one-half million by the year 2000, this church is trying to develop an effective method of influencing this very hard to reach group with the Gospel. Currently it is equipping those members as witnesses who already have contacts with Muslims. This is Paul's kind of church!

We need to care just as deeply for those who are different from us as we do for those who are dear to us. One man who felt this way was Hudson Taylor, who in 1865 founded the China Inland Mission. He certainly saw the lost as his sisters and brothers, regardless of how different from him they may have been. He labored long and hard for the evangelization of China. During the course of his mission work, some of his family passed away, including his wife, Mary. In spite of this great loss, Hudson Taylor labored on. Once, when contemplating Jesus' words, "I go to prepare a place for you" (Jn 14:2), he observed, "And is not our part of the preparation the peopling it with those we love?" Surely Hudson Taylor was referring both to his own dear family and also to the Chinese saints whom he had seen come to faith.

Is salvation only for people like us? In Romans 9 Paul tells us, "No! It's for all peoples of the earth."

Is Salvation Necessary for Good People?

Perhaps we are lacking in mission zeal because we have forgotten Paul's strong emphasis in Romans 3–5. There he clearly taught that whether Jew or Gentile, we are all saved by grace through faith in Jesus Christ, not by works of the Law. Here in Romans 9–11, Paul underscores the same point. "Christ is the end of the law so that there may be righteousness for everyone who believes" (Rom 10:4). Jesus completed the Law of righteousness for us, that is, he fulfilled it. Only by trusting in him can anyone become righteous in God's sight and equipped for righteous living.

Today, however, the modern heresy of universalism proposes that, finally, all will be saved and none will be lost—at least none of the nice people (although some who are truly evil may perish). This popular thought has led to the development of what Moishe Rosen, leader of Jews for Jesus, calls the religion of "nice-ism."

Its main tenet is that everyone should be nice to everyone else, and it doesn't matter what people believe or how they vote or even what they do, as long as they don't hurt anyone. The religion of 'nice-ism' has very few commandments: 1. Be agreeable; 2. Don't bother people; 3. Never insist that you're right; 4. Don't even say that you are right if it means saying that someone else is wrong. The only real sin against "nice-ism" is doing what really bothers another person" (Rosen 1990, 2).

This mindset runs directly counter to God's Word. God's Law upsets people because it presents us with the disturbing truth about our sinful nature and our inability to save ourselves. People don't like to hear such things. If our goal is not to disturb people, then we aren't very likely to confront them with the proclamation of either Law or Gospel. We would rather be "nice" people who let others go on thinking that all nice people will end up in heaven.

Paul, however, is not so nice. He reminds us that the Jews, with all of their spiritual advantages and all of their zeal to obey God's Law, could not be saved by their zeal. What hope is there, then, for a Muslim, Hindu, Buddhist, Communist, evolutionist, Mormon, Jehovah's Witness, or anyone else to be saved by his conduct or sincerity? There is no hope outside of Christ. Thus, Paul annihilates all forms of universalism.

Nevertheless, even after reading Paul's words in Rom 10:1–4, some Christians may still doubt that all without Christ are lost.

"The New Age" was the topic in Bible class that Sunday morning, and everyone was buzzing about the strange ideas involved in this popular movement. Pastor Martin was trying to help the class members get a handle on how to witness to friends who are involved in the New Age movement, when Dave raised his hand with a question.

"I can understand why it's important to talk to my friends who are into the New Age. Most of them are, or were, Christians. If they turn away from Christ for the New Age, I can understand why they would be lost. But what about someone who's never heard the Gospel? That's not his fault. Won't he be saved, even if no one witnesses to him?"

"That's a good question, Dave," Pastor Martin responded. "It's something all of us have wondered about at one time or another.

201

We can find the answer by looking at Romans 10 backwards."

"Backwards?" Dave looked puzzled.

"Someone read Rom 10:9–15 for us, please," requested Pastor Martin.

John started reading,

> That if you confess with your mouth, "Jesus is Lord," and believe in your heart that God raised him from the dead, you will be saved. For it is with your heart that you believe and are justified, and it is with your mouth that you confess and are saved. As the Scripture says, "Anyone who trusts in him will never be put to shame." For there is no difference between Jew and Gentile—the same Lord is Lord of all and richly blesses all who call on him, for, "Everyone who calls on the name of the Lord will be saved." How, then, can they call on the one they have not believed in? And how can they believe in the one of whom they have not heard? And how can they hear without someone preaching to them? And how can they preach unless they are sent? As it is written, "How beautiful are the feet of those who bring good news."

"Thanks, John," said Pastor Martin. "Now let's trace Paul's thought backwards from verse 15. If no one is sent, then no one will . . ."

"Preach," said John.

"Right. And if no one preaches, no one will . . ."

"Hear," added John.

"Right again. And if no one hears, no one will . . ."

"Believe," remarked Dave, thoughtfully.

"And if no one believes, no one will . . ."

"Call on the name of the Lord," Kay offered.

"Correct. And if no one 'calls on the name of the Lord' in faith," Pastor Martin concluded, "no one will be . . ."

"Saved," Dave responded. "I guess you're right, Pastor. We need to be concerned about sharing the Gospel with everyone."

Is salvation necessary for good people? Paul has told us, "Absolutely!" No one can expect to stand before God apart from his grace and mercy in Jesus Christ.

Is Salvation Needed by All?

Dave learned an important lesson from the apostle Paul that Sunday morning: It is crucial that we share the Gospel with everyone. In fact, that is precisely what Paul deliberately emphasizes in this section of Romans. In Rom 9:33, he quotes Is 28:16, which says, "The one who trusts in him will never be put to shame." Then in Rom 10:11 Paul quotes this same verse again. But in his second quotation he substitutes the word *anyone* (which is actually the Greek word *pas,* or *all*) for the word *one.* In the next three verses he goes on to use the word *pas* (all) three more times, in every form he can think of, in order to emphasize the fact that God wants all to be saved.

1. "Anyone [*pas*] who trusts in him ..." (Rom 10:11).
2. "the same Lord is Lord of all ..." (Rom 10:12).
3. "and richly blesses all ..." (Rom 10:12).
4. "for, 'Everyone [*pas*] who calls on the name of the Lord will be saved' " (Rom 10:13).

In this way Paul helps us to see that the promise of Is 28:16 is directed to every individual on the face of the earth.

Like Paul, we should learn to read the Bible with a global perspective, seeing all for whom Christ died in the inclusive terms that the Scriptures use—terms like nations, world, each, everyone, whosoever, alien, men, mankind, etc. God wants all to come to the knowledge of Jesus Christ and be saved. This means that we must work hard at proclaiming the Gospel to all mankind.

There should be no doubt in our minds about the necessity of Gospel proclamation for the salvation of all; but if you are still wondering, imagine this. You are the safety officer on the seventh floor of a large nursing home when, suddenly, a fire breaks out. What will you do? You know that there is one fire escape at the end of the main hall. Will you lead people to that one fire escape, or will you conjecture about other possible means of escape while people burn? We know that God has given us escape from sin and death through his Son, Jesus Christ. Will you lead people to that one sure escape, or will you stand around speculating whether there may be another way out, while souls are perishing? Paul knew that there was only one escape, and he labored desperately to see that everyone (*pas*) he could possibly reach would find salvation through faith in Jesus Christ (McQuilken 1981, 133–134).

Is salvation needed by all? Paul has told us, "Yes!" in no uncertain terms. He knows how desperately every person on the face of this earth needs the Gospel.

Beautiful Feet

Not too long ago in the Sunday morning service, a church was installing its Pastor of Christian Outreach along with two Christian day school teachers. During the children's message, the pastor assigned the boys and girls an unusual task. They were to be the judges in a "beautiful feet contest."

Each of the pastors and teachers then proceeded to take off one shoe so that the children could judge who had the most beautiful feet. After the children had gleefully expressed their preference based on appearance, the pastor read from Isaiah the passage that Paul quotes in Rom 10:15, "How beautiful on the mountains are the feet of those who bring good news, who proclaim peace, who bring good tidings, who proclaim salvation" (Is 52:7).

It was then that the children learned why their teachers' feet were beautiful: because they used them to stand in front of the class and speak about Jesus' love and to walk into the children's homes and witness to their families about Jesus' death on the cross for their sins. They learned that their pastor's feet were beautiful because he used them to go from house to house, calling on families to find out if they knew Jesus and because he used them to stand in the pulpit and proclaim the Gospel message.

Paul wants us as well to have beautiful feet and to use our feet for God's beautiful purposes. We won't have beautiful feet, of course, unless we really believe, as Paul did, that many will be lost without Christ. However, simply believing that some will be lost is probably not enough either. We have to move beyond merely believing the fact to caring that some will be lost. Paul cared deeply that many of his fellow Jews would be lost; but he cared deeply as well that many Gentiles also would be lost. Because he cared so much, he became the apostle to the Gentiles. In this way he could serve all, hoping that his outreach to the Gentiles would make the Jews envious and cause them to turn to call on their Messiah in whom they had failed to believe (Rom 11:14).

Grafted In to Bear Fruit

To spotlight the conversion of the Gentiles, Paul in Romans 11 uses the imagery of grafting plants. All tribes, tongues, people, and nations who confess Christ have been grafted into him. They are like wild olive shoots that "have been grafted in among the others and now share in the nourishing sap from the olive root" (Rom 11:17). This brings to mind all of the rich biblical imagery of God's planting his people (a picture of justification) and expecting them to be fruitful (a picture of sanctification and mission). God wants these ingrafted branches to bear fruit, both doing good works and also making new believers, who, in turn, will be grafted into Christ and bear fruit for him. In fact, it almost appears that Rom 11:13–24 is Paul's commentary on John 15, where Jesus spoke of himself as the vine and of us as his branches who are enabled by him to bear fruit.

Generally, Bible scholars assume that Romans 9–11 deals only with the thorny question of election. They usually view the mission emphasis in Rom 10:5–15 only as a tangent. We hope we have convinced you that Paul is not simply asking, why are some saved and others lost? Rather, he is asking, how much do you care about those who are lost? He wants to know what you and I are going to do to ensure that all people are grafted into Christ to bear fruit by grace through faith. Does it trouble you that so many are lost? A good way to measure how much you care is to see how much you're doing about it.

What Are You Willing to Do?

Paul wants each of us to ask ourselves, what am I willing to do for the salvation of all? Paul was willing to go to hell for the sake of his fellow Jews. He literally went all over the world for the sake of the lost. He let himself be sent and he sent others. Paul preached and he prayed; he suffered and he sacrificed. What are you willing to do?

Will you go to church and listen to a sermon about missions? Is that enough? Will your mere listening cause any of the lost to be saved? You will need to invest a little more effort than that. A good first step is to become informed about missions. If you are better informed, your level of caring about the lost will increase. An excellent resource to start with is the book *Joy to the World,* written by one of the authors of this book [Phil]. It may help you begin to groan for the lost, even as Paul did.

Another important thing you can do to save others is to pray. Pray for specific missionaries by name. Pray about their individual needs and challenges. Of course, this too means that you will have to become better informed about missions.

You could send someone to preach the Gospel. This means spending money for the lost—your money! Support a missionary directly or through the ministry of your local church. Join a mission organization with an important outreach to people who need the Gospel.

Better yet, like Paul, let yourself be sent! For a few, this may involve a long-term commitment to mission work. But for many more, it will mean finding a way to use your skills on a temporary basis to help the Gospel cause. Bob Johnson of Hillside, Illinois, found a way. A retired airline pilot, on his own time and at his own expense, he pilots small airplanes to missionaries in far off places on behalf of the Missionary Aircraft Ferry Service. This involves no small risk on Bob's part. Yet he believes Paul's promise that nothing can separate him from the love of God that is in Christ Jesus. (Consult the missionary organizations listed at the end of the book for further ideas of ways you can serve.)

The most important thing you can do is to speak up. Paul tells us that part of having faith is confessing with your mouth the faith which you have in your heart. Speak to those you know who don't know Jesus personally. Speak ardently and fervently, sharing your pain because they may be lost, and the love that you have for them. Keith Green told his parents how much he cared about them by writing a song for them. It's about heaven. He titled it, "I Only Want to See You There." Keith is already there, and hopefully the witness of his life and his song has influenced his parents so that they can be there too. Speaking the Gospel message to the people around you is ultimately important because "faith comes by hearing the message and the message is heard through the word of Christ" (Rom 10:17).

What if you do not share Paul's intense longing for the salvation of all? Perhaps you don't because you have been keeping Christ at a safe distance, at arm's length. Ask him to take over your heart entirely and fill you with the same kind of groaning and crying that Paul expresses in Rom 9:2! Then God will be able to accomplish the purpose of his calling in you.

Perhaps your longing for the lost lacks something because you realize that no matter how deeply you care, and no matter how much you do, not all will believe and be saved. But let that comfort rather than discourage you. No one's salvation depends on your ability to preach or to speak the Gospel effectively. The Holy Spirit works through the message of Christ, just as long as it is proclaimed, giving people faith to believe. No one's salvation depends on your energy or your ability, but it does depend on your caring enough to see that they hear the message. We all need to care enough to do something.

The fact that salvation is from God and depends entirely on his mercy is the reason that Paul concludes Romans 11 with a tremendous doxology.

> Oh, the depth of the riches of the wisdom and knowledge of God! How unsearchable his judgments, and his paths beyond tracing out! "Who has known the mind of the Lord? Or who has been his counselor?" "Who has ever given to God, that God should repay him?" For from him and through him and to him are all things. To him be the glory forever! Amen (Rom 11:33–36).

Yes, God's wisdom is unsearchable, and this side of heaven we will never be able to answer every question about the doctrine of election. But Paul has clearly answered all our mission questions. God wants *all* to hear and believe the good news of Jesus Christ! This means that you and I need to be ultimately concerned about our part in Christ's mission assignment.

Waldo Werning tells the story of Taki, a Buddhist tour guide, whom he met a number of years ago while leading a tour group through Japan. After seeing the work being done in one of the Christian schools the group visited, Taki was highly impressed and made an impassioned speech to the tour group. He told them that he had been listening to their daily devotions and had learned that Christ not only died on the cross for the whole world, but that Christ had actually died personally for him, for Taki. He said that he had guided many groups throughout Japan, but he had never seen work as exciting or a message as important as this one. They certainly had something to share with his country, Taki continued. He had only one thing more to share, Werning noted: "He could not tell us what to do or how to do it, but he said, 'Whatever you do, do something drastic!' A Buddhist challenge to Christians!" (Werning, 1986, 126f). Paul puts the same challenge to us. And now, in Romans 12 and following, he is about to tell us what drastic thing we should do.

Digging Deeper

1. How would you explain Paul's decision to discuss the doctrine of election in Romans 9–11 if justification by grace through faith is accepted as the traditional theme of Paul's letter to the Romans?
2. List verses in Romans 9–11 which you believe refer to election. List the verses that refer to mission. Which receives the heavier emphasis? How are the two concepts related?
3. Do you think this supports the authors' thesis that the theme of Romans is really the Gospel chain: revelation, justification, sanctification, mission, and glorifying God? Why or why not?
4. Describe a time or a circumstance when you have felt (even to a small degree) the passion for the lost that Paul expresses in Rom 9:1–2 and 10:1. What prompted you to feel that way? The death of an unsaved loved one? A mission fair? A presentation by a missionary? A sermon on missions or evangelism? A conversation with an unsaved friend? How can we foster Paul's kind of passion for the lost in ourselves and others?
5. Try to explain in your own words the three groanings of Paul.
   a. Groaning over his imperfection (Romans 7–8);
   b. Groaning under the burden of bearing the cross for Christ (Rom 8:18–39); and
   c. Groaning over the lost (Romans 9–10).

   Have you felt any of these groanings, and how have you dealt with them?
6. What do you think of the authors' idea that Rom 8:28–39 is basically Paul's commentary on Mt 28:20, "I will be with you always"? Do you think this limits the promise of Rom 8:39 too much or that it brings the promise into sharper focus? What

evidence can you find in these verses that this is a mission promise? See Ps 44:22.

7. What is Paul's answer to the mission question: is salvation only for people like us? Can you think of people different from yourself culturally, ethnically, or racially, with whom you have regular contact, who are in need of the Gospel? Write down their names.

8. How would you answer someone who believed that in the end everyone (or nearly everyone) will be saved? What evidence from Scripture can you give that this is not the case? You may wish to refer to Jn 14:6 and Acts 4:12. Why is the belief that everyone needs Christ's salvation so offensive to many people?

9. To what degree have you been a proponent of the religion of "nice-ism" in your Christian witness? Are there times when you have avoided offending someone when you should have spoken out for Christ? Tell about such a time. How do you feel about it now, looking back? Remember, there is forgiveness in Jesus Christ for all our sins, even for practicing the religion of "nice-ism."

10. How would you rank yourself in a "beautiful feet" contest? (Circle a number from zero to ten.)

    10   *Exceptionally beautiful*—repeatedly going to
    9   others with the message of the Gospel.
    8   *Beautiful*—but sometimes too tired to go as
    7   far as I should.
    6   A *little homely*—willing, but too often mired
    5   in the muck of the cares and worries of this life.
    4   *Very homely*—firmly planted and unwilling to
    3   move beyond the circle of my own self-interest
    2   to share the good news with others.
    1   *Downright ugly*—running away from God's will
    0   that I tell others about Jesus so they can be saved.

11. Compare Mt 13:31–33 to Rom 11:16–24. What parallels do you find?

12. What would you consider to be a drastic step towards fulfilling Christ's mission mandate at your point of life? Ask the Holy Spirit to help you decide on one action to take in order to demonstrate your increasing concern for the lost. Seek the assistance of other believers who can help you take that step forward.

11

Paul's Alter Call
Romans 12:1–8

Christian publisher Robert C. Law illustrates the latent power of the Christian church by describing a tour of Grand Coulee Dam in Washington State. In the reservoir above the dam, the water has potential, but it is not an active force. However, when the passive water enters the intake of the dam, it becomes committed. It cannot turn back. Churning and pushing, the water drives the generators, causing the whole dam to hum with energy. Nevertheless, the power does not come from the water itself but rather from its commitment (Bunkowske and French 1989, 112).

The Christian church today has great potential, just like the water in the reservoir above Grand Coulee Dam. Christ has equipped us to take his mighty Word and sacraments to all the world so that every man, woman, and child may hear his offer of salvation. Even though we have the potential, we have not yet reached the whole world. Why not? Because too many believers are only latent and passive. Like the water in the reservoir, we will not become an active force until we commit ourselves.

The Intention of Rom 12:1–2

For over three chapters, Paul has been discussing world evangelization. Now we come to a big "12," denoting the beginning of a new chapter. Seeing that number, some have traditionally believed that Paul has concluded his discussion of Gospel outreach and is now setting a course in a new direction. Nothing could be farther from the truth.

Rom 12:1–2 climaxes the entire letter to Rome. Paul has been building up to these lines for 11 chapters. The five remaining chapters look back to these two verses. Here Paul sounds his alter call.

Note, it is not an *altar* call, but an *alter* call, urging us to alter our attitude and lifestyle and commit ourselves to calling people from among all the nations to the obedience of faith.

> Therefore, I urge you, brothers, in view of God's mercy, to offer your bodies as a living sacrifice, holy and pleasing to God—which is your reasonable act of worship. Do not conform any longer to the pattern of this world, but be transformed by the renewing of your mind. Then you will be able to test and approve what God's will is—his good, pleasing and perfect will [Authors' translation].

Traditionally, Bible students have considered Rom 12:1–2 a call to discipleship *in general* but not a call to engage in world evangelization *in particular*. They virtually ignore the close connection to Paul's mission discussion in the previous chapters. On what grounds has this derailment of Paul's argument been permitted? The answer revolves around the phrase "in view of God's mercy." With these words Paul is clearly pointing back to something that he has written earlier in the letter. Many Bible scholars have claimed that there is no preceding reference to "God's mercy" in the immediate context of Romans 11. Therefore, they conclude, Paul must be referring all the way back to Romans 3–5, where he described God's mercy in declaring us righteous through the atoning sacrifice of Jesus Christ.

Is it true that there is no reference to God's mercy in Romans 11? The authors don't think people have searched thoroughly enough. Take a look in your own Bible. Sure, you won't find mercy mentioned in the doxology of Rom 11:33–36, but look back a little farther. There! Do you see it? In Rom 11:30–32, Paul speaks of mercy four times. Surely here is the antecedent of "in view of God's mercy" that we find in Rom 12:1. Furthermore, Rom 9:14–23 contains six more references to the mercy of God. These ten occurrences of *mercy* compel us to conclude that there is a critical connection between *God's mercy* in Rom 12:1 and the immediately preceding context of Romans 9–11, which speaks of God's mercy to the nations.[1]

Bible scholars are not to be faulted, however, for recognizing a connection between Rom 12:1–2 and Romans 3–5. This connection surely exists, because the phrase "in view of God's mercy" calls to mind not only Romans 9–11 but everything that Paul has taught in the previous 11 chapters about the Gospel and its goal.

When the apostle says "in view of God's mercy," he is reminding us of our lost state without God's mercy, the very theme he elaborated in Rom 1:18–3:20. When Paul says "in view of God's mercy," he is also referring to the glorious grace of God in sending Christ to redeem us, the subject developed in Rom 3:21–5:21. In addition, when Paul writes "in view of God's mercy," he has in mind God's miracle of the new self and our rescue from the reign of sin by the Spirit who gives us life. This is what he developed in Romans 6–8. Finally, when the apostle writes "in view of God's mercy," surely he is also referring to Romans 9–11, where he passionately reveals our responsibility to preach the saving message of Christ to the nations so that they too may know God's mercy.

Realizing that all of the above is included in the words "in view of God's mercy," ponder again the full import of Paul's *alter call.*

> Therefore, I urge you, brothers, in view of God's mercy, to offer your bodies as a living sacrifice, holy and pleasing to God—which is your reasonable act of worship. Do not conform any longer to the pattern of this world, but be transformed by the renewing of your mind. Then you will be able to test and approve what God's will is—his good, pleasing and perfect will [Authors' translation].

Surely, here is the climax of Paul's missionary letter to the Romans and to us. The apostle is seeking nothing less than total commitment to God's global enterprise of saving people from every tribe, tongue, people, and nation. Indeed, he is calling you and every Christian to dedicate your life to obedience, missions, and the glorification of God.

Wanted: Personal Commitment

At the end of the previous chapter, we referred to Taki, the Japanese tour guide, who urged Christian believers to do something drastic. Well, this is it! In Rom 12:1–2, Paul, like Uncle Sam, looks you straight in the eye and with compelling finger declares, "God wants *you!*"

His alter call is disconcerting, to say the least. It's all too personal, too demanding, too honest. We each feel like sticking a finger in our collar to allow an uncomfortable gulp to clear our throat. Why does Paul's exhortation upset us so? It's because we have always assumed that commitment to evangelism and mission was merely one option among many choices that a believer could make. A few crazy, or brave, members of each congregation get excited about outreach, while we opt for "safer" activities such as teaching Sunday school or ushering. With this attitude we fail to see that outreach is the overarching option intended to influence everything we do in the church, even teaching Sunday school and ushering.

One of the greatest chapters in mission history concerns the Student Volunteer Movement. In 1886, Evangelist Dwight L. Moody sponsored a Christian Student Conference at Mount Hermon, Massachusetts. On the final day of the conference, Robert Wilder of Princeton delivered a fervent message about the need for mission workers. He concluded by calling for a personal commitment from the students. The Holy Spirit was surely working, for one hundred of those present responded by signing the following pledge: "I purpose, God willing, to become a missionary." This spark of mission commitment spread throughout North America and Europe. Over the next few decades, over 100,000 university students signed the pledge and joined the Student Volunteer Movement. More than 20,000 of them were led by God to serve as overseas missionaries, while the remainder supported their efforts with financial resources and prayer. Miracles happen when God's people commit themselves to his purposes. Spiritual power is released that touches other people.

Paul's alter call in Rom 12:1–2 brings to a climax his teaching about the goal of the Gospel. In view of God's mercy to us and all the nations, how will you respond? This is not an academic question. God is seeking your personal response and commitment. When we preached on this text at our church, we wanted to make clear to the worshipers the personal nature of Paul's alter call. So we printed this card for each person to consider prayerfully (see next page).

Paul's Alter Call

Therefore, I urge you, brothers, in view of God's mercy, to offer your bodies as living sacrifices, holy and pleasing to God—which is your reasonable worship. Do not conform any longer to the pattern of this world, but be transformed by the renewing of your mind. Then you will be able to test and approve what God's will is—His good, pleasing and perfect will (Rom 12:1–2).

On this day, _____, in view of God's mercy to me, I offer to Him my body, soul, and mind as a living sacrifice, for Him to use in His plan to bring Christ's mercy to all the peoples of the earth.

Signed: _____

About one-fourth of the congregation signed the card and now keep it in their Bibles as a remembrance of their mission covenant with God. We urge you to ask God to show you how he wants you to respond to Paul's alter call. If the Lord leads you to do so, sign your name in the space provided. How can God dare require such a sacrifice from you? You have seen the answer: Because of his mercy toward you and his desire to touch all the nations with his mercy. In the following pages we will see even more reasons to respond affirmatively.

Details of Paul's Alter Call

A closer look at Paul's words will reveal that the authors are not overstating the intent or intensity of Paul's alter call.

"I urge you"—the Greek word is *parakaleō*. In classical Greece, military commanders used this word to exhort their troops before marching into battle. This brings to mind the old hymn: "Onward, Christian soldiers, marching as to war, with the cross of Jesus going on before." Paul is recruiting Christians to take up arms and fight on God's side in the battle against Satan and the evil forces of this present world.

"To offer your bodies as living sacrifices"—this phrase takes us back to Paul's counsel in Romans 6:

> Do not offer the parts of your body to sin, as instruments of wickedness, but rather offer yourselves to God, as those who have been brought from death to life; and offer the parts of your body to him as instruments of righteousness (6:13).

The amazing thing about a living sacrifice is that when you give yourself to God, you don't die. Instead, you are more alive than ever before. People who have dedicated their lives to Christian outreach testify that this is absolutely true. A missionary to Egypt rejoices,

> Some folks back home think that I am sacrificing so much to be here in Egypt, but I consider being here a marvelous privilege. In the last five years, I have shared God's Law and Gospel with about 250 Muslims. In most cases, I was the first person ever to witness to them about Jesus Christ. Think of that! What higher privilege can there be than to be the first to tell a precious person of the precious Savior?

Yes, sacrificing one's life is the key to real living. Paul's words should not surprise us, because they parallel Jesus' statement:

> If anyone would come after me, he must deny himself and take up his cross and follow me. For whoever wants to save his life will lose it, but whoever loses his life for me and for the gospel will save it (Mk 8:34–35).

Paul could have urged us to offer our thoughts or our good intentions. Why did he say instead, "offer your bodies"? One can make a mental commitment without anything actually happening, but Paul is looking for action, for results. For missionaries to be wholly involved in reaching the lost, their bodies must participate. And it is the same for us who live in our own homeland. When we drive a newly arrived refugee to the grocery store, our whole body is involved. When we pray God's blessing on believers of other continents, heads are bowed and hands folded. Our eyes read about Islam so that we can witness better to the Pakistani who moved into our neighborhood. Our hands print, punch, and collate the Braille Scripture portions so that the blind can see and believe in the Son of Man. Our lips smile on the atheistic international student whom we have invited over for dinner. Our mouths speak the life-giving word of God to a lost person. Such are the bodily activities performed by a redeemed sinner who has offered his or her body to God as a living sacrifice.

"This is your reasonable act of worship," Paul assesses the commitment that involves our bodies. Although some translations have the word "spiritual" in place of "reasonable," the authors believe that Paul had the latter word in mind. Here is why. The Greek word translated as *reasonable* is *logikos*. You can see its similarity to our word logical. More importantly, *logikos* comes from the same root as *logizomai,* one of the key verbs found in Romans. In Rom 4:3–8, you will recall, God reckons (*logizomai*) us as righteous apart from works of the Law. In light of this Gospel reality, to offer our bodies as living sacrifices is logical and reasonable. Then in Rom 6:11, Paul advises us to reckon (*logizomai*) ourselves "dead to sin but alive to God in Christ Jesus." In light of the reality of the new self in us, to offer our bodies as a living sacrifice is logical and reasonable. Therefore, when Paul declares, "This is your reasonable (*logikos*) act of worship," he is saying, "Add it all up!"

Salvation from sin's condemnation +
Deliverance from sin's power =
Offering ourselves to God

To help us reach this conclusion, the Lord informs our minds by his promises and motivates our wills by his mercy. Our Father is not a slave driver who insists with threats and penalties. Instead, with the beauty and kindness of his mercy, he allures and incites us to dedicate our redeemed lives to him. You see, he wants no unwilling works and reluctant obedience; he desires only joyful and delighted service, body and all.

Called to Sacrifice Together

The wording of Rom 12:1–2 reveals that commitment to Christian outreach should be a group activity. In the original Greek, he writes, "Offer your bodies [plural] as a living sacrifice [singular]," indicating that we should offer our bodies together in united efforts. Here is an example.

In the city of Maturin, Venezuela, three young Christian men played baseball on the same team. Each of them was concerned about witnessing to other players on the team, but at first they met with little success. How come? They were working at it separately, each witnessing to and interceding for the unbelievers on an individual basis.

Then one day at church, the three fellows discovered their mutual concern and frustration. Sensing God's leading, they covenanted to work together in their evangelistic witness to the baseball team. Up to this time they had been dedicated to solo witnessing, but now they offered their bodies together as one living sacrifice. The result: in a few months the first baseman came to know Christ through their proclamation of the Word. Now there were four—united in offering a single, living sacrifice.

These young Christians discovered the same strategy that Paul used throughout his missionary career. He always worked in tandem with others, because he viewed witnessing as a team sport. Unfortunately, we tend to view it as an individual sport, struggling on our own. Unable or unwilling to admit our weaknesses or failures, we become overwhelmed and discouraged by obstacles we meet along the way.

Thank God, there are several new approaches to witnessing that help us overcome evangelistic individualism. "Heart to Heart" helps Christians work together in learning how to share their personal testimony of how Christ has worked in their lives. "The Master's Plan for Making Disciples" trains believers to work together in sharing the love of Christ with friends, family, neighbors, and coworkers. Both methods can add the power of numbers to your church's witness. See the resource list, Win and Charles Arn (page 264), for details about these and other ways for united witnessing.

Specifically in world mission outreach, teamwork is essential. It takes loads of boldness to witness to people who are different from us. When we share this difficult challenge with others, the burden is lightened. For example, you may have near your home international students who do not know Christ. To reach out and befriend one or two of them will take a great effort. Few Christians have been willing to do this alone, but if they had even one other Christian who shared the same concern, they would be much more likely to accept the challenge.

The same principle applies to mission work in other lands. What gives people the gumption to live in another culture and share the Gospel there? Certainly, the Holy Spirit has led such people to accept such a call, but do not underestimate the importance of group support. Many missionaries were led to their vocation by participation in a world Christian study group. These are circles of Christians who focus on the spiritual needs of the world. Studying the Scriptures together, they learn about God's global mission. They pray for unreached people who have little or no Gospel witness among them. They seek opportunities to share Christ with ethnic groups in their immediate area. They ask God to help the group focus on one or two particular unreached groups. Perhaps such a group already exists in your church. If not, talk to your pastor and others about starting one.

As the world Christian study group engages in these activities over months or years, do you know what the Holy Spirit often does? First, he works in the hearts of one or two in the group to actually go to the unreached people on whom the group has focused. Secondly, he works in the hearts of the rest of the group to assist the ones called to be missionaries by supporting them with their prayers, gifts, and concern. In a world where 2.5 billion have not yet heard the Gospel, thousands of world Christian study groups are urgently needed. So ask yourself: "Does the Lord want me to participate in such a group where we may offer our bodies as a single, united, living sacrifice?"

Together, Yet Uniquely Different

Paul's advice to work in unison is graphically illustrated by the following "visual poem" (attributed anonymously):

The Wall
brick   brick   brick

brick   brick   brick   brick

brick   brick   brick   brick   brick

brick   brick   brick   brick   brick   brick

brick   brick   brick   brick   brick   brick   brick

218

As we individually lay down our lives for the cause of world evangelization, the structure is eventually completed, to the glory of God. On second thought, however, the "visual poem" contains a major inaccuracy. Christians are not like factory-made bricks, with the same dimensions and density. The wise Creator has made us each uniquely different, as Elizabeth O'Connor observes:

> Because our gifts carry us into the world and make us participants in life, the uncovering of them is one of the most important tasks confronting any one of us. . . .

> We ask to know the will of God without guessing that his will is written into our very beings. We perceive that will when we discern our gifts. Our obedience and surrender to God are in large part our obedience and surrender to our gifts (O'Connor 1971, 14–15).

This is why Paul proceeds directly from his alter call to a discussion of spiritual gifts in Rom 12:3–8. In bringing Christ to the nations, we do not all play the same role. God has granted us different gifts and abilities to use in our own unique manner. As we unite our multiple efforts, we will see the huge task of world evangelization steadily approach its completion.

Paul's emphasis on spiritual gifts will help us avoid possible frustration and burnout due to unrealistic expectations. When we ponder the worldwide mission task, we ask, "What shall I do, Lord?" (Acts 22:10). Because there are so many billions who face a Christless eternity, the possible challenges may overwhelm you. Does he want me to witness to a million people? Does he want me to translate the Bible single-handedly into an until-now unwritten language? Does he want me to be a missionary to a hundred villages in India?

The answer to all these questions is probably not. Why? Because there is a logical flaw in all these possible scenarios. They are simply too much to expect of any one human being. Therefore, when you ask, "What shall I do, Lord?" you should be much more realistic. You need to think in terms of a one-person-sized role as you work in tandem with other believers who are also doing a one-person-sized job.

How do you determine what your one-person-sized role should be? One key is to discover your spiritual gifts. The resource list (page 264) at the end of this book mentions some effective courses

219

that can help you and fellow believers discover your spiritual gifts and put them to use. In particular, the authors recommend the books by Ralph Mattson and Arthur Miller. We have used their concepts in our own congregation and found them to be a unique and highly accurate method of discovering how God has gifted each one of us.

As you learn to use your gifts and joyfully do your one-person-sized job, other Christians will do the same. Together you will discover that you are building blocks in the kingdom of God as illustrated below:

The Kingdom Wall

Diamond Diamond Diamond

Pearl Silver Onyx Gold Sapphire Ruby

Bronze Lead Platinum Tin Bronze Sandstone

Brick Slate Concrete Brick Concrete Brick

Granite Marble Granite Quartz Limestone Granite

We, "like living stones . . . are being built into a spiritual house to be a holy priesthood, offering spiritual sacrifices to God through Jesus Christ" (1 Pet 2:5).

What Will the Future Hold?

As you consider offering your life as a sacrifice to God, you may be asking yourself, "Isn't this sort of risky? God only knows what will happen if I do that!" But isn't that the point? God does know! To encourage us to take this step of faith, in Rom 12:1–2 Paul gives us a general overview of what will happen.

"Do not conform any longer to the pattern of this world, but be transformed by the renewing of your mind" (Rom 12:2). The Greek word for *transform* is *metamorpheō*, from which we get our word *metamorphosis.* When we sacrifice our bodies to God for his purposes, he will start working changes in our attitudes and lifestyles. One thing that will change is the emphasis on meeting our own needs and desires. Have you seen the slogan "Born to Shop"? That phrase aptly describes "the pattern of this world" in affluent

North America. As you and your group of mission-minded believers learn to give top priority to reaching the nations, you will come to understand that you were not born to shop. You were born to be a blessing to the tribes, tongues, peoples, and nations that do not yet know the joy of salvation in Jesus Christ.

Such changes, Paul says, will occur "by the renewing of your mind." Does this mean that we have to work the changes by some kind of mental gymnastics? Not at all. Paul uses the Greek word *nous* (mind) as a synonym for the new self, the new spirit placed in us at baptism. "The mind (*nous*) controlled by the Spirit is life and peace" (Rom 8:6). So, rather than urging us to pull ourselves up by our mental bootstraps, the apostle assures us that God the Holy Spirit will indeed work his miracle of renewal and transformation in our minds and lives. Often young people are asked, whom do you want to be like when you grow up? As adult believers with a childlike faith, we can ask ourselves, whom do I want to be like when I grow up? The answer is, I want to be more like Jesus! And, wonder of wonders, this is just what the Holy Spirit has planned for us. "We . . . are being transformed into his [Christ's] likeness with ever-increasing glory" (2 Cor 3:18). What a marvelous prospect for all who answer Paul's alter call!

What else will the future hold for those who offer their life as a living sacrifice? "Then you will be able to test and approve what God's will is—his good, pleasing and perfect will" (Rom 12:2). This is an existential promise. Every day, every moment, you will be running an ongoing experiment to determine if God's will is good or bad. You can test his will by doing good, and lo and behold, every time God's will will prove itself to be perfect.

Interestingly, the Greek word for "perfect" is *teleon*. This is the adjective form of the word *telos* (goal), which we studied way back in chapter one when we first considered the goal of the Gospel. God's will for you will reach his intended goal.

To fathom fully the meaning of Paul's statement here, we need to view it from the perspective of the big picture. Adam and Eve could test God's will either by doing good or by doing evil. We who have been redeemed by Christ and equipped for righteous living can also put God's will to the test. Commandment by commandment, moral decision by moral decision, we can discover for ourselves and demonstrate for others that God's will is indeed good, pleasing and perfect. Like Mr. 119, the author of Psalm 119, we will exult, "Your promises have been thoroughly tested, and your servant loves them" (Ps 119:140).

Why will this daily experiment and approval be so satisfying? Because we were created to obey our Creator, finding joy and fulfillment in the doing his will—his good, pleasing, and perfect will.

Will You Answer the Call?

Paul directs his alter call to every Christian who reads his letter to the Romans. In view of God's mercy to you, offering yourself as a living sacrifice for the sake of the lost is a reasonable act of worship. How will you personally respond to Paul's alter call?

If in the past you have already made such a commitment to God's world mission enterprise, praise God. May he continue to bless your efforts on behalf of lost unbelievers.

If the Spirit moves you to make this personal offering now, praise God! In the coming months and years, he will begin doing marvelous things in your life. Without a doubt, you will discover how good, pleasing, and perfect it is to do God's will.

If you are not ready and willing to make such a commitment now, please don't sign the form on page 214. However, please keep in mind that God is seeking such a freewill offering. His goal in calling you to faith in Christ was not only to save you, but also to equip you for righteous living, to use you and all believers to convey to all peoples his message of mercy in Christ, and to bring glory to himself by all that you do. This is the goal of the Gospel, and it is God's goal for you personally.

Digging Deeper

1. Does your church ever have altar calls? Why do the authors say that Rom 12:1–2 is Paul's alter call? To whom is his alter call directed? How does it make you feel?
2. How does Rom 12:1–2 bring to a climax the preceding eleven chapters?
3. "In view of God's mercy" is a phrase full of significance. Recount the many ways that God has shown his mercy to you.
4. Compare and contrast the following texts with Paul's alter call:

Mk 8:34–35; 1 Cor 15:58; 2 Cor 3:18; and 1 Pet 2:5, 9–10.

5. With yourself or another person, debate this question: Is it reasonable or unreasonable to offer my body to God as a living sacrifice?

6. Why does Paul urge us to offer our bodies and not just our good intentions? Brainstorm for a couple minutes, thinking of ways you can use your body to bring the Gospel to others.

7. A caterpillar concludes its stage of development by wrapping itself in a chrysalis. Imagine that a certain caterpillar is unwilling to entomb itself in its chrysalis. What fears and apprehensions might motivate such reluctance? Now imagine that another caterpillar is aware of a bright, butterfly future to follow. With what kinds of emotions might it enter the chrysalis? With which caterpillar do you identify as you consider Paul's command to be "transformed (metamorphosed) by the renewing of your mind" (Rom 12:2)? If you are in a group, two people could portray these caterpillars in a pair of brief skits.

8. Consider your approach to personal witnessing. Is it more like a team sport or an individual sport? Which would you prefer? Why?

9. Do you know people who have participated in "Heart to Heart," "The Master's Plan for Making Disciples," or some other team approach to witnessing? If so, ask them to describe their experiences.

10. If you could participate in a world Christian study group, what effect would it have on your personal mission commitment? How could you go about forming such a group? Remember, you need only one other person for it to be a group (Mt 18:20).

11. What is meant by a one-person-sized role? How does this concept help you to cope with the massive nature of God's global mission task?

12. What gifts have you recognized in other Christians? What gifts have other Christians recognized in you?

13. How can you use your unique mix of gifts to call people from among all the nations to the obedience that comes from faith?

14. If you could participate in a world Christian study group, what do you think the future would hold for your group? What transformation and renewal of your minds might occur?

Note

1. The word for *mercy* in 12:1 is *oiktirmon,* a noun. In Romans 9 and 11, a verb form is used: *eleasa.* Although these words do not come from the same Greek root, their meanings are sufficiently similar to conclude that Paul is treating them synonymously.

12

Unity in a
Multicultural Church
Romans 12:9–15:13

Love Is Key

Love is what the Gospel of Jesus Christ is all about. "For God so loved the world that he gave his one and only Son, that whoever believes in him shall not perish but have eternal life" (Jn 3:16). Jesus demonstrated love beyond compare. "Greater love has no one than this, that one lay down his life for his friends" (Jn 15:13).

Since love is such an integral part of the Gospel, it should not surprise us to find love at the heart of the goal of the Gospel either. How could Paul write with such fervor and passion about becoming more and more like Christ and spreading the Gospel so that all might be saved, without including a section on love? In Rom 12:9–15:13 he speaks about love and its connection to the links in the Gospel chain of obedience, mission, and glory.

An elderly couple walked through the door of a small florist shop and asked about floral arrangements for a funeral. As they considered the various baskets and bouquets, the thoughts of the young woman behind the counter were on closing the shop a little early in order to go waterskiing. Why were they so slow? With each passing minute she became more frustrated and angry. At last they seemed to make up their minds. She went back to the workroom and prepared the bouquet, designed for a child's casket, stuffing it with twice as many flowers as usual to add to her profit. She brought it out and placed it on the counter before the couple, who just stared at it. Again she felt impatient, anxious to get on with her plans for the afternoon. Finally the man began to write a check for the arrangement. As he did so, he looked up at the shopkeeper with tears in his eyes and said, "He would have been our first grandson, but he died!" At last, the young woman started to regret her impatience. She felt sick with herself for thinking only of her wants. Now she deeply regretted her angry frustration. How it pained her that she had not taken advantage of this crucial moment to show Christlike love to these two people, so deeply in need of love and understanding (Barry 1990, 21).

That is where love is so badly needed, in the real world of everyday pain and sorrow where, as Paul put it, "Love must be sincere" (Rom 12:9). How often we have all failed, just as this young lady did, to show sincere love for someone who desperately needed it. Love in action is at the heart of sanctification. What one command did Jesus give to his disciples? "Love one another as I have loved you." Paul says as much in Rom 13:9–10:

> The commandments, "Do not commit adultery," "Do not murder," "Do not steal," "Do not covet," and whatever other commandment there may be, are summed up in this one rule: "Love your neighbor as yourself." Love does no harm to its neighbor. Therefore love is the fulfillment of the law.

Love in action is what witnessing and world mission are all about. If we fail to demonstrate love for those we are attempting to win to Christ, how will they ever know that Jesus loves them? Evangelism and missions are 90 percent love (Peterson 1980, 107). Presenting the Gospel without love is like sharing the words of a song without the music. The "music" of the Gospel (love) must precede the words of the Gospel (Aldrich 1981, 20–21). As we love others we will become "little Christs" to them and win them to him. That's why Paul says to "clothe yourselves with Jesus Christ" (Rom 13:14). And so Paul tells us to "be devoted to one another in brotherly love" (Rom 12:9). He goes so far as to admonish us to love our enemies and to bless those who persecute us. And at that point Paul's thoughts take a curious turn.

Love in the Face of Persecution

Immediately after telling his readers to love their enemies, he turns to the subject of submission to the governing authorities. Why? In Paul's time and in many parts of the world today, the governing authorities are included among the enemies whom Paul commands us to love. Paul himself had experienced much persecution at the hands of the authorities. Village councils ran him out of town; he was arrested and tried before provincial governors. Ultimately, he appealed to Caesar and came under the jurisdiction of the Roman emperor (Acts 25:11). Whenever arrested, Paul was aware of his legal rights as a Roman citizen and made full use of them for his benefit. At the same time, however, he was always respectful and submissive. Imagine Paul spending nights in prison, in between hymn stanzas praying for those who had put him there! This is love in action. And this is the kind of action to which Paul calls us today.

Around the world, Christians persecuted by their governments are rising to the challenge to love their enemies. Until 1990, East Germany was locked in the grip of communist rule. Communism failed, however, and East Germany's government collapsed. Former party chief, Erich Honecker, found himself without a job, without a home, without a pension, and without a friend in the whole country except for his wife, Margot.

In spite of the nationwide hatred of this former dictator, Pastor Uwe Holmer took the Honeckers into his own home to live with him and his family. During their stay, Erich and Margot had the opportunity to listen in on the Holmers' family devotions and to hear expressions of their faith in Jesus Christ, which motivated their act of loving compassion.

This example of love is highlighted by the fact that Pastor Holmer's oldest son, Johannes, was denied the opportunity to study in the university because of his faith. That denial was approved by the former Minister of Education, Margot Honecker herself! Pastor Holmer did exactly as Paul commanded. He blessed the ones who persecuted him, and he did so in a very personal manner. His act of Christian love brought glory to God, because it came to the attention of the entire world.

In his book *Speaking the Gospel Today,* Robert Kolb explains the significance of acts like those of Pastor Holmer.

> Agape, as God channels it through us, is directed at specific individuals and groups, not at humanity in general. We must be prepared to do good to all, but we actually do good to specific neighbors. Jesus did not say that the neighbor was anybody and everybody but was a beaten stranger by the side of the road (Lk

10:30). Among those individuals whom we are to love are even those who exhibit hostility and hatred toward us (Kolb 1984, 198).

Pastor Holmer was not afflicted with the problem some Christians suffer from. They claim to love people everywhere, yet they hate the person next door or at the next desk. If we can't love specific people on specific occasions, then we don't really know how to love.

Now Is the Time for Love

After urging us to love sincerely and to bless those who persecute us, Paul adds, "And do this, understanding the present time. The hour has come for you to wake up from your slumber, because our salvation is nearer now than when we first believed" (Rom 13:11). The apostle is urging us to make the most of every opportunity to love, because time is fleeting, and the day of Christ's return is drawing nearer. If Paul could say that in his day, how much more true it is today!

When Paul said, "And do this, understanding the present time," he used a very significant word for *time*. The usual Greek word for time, *chronos,* denotes the passage of time. Our word *chronology* comes from *chronos.* However, when Paul challenged us to love, "understanding the present time," he used a different word for time, *kairos. Kairos* refers to a singular moment in time, a unique occasion, an opportune moment. Paul's usage of the word *kairos* sheds light on the urgency of showing forth God's love and evangelizing the world in each generation. Now is the time for us to be a light shining in the darkness. The young lady in the florist shop realized her opportune moment to demonstrate love, only after she had missed it. How she regretted it! Pastor Uwe Holmer made the most of his opportune time to demonstrate love to the Honeckers. What will you do with your opportune time?

Convicts often speak of "doing time." For most of those in prison, this simply means marking time or killing time, waiting to get out. The only time they feel good about doing time is when they become "short-timers" who are almost ready for release. In Michigan, however, a group of convicts is making the most of "doing time." They have formed a prison ministry, giving it the name, *Kai-*

ros. They see their time in prison as a special opportunity to demonstrate the love of Jesus Christ to fellow inmates by sharing the Gospel with them. They have turned "doing time" into God's time, their opportune moment, their *kairos* for the Lord.

These men are in prison, their freedom limited, yet they are making the most of every opportunity to glorify God. You and I who are free also have a *kairos*, our time to proclaim the Gospel by the way we live. Will you make the most of it? Now is the time to exercise the obedience that comes from faith. Now is the time to "let your light shine before men, that they may see your good deeds and praise your Father in heaven" (Mt 5:16).

God Loves Variety

Paul goes on to make it clear that love must be sincere, not only toward those who are outside the church, those whom we would win to Christ, but also to those within the church. Love is so necessary within the body of Christ because God loves variety.

Have you ever been to a large public aquarium, like the Shedd Aquarium in downtown Chicago? Several years ago I [Bob] took my family there, expecting to be bored. I thought only fishermen could really enjoy an aquarium, and even they would find it frustrating, since they couldn't catch anything! What I found at the aquarium surprised me. In those tanks were fish and other amazing creatures from the sea, of all shapes, sizes, colors, and descriptions! Then I began to wonder. Why did God create all these beautiful, colorful creatures that, most of the time, no one can appreciate? Have you ever wondered why? Especially, why all the colors? Who can appreciate the differences—a few other fish? Then it hit me. God appreciates them, that's who! God can see all of his creatures at all times, and how delighted he must be by all the incredible shapes and sizes and colors in the sea. I came to an inescapable conclusion. God loves variety! He loves people—in all the shapes, colors, intellects, and personalities that we come in. He loves the persons behind the variety. He has created and redeemed all of us.

Just last summer I did something that I had been meaning to do for several years. I took my family downtown on the train to attend the Windy City's food and music festival called "Taste of Chicago." I had put off going to the "Taste" because of the crowds of people one always heard were present. Well, I wasn't disappointed. Probably a million people jammed Grant Park on the shore of Lake Michigan that Friday evening, but it turned out to be every bit as fascinating as my trip to the Shedd Aquarium.

First of all, we could purchase food of every ethnic variety imaginable, all of it tasting great! Yet, even more interesting were the people, people from different cultures and nations demonstrating their uniqueness through music or acrobatics. One group of young men twirled and tossed sticks in the most amazing fashion, holding two ordinary sticks in their hands. I attempted it, only to succeed in dropping the sticks on the ground try after try. Here I had put off going to "Taste of Chicago" for years because of the crowds of people. Now that I was finally there, I learned that the people were the main attraction!

After wandering through the park for a while, we stopped at a music stage as people gathered for a show. As we watched, a young man strode up in a pair of blue jeans filled with holes at his thighs, on his knees, and down by his ankles. He wore a black leather jacket proudly emblazoned with the emblem of a rock group. His head was shaved bald except for a central strip of hair, which stood straight up in the air about ten inches high. It was dyed green. He was wearing earrings, not unusual in this era, but he also had safety pins in his cheeks!

Needless to say, he was attracting much attention, especially after a female of similar description joined him. I was standing next to a man who had not yet noticed this couple, but when he did, his jaw dropped. He looked at them and then he looked at me and just shook his head back and forth. Now, this gentleman was not of the same ethnic background as I. He was black, but it was obvious that the cultural gap between the two of us was much smaller than the gap between either of us and these two young punk rockers. I leaned closer so I could speak to him over the sound of the music which had now begun, and I said to him, "God loves variety." We both smiled.

Yes, just as God loves variety in fish, so he also loves variety in people *because they are people, his creation, which has also been redeemed.* God has created all kinds of people from all kinds of nations with all kinds of cultures. In the Great Commission Christ has told us to make disciples of all of them, and he has told us to do so by *going*. This is a significant Greek word. *Poreuthentes* means *to depart, to leave, to cross boundaries.* What sort of boundaries does Jesus want us to cross? Certainly he had in mind geographic boundaries, but the Savior also recognized we would need to cross sociological, racial, linguistic, and cultural boundaries in order to bring the Gospel to all people. Obviously the worldwide Gospel mission takes us beyond many barriers, but so does our mission closer to home.

We live in a society with many differences. About 100 years ago, the community in which this author ministers was made up almost exclusively of German Lutheran immigrants. This remained largely the case until after World War II. Then things began to change. Today many Italian Catholics live in our neighborhood, far outnumbering the German Lutherans. In recent years even more change has come about. Several Asian Indian families live within a few doors of my home. We now have blacks and Hispanics moving into our neighborhood in increasing numbers. Each of these groups brings with them a different culture, a different sociological background.

What's true of the neighborhood is true of our local church. Now whites, blacks, Hispanics, and people with Lutheran, Roman Catholic, and Baptist heritages, all worship together. Each group brings different attitudes and ideas about certain cultural matters— which means we have different ways of doing things and different customs. We even have some different values. When we all try to live together in one family—that is, as we try to be the church— these differences may become an issue, causing conflict within the body of Christ.

Loving Those Who Are Different from Us

Paul's discussion of weak and strong Christians in Romans 14 and 15 must be viewed as an example of the conflict that was already occurring in his time and will continue to arise between Christians from different cultures. How can the unity of the body of Christ be maintained in the face of such variety? It is impossible for Paul in this brief discussion to settle every debate over culture that will occur in the history of the church the world over. Instead, he lays down *principles* for dealing with such issues in an atmosphere of brotherly love and acceptance.

We are not speaking here of differences over the clear teachings of Scripture, but over matters not plainly spoken of in Scripture. Such matters sometimes are called *adiaphora*, "indifferent things," or genuinely disputable matters. Paul says that in such things we should not judge one another but be willing to accommodate each other if we are to live together in harmony and unity in the church.

What are some examples of disputable matters? Paul mentions several in his letters. They involve questions about the eating of certain foods, about ritually clean and unclean foods, and about vegetarianism versus eating meat. They revolve around days of the week for worship, whether the Sabbath (which is Saturday) or the Lord's Day (which is Sunday) is the proper day for worship. Another disputable matter among Christians is drinking or not drinking alcohol. Even though the Scriptures clearly condemn drunkenness, they do not forbid the moderate use of alcohol. Manners or customs of worship have always been issues for dispute in the church, because the Scriptures contain no set form of liturgy or note of music.

So, how may we accommodate one another in order to get along in the multi-cultural church of today with its diversity of people? Paul gives us good advice as he speaks to both weaker and stronger brothers and sisters in the faith. The weaker believer is the one who is bound by an overly cautious conscience, perhaps based on cultural taboos, which will not allow him the freedom to do certain things that the Scriptures do not forbid. The stronger Christian is the one who understands and accepts the limits placed on his conduct by the Word of God, but feels at liberty to practice the freedom from man-made rules and regulations that he has in Jesus Christ.

Paul speaks to stronger Christians, giving them permission to exercise their freedom. "Happy is the person who does not feel guilty when he does something he judges is right" (Rom 14:22 TEV). He advises weaker Christians not to judge or condemn the stronger ones for exercising their freedom under the Gospel in certain matters.

But Paul seems to lay a special burden on the stronger Christians precisely because they are stronger. He says that the stronger believer should not cause his weaker brother to stumble by knowingly doing something the weaker brother would consider wrong. By doing so, he would mock the conscientiousness of the weaker brother. He might also put pressure on the weaker brother to go against his conscience and so fall into sin. The stronger brother also needs to bear patiently the criticism of the weaker brother. Even Christ was criticized for the way he lived and the freedom he exercised. He set an example for us when on the cross he bore insults silently.

Overcoming Cultural Barriers with Love

Paul's principles apply in today's church as much as in his own time. Christians of different ethnic or cultural backgrounds are free to live out their faith, expressing it in their own cultural terms, as long as they do nothing contrary to Scripture or their conscience. However, when a weaker Christian views a certain practice as sinful and in violation of his conscience, then the stronger believer should accommodate the weaker when they are together. At the same time, the weaker Christian should not condemn the stronger one for his freedom under the Gospel.

Too often we have been guilty of condemning fellow Christians for exercising their freedom. We have let our faith become so bound up with our culture that we consider any faith expressions that flow out of a different culture to be an assault on our faith. A look at one church's history bears this out.

Worship

A couple of generations ago, many Lutherans in America went through a crisis in culture when they switched from the German language to English in worship and in their schools. Some thought that when German was left behind the pure Gospel would be lost as well. These few fought vociferously for their language, and in some congregations the German worship service didn't die until the last German speaking member of the congregation had been laid to rest in the church cemetery. Today, a new controversy is raging in many Lutheran congregations. This crisis concerns the use of contemporary American styles of worship as opposed to a more traditional, liturgical style of worship.

Over 100 years ago, German immigrants to the Midwest founded Fortress Lutheran Church. Today it sits in a growing suburb of a large metropolitan area. The congregation still serves many older members of German descent. They tend to be rather formal, conservative, and traditional in their lifestyle. At the same time, many young families and single professionals are moving into the area and into the congregation. They tend to be more informal and contemporary in their style of living. Quite naturally, this mix of members has led to a difference of opinion about styles of worship. The older, long-standing members of the congregation want to retain their more formal, traditional, and liturgical worship service. They have used it all of their lives and are quite comfortable with it. The younger members prefer a freer, less formal atmosphere of worship with contemporary music.

In a spirit of compromise and harmony, Fortress' members have decided to retain the traditional liturgical forms at the early Sunday morning service to be held in the sanctuary of the church. However, the later worship service, of a more contemporary style, is relegated to the fellowship hall, because many of the congregation's more conservative members think that such a style of worship would be inappropriate in the church itself.

At first, many more worshipers attended the traditional rather than the contemporary service. Interestingly, however, within two year's time, the contemporary service has replaced the traditional liturgy as the primary form of the congregation's worship. A change has been made which reflects the changing culture in which this congregation is seeking to minister. It has not divided the congregation, nor has it robbed the church of the pure Gospel message it is seeking to proclaim. Instead, it has given the church an avenue of outreach to many more residents in its community than it ever had before.

This same tension has been and is still being experienced in Lutheran churches all over America, as well as in some other denominations which have traditionally used a more formal, liturgical style of worship. The results have been varied. A few congregations have been able to maintain a vibrant liturgical style of worship by educating their members about the meaning of the liturgy and by using it innovatively. Some have found variety to be the key to serving the differing needs of the broad spectrum of people who worship in their midst, alternating from week to week between more formal and more contemporary styles of worship. Sadly, other congregations have painfully divided over styles of worship. And still others, who feel totally tradition-bound, have watched their ministries decline in the face of changing cultural patterns.

Music

Perhaps the next stage in differences over worship styles will involve music. Hymns, praise songs and choruses, and some other more contemporary forms of music have gained a broad acceptance in the North American church. But Christian contemporary music and Christian rock have been limited primarily to concert settings and Christian broadcasting. Does a Christian rock band like "Petra" have a place alongside Bach in Christian worship? At least a few congregations have concluded that it does, some forming their own "rock" bands to perform Christian contemporary music in worship. One church calls its group "The Spiritual Rock," based on 1 Cor 10:4, to indicate that they proclaim Christ, the spiritual Rock who accompanied Israel on its wilderness wanderings and who is with us to the end of the age, and to identify the style of music which they use to proclaim him.

Some believe that using Christian rock music goes beyond disputable matters, but the truth is that Scripture is silent on the form our music should take when we worship and praise our God. Certainly most North American Christians would be very uncomfortable with the music Christians in Africa or India play to praise the Lord. Does that make their expression wrong? No, it only means it is different. It is a matter of culture, and in such matters Paul tells us that we need to be accepting of one another. God loves variety— he loves people regardless of their differences.

Culture

Perhaps Christians in America today need to scrutinize areas of our own culture more carefully. While we are quite conscious of and uncomfortable with certain cultural expressions of worship that are foreign to us, we may be blind to certain aspects of our own culture with which we are quite comfortable, though they may not be pleasing to God.

For example, we ought to examine our affluent lifestyles in the face of the homelessness and poverty that exist not only in the third world but even in our own land. We ought to evaluate our use of television, films, and music in the light of Paul's warnings against even a hint of sexual immorality, obscenity, foolish talk, or coarse joking (Eph 5:3–4). We ought to investigate whether some of our extravagant American funeral customs line up with our faith in a risen Christ and our hope of the resurrection. These examples, and many others, illustrate that we should be cautious about criticizing the culture of others when we have not even carefully assessed our own.

At times, Christians have thought that their music, architecture, or some other cultural expression was essential to communicating the Gospel in another land. However, in Romans 14 and 15, Paul reminds us that calling people to Christ "from among all the Gentiles" will result in a wide variety of cultural expressions of faith. Forms of worship, Christian lifestyles in different lands, and even the theological concerns that Christians must address and resolve, will differ from culture to culture. For instance, most North American Christians have never struggled with issues like the veneration of ancestors or polygamy, but in Japan or Africa these are very pressing and important questions to Christians. Can't we give Christians in other cultures the freedom to work out such conflicts and express their Christian faith in their own way, as long as they are within the bounds of Scripture?

I recall the story of missionary Bruce Olsen and his first convert among the Motilone Indians on the Colombian-Venezuelan border. Olsen was disappointed that this man did not immediately witness to the other people of his tribe. He was certain that this man would have a much more positive effect in converting others to Christ than would his own witness to the Motilones. One day, a special festival was being held. The event included the performance of lengthy narrative songs by individual Motilone tribesmen. To the missionary's surprise and delight, this new believer, who up to this point had been so silent about his new-found faith, sang the entire story of salvation to his people in a manner which was absolutely appropriate for their culture.

In another part of the world, former Muslims who have now become Christians still pray five times a day and worship on Friday, according to the Muslim custom. About these practices, Ralph Winter comments,

> Jesus died for these people around the world. He did not die to preserve our Western way of life. He did not die to make Muslims stop praying five times a day (Winter 1981, 311).

Winter also commented on the cultural richness and diversity within the Christian church.

> If the whole world church could be gathered into a single congregation, Sunday after Sunday, there would eventually and inevitably be a loss of a great deal of the rich diversity of the present Christian traditions. Does God want this? Do we want this? (Winter 1981, 311).

Certainly we know that God does not want this. Hopefully, we do not want it either. God loves variety. Hopefully, we can accept one another with our cultural differences and accommodate one another within the body of Christ, not for the purpose of having an acceptable quota of ethnics in our church, as though variety itself was the goal, but because God created everyone and Christ sacrificed himself for them all.

Why Love Is So Important

Paul writes about mission in Rom 9–11. In chapters 12–15, he follows with detailed instructions about love, in particular regarding acceptance of the cultural practices of other believers. In this manner the apostle reveals the essential connection between the church's mission and its expression of love and acceptance. Let us briefly consider several reasons why love is so important to mission.

1. God loves all human beings and cultures and desires to see them represented in heaven. Regarding our eternal home, the Lord Jesus revealed to John that "the kings of the earth will bring their splendor into it. . . . The glory and honor of the nations will be brought into it" (Rev 21:24, 26). The Lord will transfer human beings with their cultural riches to the new heaven and the new earth. Since this is so, as we introduce the Gospel to those in another culture, rather than shunning everything in that culture, we should be encouraging these new believers to express their faith in and love for the Triune God in ways that are culturally meaningful to them.

In Elmhurst, Illinois, there is a small but surprising museum called the Lizzadro Museum of Lapidary Art. It is filled with all sorts of beautiful gemstones carved into intricate vessels and figures, formed into beautiful mosaics, and cut into dazzling shapes. In this museum, as in the Shedd Aquarium, one is struck by the rich variety of creation. Even the mineral world is filled with all sorts of colors, textures, shapes, and sizes. The rock collector, or rock hound, scrutinizes outwardly drab rock formations in search of the beauty which the Lord has hidden within them. The lapidary artist then molds and shapes the rocks to form objects that are both strikingly attractive and surprisingly useful.

The parallel between rocks and cultures is amazing. Cultures not yet influenced by the Gospel are like the gem stones that lie hidden in the ground. Missionaries are holy rock hounds who hunt for all the gems of culture that God has created. Then the missionaries help the believers of each culture become lapidary artists, as they mold and shape their own culture so that they can use it to praise and glorify God.

Since the Lord loves all people with their cultures and longs to see them enjoy their redemption in Christ Jesus, can we love them any less?

2. Evangelism in North America is a cross-cultural activity. This is true not only because more and more people from differing cultural backgrounds are making their home in America but also because the cultural consensus which existed in America in the past is largely gone.

The punk rockers at "Taste of Chicago" may be an extreme example, but they are evidence of a much broader range of cultural opinion and expression present in America today than there was 40 or even 30 years ago. In the 50s and early 60s, most people adhered to a form of "civil righteousness" whether they were part of the church or not. Outwardly, their lives conformed quite closely to the morality espoused by Christians. When they were exposed to the Gospel and came to know Christ, they were changed dramatically on the inside, but outwardly they did not have to undergo a drastic change in lifestyle.

Today we live in a more outwardly pagan society. Morality is no longer commonly agreed upon. People with very different ideas of right and wrong, with very different standards of conduct, live right next door to us. God's love for our diverse population compels us to present the Gospel in Word and sacrament to them in a way they can identify with culturally. Furthermore, we will have to expend much more effort to bring their hearts and minds and lives into conformity with the Word of God. Such effort will only be made when we are moved by Christlike and Christ-inspired love.

3. Sometimes the biggest barrier to reaching the lost is our own lack of love. During his 1990 concert tour, Christian singer and songwriter Wayne Watson made a bold confession. He told his audience (which included me—Bob) that in prayer with the Lord he had discovered what his greatest spiritual difficulty was. The crowd grew silent, wondering what kind of personal problem this respected Christian artist was going to confess. They were more stunned than they expected to be when Watson spilled out his greatest spiritual problem in one word: "Madonna!" No, it was not what everyone immediately thought. Watson was not consumed by some sinful passion for the leading secular rock star, Madonna. Instead, he confessed that he despised her, considered her vulgar, immoral, and profane, and didn't want her to be in heaven with him. Then he confronted his audience, asking who it was that they did not want to see in heaven. Finally he prayed, asking that his heart and the hearts of his audience would be filled with love rather than contempt for the lost, and that God would touch the hearts of the people they did not want to see in heaven so that they too would indeed come to know Jesus and be saved.

This is why love is so essential to the mission of proclaiming the Gospel. We may not really care to be in heaven with fellow sinners who are so vastly different from ourselves. Only the love of Jesus can overwhelm our lovelessness, move us off dead center, and help overcome the cultural gap between us and them so that we can proclaim to them in a meaningful way the good news of salvation through faith in Jesus Christ.

4. Finally, Paul also advocates openness to cultural variety to help us realize that we are all saved by grace through faith, not by what we eat or drink or by the manner in which we worship. Before God and by his grace, we are all on equal footing. We do not make ourselves more acceptable to God by the customs we observe. No one can stand before God except by grace through faith in Jesus Christ.

God's love has saved us all, and his love in Jesus Christ must be the glue that holds together all the diverse elements of one body. Whether Jew or Gentile, Greek or Roman, Italian or German, black or white, love is the key to our unity and harmony. Only as we exercise love toward one another will we be able to maintain the unity and harmony which we must have to be able to win the great variety of people around us to Christ.

> Accept one another, then, just as Christ accepted you, in order to bring praise to God. For I tell you that Christ has become a servant of the Jews on behalf of God's truth, to confirm the promises made to the patriarchs so that the Gentiles may glorify God for his mercy (Rom 15:7–9a).

Let us be tolerant of our differences, living together in love and unity, in order to win the world for Christ.

In Spite of the Obstacles, Keep on Hoping

Does winning the world for Christ sound like a tall order? Perhaps it sounds more like "Mission Impossible." Nevertheless, Paul concludes this section of Romans assuring us that it is *Mission Possible*. Indeed, God has given us some challenging goals: To evangelize the world in our generation, and to maintain the unity of the Spirit in the bond of peace with everyone who has been evangelized. How can we ever hope to achieve such results? Think of all the cultures and peoples in this world in need of the Gospel. Think of all the differences between them—racial, ethnic, linguistic, social, economic, and cultural.

Introducing people of a new culture to Christ is a monumental task, like climbing a mountain. When General Fremont discovered Pike's Peak, his vision was to climb it. After failing in the attempt, he declared that no one would ever reach the summit. Today, hundreds of successful climbers have ascended Pike's Peak in spite of General Fremont's pessimistic prediction. Like those mountain climbers, we need to have an optimistic vision that we can fulfill the Great Commission, to make disciples of all nations, by obeying the Great Commandment, to love others as Christ loved us. With God's help we can overcome cultural barriers and evangelize the nations!

So that we do not lose heart in striving for these goals, Paul cites several Scriptures that speak of the attainment of these goals.

1. "I will praise you among the Gentiles" (2 Sam 22:50).
2. "Rejoice, O Gentiles, with his people" (Deut 32:43).
3. "Praise the Lord, all you Gentiles" (Ps 117:1).
4. "The Gentiles will hope in him" (Is 11:10).

These promises from God's Word show us that people from all over the world, from every race and culture, will be trusting and praising God along with his chosen people Israel. No barrier is too big for the power of God's promises to overcome. Thus, as Paul said, "Through endurance and the encouragement which come from the Scriptures we ... have hope" (Rom 15:4). This hope enables us to continue faithfully in the work of calling people from among all the Gentiles to the obedience of faith. At times, this may seem to be an impossible challenge, but Hudson Taylor knew otherwise: "There are three steps to every work of God," he observed. "First it is impossible. Then it is difficult. Then it is done."

Digging Deeper

1. Why is love of such great importance to the goal of the Gospel? What role does it play in:
   a. the Gospel itself?
   b. the goal of obedience?
   c. the goal of missions?
   d. the goal of glorifying God?
2. Have you heard of any recent examples of the persecution of Christians by the government, either in your own land or around the world? What happened? How would you respond if you found yourself (or are!) in such a situation? What would love compel you to do or to say in that situation?
3. What does Pastor Uwe Holmer's act of kindness toward Erich Honecker have to do with the goal of the Gospel? Can you think of ways in which all three aspects of the goal of the Gospel were fulfilled by this act of love?
4. Why is *now* a crucial time in your life to fulfill the goal of the Gospel? What is happening in your life now that makes this a

kairos for you? Can any *now* become a *kairos* if we place it in God's hands?

5. Think of the variety of people in your church. How would you describe them? How are they different? How are they all alike?

6. Now think of the variety of people in your neighborhood (or the neighborhood around your church). How would you describe them? How are they different? How are they all alike?

7. Do you see greater variety in your neighborhood than in your church? Why might this be? How can your church reach out to the variety of people in its neighborhood? What is the key?

8. Can you think of any differences that have arisen between Christians in your church over "indifferent things," that is, matters which are not spoken of directly in Scripture? How could these differences be resolved by applying the principles that the apostle Paul give us in Romans 14–15?

9. How do you feel about the worship or music in your church? How would you like to see it changed, if at all? How appropriate do you think it is to today's culture? Is it proper for Christians to accommodate our culture in our styles of worship or music? Does worship have to be culturally irrelevant in order to be God pleasing? On the other hand, is it proper to help others understand your worship tradition and its positive benefits?

10. Do you think our society's standards or values are generally different today from a generation or two ago? How have they changed? Why does this present us with a greater evangelism challenge than we have faced in the past? How can we meet this challenge? What role can a proper understanding of the goal of the Gospel play in meeting this challenge?

11. Can you identify with Wayne Watson's confession about the person he did not want to be with in heaven? Can you think of someone you know personally, but dislike so intensely that you would just as soon not spend eternity with them? If so, offer a prayer of confession and ask God to change your heart toward that person. Pray that God would help you do what he wants in order to help lead that person to Christ.

12. Have you ever felt that there was no hope of fulfilling the Great Commission? When and why? How do Paul's words in Rom 15:1–13 and his use of the Scriptures in this section offer hope?

13

To the Ends of the Earth
Romans 15:14—16:27

In Rom 12:1–2, Paul sounded his alter call in the *general* appeal, "Offer your bodies as a living sacrifice." Now, at the end of his letter the apostle states the *specific* world evangelization action he wants the Romans to take.

Paul certainly does not write a letter in typical North American style. When we want someone to do something, we usually get right to the point. "Dear Charles: Next Tuesday I want you to. . . ." Although Paul desires the Roman Christians to take a certain action, he is a paragon of patience, laying a foundation of motivation for over 14 chapters as he writes "quite boldly on some points" (Rom 15:15): Scripture, salvation in Christ, obedience, outreach to the nations, and the glory of God. With all the motivational information now in place, Paul calls the Romans—and us—to action and commitment. Exactly what does he want us to do? That is what we will learn in this chapter.

Headed for the Ends of the Earth

Perhaps some readers of this book are tired of hearing about obedience and missions. Maybe you feel that we have overdosed on these teachings. "Thank God," you may be thinking, "only one more chapter to plow through, and then I can take a rest from all this intense emphasis on discipleship and outreach. I've had enough of courageous obedience for a dying world. Let's get on to other topics and activities in the church."

Even though at times we feel as if we have had enough of these subjects, consider this: Paul had not yet had enough. Note his evident eagerness in Rom 15:17–24, where he charts his future plans:

Therefore I glory in Christ Jesus in my service to God. I will not venture to speak of anything except what Christ has accomplished through me in leading the Gentiles to obey God by what I have said and done—by the power of signs and miracles, through the power of the Spirit. So from Jerusalem all the way around to Illyricum, I have fully proclaimed the gospel of Christ. It has always been my ambition to preach the gospel where Christ was not known, so that I would not be building on someone else's foundation. Rather, as it is written: "Those who were not told about him will see, and those who have not heard will understand." This is why I have often been hindered from coming to you.

But now that there is no more place for me to work in these regions, and since I have been longing for many years to see you, I plan to do so when I go to Spain.

Paul glorifies God for the successes he and his missionary teams have realized in the Eastern Mediterranean. From Jerusalem around to Illyricum (present day Albania and Yugoslavia), they had planted congregations, like lighting one beacon after another, until that whole region glowed with "the light of the knowledge of the glory of God in the face of Christ Jesus" (2 Cor 4:6). Those new congregations were now responsible for spreading the light to all unevangelized people in their environs.

With this great accomplishment behind him, why didn't Paul take it easy? He could have coasted to the finish line. He could have claimed his age as his exemption from further service, for we know that he was past fifty. His poor health would have been a legitimate excuse; we know that he suffered from some ailments (2 Cor 12:7–10; Gal 4:13–15). Yet, in spite of these reasons to relax or even retire, it was still Paul's ambition to preach the Gospel where Christ was not known. Thus we find him informing the Romans of his next missionary expedition—"I'm headed for Spain!"

What Motivated Paul?

What prompted the veteran missionary to head for Spain on yet another foray into territory held by Satan? He was motivated by the only thing that should motivate Christians: the Word of God. In particular, Paul refers to one verse that influenced him. "Rather, as it is written: 'Those who were not told about him will see, and those who have not heard will understand' " (Rom 15:21). Our purpose in this section is to grasp why Paul selected this verse.

Rom 15:21 is one of four quotes in Romans from Is 52–53. You may want to take a minute to turn to Isaiah in your Bible and glance over these chapters.

Rom 2:24 refers to Is 52:5, which reads, "All day long my name is constantly blasphemed." Earlier in chapter 7 we discussed how Is 52:5 and Ezek 36:22 portray the failure of the Jews to glorify God before the nations of the world.

Rom 10:15 quotes Is 52:7, "How beautiful on the mountains are the feet of those who bring good news." And Rom 10:16 repeats the question stated in Is 53:1, "Who has believed our message?" These two citations appear at the very pinnacle of Paul's argument about the necessity of Gospel proclamation for the salvation of both Jew and Gentile.

Now in Rom 15:21 Paul quotes Is 52:15 as his motive for pioneer mission work: "So will he [Christ] sprinkle many nations, and kings will shut their mouths because of him. For what they were not told, they will see, and what they have not heard, they will understand." Obviously, Paul considered Isaiah 52–53 to be as filled with mission themes as there are chocolate chips in your grandmother's cookies.[1] What is the good news to be proclaimed by those with beautiful feet? What information will be seen and understood that was not told or heard before? What is the message that is to be believed?

Paul is a genius when it comes to quoting Scripture. He found his key mission verses in the very place that the Lord foretold Christ's salvation ministry in the greatest, most poignant detail. Read Is 53:2–6 with new eyes, with mission eyes. We have italicized the all-inclusive words to indicate the global implications of the saving work of love Isaiah prophesied:

> He grew up before him like a tender shoot, and like a root out of dry ground.
>
> He had no beauty or majesty to attract *us* to him, nothing in his appearance that *we* should desire him.
>
> He was despised and rejected by *men*, a man of sorrows, and familiar with suffering.
>
> Like one from whom *men* hide their faces he was despised, and *we* esteemed him not.

Surely he took up *our* infirmities and carried *our* sorrows, yet *we* considered him stricken by God, smitten by him, and afflicted.

But he was pierced for *our* transgressions, he was crushed for *our* iniquities; the punishment that brought *us* peace was upon him, and by his wounds *we* are healed.

We all, like sheep, have gone astray, *each* of *us* has turned to his own way; and the Lord has laid on him the iniquity of *us all*.

Although not as many all-inclusive terms appear in verses 7–12, the emphasis is clear that "he bore the sin of *many,* and made intercession for the *transgressors*" (Is 53:12).

Christians treasure Isaiah 53 with its sublime depiction of Jesus, the suffering servant of God. Every Good Friday, believers around the world read this chapter and sing hymns such "Stricken, Smitten, and Afflicted," finding great consolation and assurance in the marvelous message of atonement and salvation in Christ. We love Isaiah 53 because there we find 24-carat Gospel.

But have we seen all that there is to be discovered in Isaiah 52–53? Not if we overlook the themes that Paul stresses in Romans. His quotations from the first half of Isaiah 52–53 speak of proclamation to the nations. In contrast, we overwhelmingly quote from the second half, the marvelous Suffering Servant text with its beautiful Gospel. However, if you love Isaiah 53, then you must share it with the world, as Isaiah 52 stresses. We need to sing "Stricken, Smitten, and Afflicted," in medley with "I Love to Tell the Story" "till all the world adore his sacred name."

So what motivated Paul to go to Spain? The full Word of God, including both the Gospel and the goal of the Gospel. This Word, full of grace and truth, is what should always motivate the church to loving action.[2]

"Come with Me to the Ends of the Earth"

Paul is headed for the ends of the earth. He informs the Romans of his goal in order to invite them to come along.

But now that there is no more place for me to work in these regions, and since I have been longing for many years to see you, I plan to do so when I go to Spain. I hope to visit you while passing through and to have you assist me on my journey there, after I have enjoyed your company for a while (Rom 15:23–24).

This request for assistance is what Paul has been driving at throughout the letter to the Romans.

Hmmmm. Does this mean that all of his glowing talk about salvation, obedience, and mission is nothing more than the prelude to a crass appeal for funds? What a disappointing anticlimax that would be!

However, Paul is not looking to Rome for mere dollars. He is looking for committed hearts. "To have you assist me on my journey" is a broad phrase that includes many kinds of support. More important than funds, he needs information about Spain from those acquainted with that province of the Roman Empire. He was eager to receive letters of recommendation to people in Spain whom the Romans knew personally. With such letters, Paul would have an open opportunity to proclaim Christ in their households.

However, the most important items on Paul's "Mission Expedition Shopping List" were people themselves. Remember, Paul always worked with a team of missionaries, training young people like Timothy and delegating key ministries to seasoned veterans like Titus, Luke, and Silas. Here he asks the Romans to consider volunteering to join his team as it heads for the ends of the earth. So, you see, Paul is not simply asking the Roman Church to take up a mission offering and pray now and then. He is urging them to become partners in the mission of spreading the Gospel, as the logical conclusion of his theme statement in Rom 1:5: "Through him and for his name's sake, we received grace and apostleship to call people from among all the Gentiles to the obedience that comes from faith."

In Romans 15, Paul calls the Romans to live up to their reason for being, to strive toward the triple goal for which the Lord founded his church: obedience, mission, and the glory of God. The apostle issues the same challenge to every Christian who down through the centuries reads Romans: "I'm headed for the ends of the earth! Won't you please come along?"

Views of Serving God

A June afternoon could not be better than the one the Wilbertson clan was enjoying together. Young Mike Wilbertson was the focus of the family gathering as grandparents, aunts, uncles, and cousins arrived from four states to celebrate his graduation from college.

After a delicious picnic and a rousing softball game, some of them relaxed in lawn chairs, sipping lemonade and enjoying the soft breeze. Seated near Mike were his Grandma Norris, Uncle Dave, and Mike's eleven-year-old kid sister, Jenny.

For a while, the conversation centered on Mike's future in computer programming, but then Mike tired of talking about himself and changed the topic. "How are things going at your church these days, Uncle Dave? You are still an elder, aren't you?"

"Well, Mike, some good things are happening since Pastor Dawson arrived. As far as me being an elder goes, the election of officers is coming up next Sunday, but I don't know if I feel like running for any position."

"How come?" Mike asked. Grandma Norris also appeared interested in hearing Dave's reply as she aimed her good ear in his direction.

"I've been thinking about this for quite a while. For the last 15 years, I've been mighty busy at Faith Chapel, what with teaching Sunday School, a term as a trustee and three terms as an elder. Maybe it's time for me to retire and let someone else do the work."

"David," Grandma interjected, "how long have you been a foreman at the mill?"

"Thirty-one years, Mom."

"And how much longer are you going to work there?"

"I don't know. Till I retire I guess."

"Oh, then you're retiring next week, David?"

"Of course not!" Dave answered with a laugh. "Why in the world would I retire when I'm only 52?"

"That's exactly what I'm wondering, David. You said that next Sunday you hope to retire."

"You misunderstood, Mom. I was talking about church, not work."

"I don't see the difference. If you can keep serving yourself by working, you can keep serving the Lord." Her warm smile assured Dave that she was not angry at him, only trying to share her personal convictions.

"Don't you think there comes a time when the reins need to be turned over to young adults, like Mike here?"

"David, if you don't wish to continue as an elder, that's fine. Just find yourself some other way to serve. Remember your father's example. He retired from work at age 65, and in the four years before the Lord took him home, he got more involved at church than ever before because he tried new things."

"I guess you're right, Mom," he replied. "I remember Dad talking my ear off about the fun he was having as an evangelism caller. He thought he could never do that, and when he learned how, boy, was he excited." Dave took a sip of lemonade and then winked at his mother. "I'll call up Pastor Dawson when I get home and ask him about alternative ways to serve."

"Good!"

After a pause, Mike ventured, "Grandma, don't you think people my age can contribute to the leadership of a church?"

"Of course they can, Son. I'm sorry if I gave you that impression. My point is that Christians of all ages can and should be actively living for the Lord as long as he gives them breath. By your involvement in various church activities and Bible classes over the years, Mike, you are well prepared to serve now that you're grown."

Having silently followed every word of the conversation, Jenny piped up, "I want to be a missionary when I grow up!"

"Why, that's wonderful, Honey," Grandma Norris smiled. "I hope your dream comes true."

"It's not just a dream, Grandma. I can't think of anything I would rather be."

"When the time comes, young lady."

"I know I have to wait, but isn't there something I can do now to prepare for being a missionary?"

Grandma Norris, Uncle Dave, and Mike fell silent, not knowing how to advise the pre-adolescent volunteer.

Finally, Mike joked, "Hey, Jenny, someday when my company sends me to Japan or Singapore on a business trip, you can stow away in my luggage. Okay?"

A Mission for All Seasons of Life

Have you ever been asked to read a Bible passage at church? Even though you may be shy about reading out loud, the assignment is bearable as long as you do not encounter any difficult foreign names. Now we turn our attention to Rom 16:3–15, one of those Bible sections that people dread reading in public. Here Paul greets everybody and his uncle, it seems. All together, Paul mentions 26 individuals. Some have easy names, like Mary and Julia, but how does one pronounce Stachys, Apelles, and Nereus? Your guess is as good as ours, though a Bible dictionary helps.

Although these names sound unfamiliar to us, to Paul each one of them represented a dear friend with whom he had shared profound experiences. For example, Andronicus and Junias were relatives who had been imprisoned with him (Rom 16:7), and Rufus's mother was so dear to Paul that she seemed like a mother to him (Rom 16:13). His list of friends encompasses even more people than the folks he mentions by name, because he repeatedly greets whole households, which would include many relatives and servants—people of all generations.

What significance do these greetings have for the goal of the Gospel? It is possible for someone to hear Paul's call to holiness, to mission, and to glorify God, and yet respond with the thought, "Oh, Paul didn't mean for me to do that, did he? His appeal to offer one's body as a living sacrifice must be for someone else. His request to assist him in the mission must be intended for someone else, perhaps for someone a different age than I."

Rom 16:3–15 bursts the bubble of such rationalizations. Paul's greetings demonstrate that his letter was written to everyone, not just the leaders or the elders, but to everyone in Rome who knew the name of Jesus Christ. We today need similar assurance that the goal of the Gospel is for all of us, no matter who we are. At every stage of life we can bring glory to God. In fact, every age group in the North American church today has a unique contribution to make to world evangelization.

The Veterans

Older Christians in North America have experienced a unique adventure that qualifies them to be effective world Christians.

"Here at WBTL we have time for one more phone call before we sign off," barked radio talk show host Sid Pierson. "I have on the line Milt Horvath, calling from San Clemente. Hi, Milt."

"Hello, Sid. I'm not much for words, but with Veterans Day

coming up next week, I just wanted to say something."

"Shoot, Milt. We're all ears."

"During World War II, I served in a bomber squadron flying missions over Europe. As I think back on those tense days, I have to say that participating in the war was a great honor. I guess it was the most significant thing I ever did in my life."

Always looking for an angle, the host argued, "You're overstating things a bit, aren't you, Milt? Do you really mean you haven't done anything important since 1945?"

"Of course I have," the vet replied. "But winning the war was more important than getting married, raising kids, or working for 40 years."

"Now look, Milt. I'm a Korean vet, but there is no way I would ever say that the years I spent shooting Commies were the best years of my life."

"I can't speak for you, Sid. All I know is that the most important thing I ever did was to play a small role in the conflict that freed millions of people from the menacing oppression of Hitler's Germany and Hirohito's Japan."

A sizable portion of the members of many churches can recall World War II. In fact, in some congregations the "veterans" outnumber all other age groups. Whether they were ever on the battlefield is not important, because it was a "total war" that involved practically every civilian. Many households contributed a brother, son, or husband to the war effort. Women took their post on factory assembly lines. Even children helped gather scrap iron, aluminum, nylon, and other resources. Everyone rationed gasoline and food. Others were civil defense volunteers running air raid drills or combing the sky with binoculars on the lookout for attacking planes.

What has all this to do with world missions? The shared experience of World War II has equipped the veterans in our churches to be effective world Christians. The worldwide preaching of Christ is a total war dedicated to saving people from the oppression of sin, death, and the devil. If we are going to be the church of God, we have no choice but to participate in the Lord's war, as C. F. W. Walther observed:

> The church is not a kingdom that can be built up on peace; for
> it is located within the domain of the devil, who is the prince of

this world. Accordingly, the church has no choice but to be at war. It is *ecclesia militans,* the Church Militant, and will remain such until the blessed end. Wherever a Church is seen to be, not *ecclesia militans,* but *ecclesia quiescens,* a Church at ease, that—you may rely on it!—is a false Church (Walther 1928, 266).

Most older Christians are uniquely suited for service in this spiritual combat, because they have personally known full-scale war and the massive effort required to realize victory. They know that sacrifice and dedication are essential to attain a goal of global magnitude. Now is not the time to retire from the church, as Grandma Norris warned Uncle Dave earlier in this chapter. With their war experience, veteran believers should be in the vanguard of world Christian activity. Never in the history of the world has there been an older generation as healthy, as well educated, and as well-to-do, as the generation that now receives senior citizen discounts. If you are over 55, ask yourself:

Why has God given me these extra years—to spend them on myself, or to devote to the millions who do not know Jesus as I do?

Why has the Lord given me my skills and experience—so that I can bury them like an unused talent, or to put them to use in the worldwide mission enterprise?

Why has God granted me financial security—simply to get myself a piece of the rock, or to lead my lost brothers and sisters to everlasting security in Christ the Rock?[3]

Baby Boomers

After the insecurity of World War II, many young couples started raising families, resulting in the Baby Boom from 1945–63. This bulge in the population has had a constant impact on North American society and economy. Couldn't Baby Boomers also be an influence for world mission outreach?

In the late 1960s and early 1970s, many Baby Boomers viewed themselves as the Woodstock Generation, an idealistic legion of youth intent on changing the world. The Peace Corps, antiwar demonstrations, civil rights marches, and other social causes attracted their energies. Protest songs filled the airwaves with messages of loving one another and bringing peace on earth. Paraphrasing one of those popular songs, we can ask:

Where have all the protesters gone?
Gone to looking out for Number One.
Where have all the young idealists gone?
Gone in search of affluence and fun.

The Woodstock Generation deplored their elders' values of personal peace and affluence until they grew older themselves. Then they discovered that changing the world was a lot more difficult than they had thought. Little by little that dream was snuffed out and replaced by the daily struggle of making a buck.

North American churches are filled with Baby Boomers who once thought they could change the world, until they found out that it takes more than naive idealism to combat evil. The Baby Boomer crop of Christians needs to learn two things. First, the Woodstock idealists failed because they rejected God and his Word, putting their faith in an assortment of idols such as drugs, free love, Eastern religions, rock stars, political ideologies, and rebellion against parents. Such a man-centered foundation could not help but crumble under the pressure.

Second, if you are a Baby Boomer, God still wants you to be an idealist, living according to the Savior's words, "Love one another." He still calls you to change the world, this time by playing your part in spreading the life-changing and society-changing Gospel of Jesus Christ. And, best of all, the Lord has equipped you for this righteous crusade by the gift of your new self and the power of the Holy Spirit within you.

With a resurgence of Spirit-empowered idealism, the Baby Boomer generation could be a mighty force in God's plan to save the world.

Young Adults and Teens

Kathryn was a bright young Christian. At her church she showed signs of maturity and often spoke with interest about a career of service to the Lord. Then she met some new friends and, under their influence, started to drift away from the truth.

One day Kathryn received a long white box in the mail. The

card on the outside stated that it was a gift from Annie Harbin, an elderly woman at church. "When I saw these flowers, I thought of you," Annie had scrawled with a black fountain pen.

"What a sweetheart," Kathryn cried as she opened the box to discover a dozen long stem roses—all withered and brittle. Assuming there must have been a mistake, she forgot about the whole thing until the next Sunday at church when Annie approached her.

"Good morning, Kathryn. How did you like the wilted roses?"

"You mean you sent them that way on purpose!"

"Of course, my dear."

"Why?"

"Because they reminded me of you. Remember, I told you that in the note."

"I'm sorry, Mrs. Harbin. I don't follow you. Why would those withered roses remind you of me?"

"Kathryn, your faith and youthful energy are like bright, fragrant flowers in our church. Lately, however, I have noticed you are spending time with friends who are not concerned about doing the Savior's will. When I saw those faded flowers at the florist shop, they made me think how your youth may be squandered on worthless pursuits, if you follow the lead of your new friends."

Youth is a gift from God to be dedicated to his glory. Historically, young adults have contributed significantly to world evangelization. Every generation needs a new wave of youth committed to reaching the nations with the Gospel. Young adults are uniquely suited to the mission of the church for several reasons. Single youth may be free of family commitments. Many are still in the academic world and will not shrink from the intellectual challenge of learning another language and culture. With their great energy and idealism and their whole adult life before them, the world is theirs to claim for Christ.

Children

According to a popular account, Dwight L. Moody was asked after one evangelistic meeting, "How many were saved tonight?"

With a sense of humor he replied, "Two and a half."

"Oh, you mean two adults and one child?"

"No," Moody retorted, "I mean two children and one adult."

"How do you figure that?"

"The adult has only half his life remaining in which to serve his Savior. The children have almost their whole lives."

Of all the age groups that need to participate in the church's mission, children are perhaps the most important and yet most often overlooked. Do you recall when eleven-year-old Jenny told Grandma Norris, Uncle Dave, and Mike about her desire to be a missionary? The adults hardly took her seriously. Unfortunately, such indifference is not rare.

The majority of today's missionaries report that the Holy Spirit gave them the desire to become missionaries when they were in the 5th or 6th grade. In light of this finding, our Sunday schools and parochial schools ought to be centers of mission education and recruitment. The libraries of churches and Christian schools should be well stocked with children's mission books. Mission clubs should be organized, meeting once or twice per month to inform and motivate children about God's global task and give them an opportunity to participate in it right now. Make an honest appraisal of your church's elementary mission curriculum. What efforts are being made to give to the Jennies of your church a heart for the world? For your assistance a free list of children's mission books and resources is available from the Board for Mission Services of The Lutheran Church—Missouri Synod. Consult the list of mission organizations at the end of this book for the address.

Obedience, mission, and glorifying God are activities for all seasons of life. All generations need to be working together so that all the nations of the world may be blessed with the Gospel. When the Lord calls us home, people of all ages should be able to say, "Since my youth, O God, you have taught me, and to this day I declare your marvelous deeds. Even when I am old and gray, do not forsake me, O God, till I declare your power to the next generation, your might to all who are to come" (Ps 71:17–18).

Orthodoxy and Orthopractice

Good Shepherd Church had been so sharply divided by doctrinal controversy that finally their pastor left to serve elsewhere. The pulpit committee interviewed several ministers, hoping to find someone who could pull their church together. The most unusual interview occurred with a Pastor MacKenzie.

After several preliminary questions, Bill Sadler voiced the key question: "Pastor MacKenzie, if you were to serve here, how would you work to make peace between the warring factions in our church?"

Pastor MacKenzie confidently strategized, "First, I would preach a series of sermons and conduct Bible classes on the world mission responsibility of this congregation. Second, I would lead a group of members on a tour to one of our mission fields. Seeing the work firsthand will give them a heart for the world. And third, I would form a mission committee to maintain the momentum that would have begun."

"What good would that do?" Bill Sadler queried. The expressions on the faces of the rest of the committee showed that they were just as nonplussed as Bill.

The minister replied, "I don't believe this church will ever have the spiritual maturity to resolve its doctrinal differences until it rediscovers and recommits itself to obey Christ's final orders."

The pulpit committee put many other questions to Pastor MacKenzie until 9 p.m. when they thanked the minister and bid him good evening. Two hours later, they were still debating whether or not to call Pastor MacKenzie. Although generally impressed with his credentials, the issue they kept returning to was his answer about missions as the solution to dissension in the church. They could not make up their minds. Was Pastor MacKenzie right or wrong?

Pastor MacKenzie recognized that proclaiming the Word of God and putting it into practice are as important as defending his Word. Paul addresses this very topic after his numerous greetings in Romans 16:

> I urge you, brothers, to watch out for those who cause divisions and put obstacles in your way that are contrary to the teaching you have learned. Keep away from them. For such people are not serving our Lord Christ, but their own appetites. By smooth talk and flattery they deceive the minds of naive people. Everyone has heard about your obedience, so I am full of joy over you; but I want you to be wise about what is good, and innocent about what is evil.

The God of peace will soon crush Satan under your feet.

The grace of our Lord Jesus be with you (Rom 16:17–20).

First, Paul warns against false doctrine in the church. Whenever someone is spouting heresy, we turn to this text (among others) to determine how to deal with false teachers. Time and again Christians have needed to act upon this warning in order to maintain orthodoxy (right doctrine) in the church.

We authors concur that concern for orthodoxy is a proper application of the text. Yet, Rom 16:17–20 calls for action beyond the intellectual and theological exercise of defending orthodox teaching. When Paul says, "Everyone has heard about your obedience," he is speaking of right living as much as right believing. The divisions and obstacles Paul cautions us to watch out for are not limited to false doctrines; they also include actions and lifestyles contrary to God's will. The prefix *ortho* means straight, upright, proper, and correct. In addition to orthodoctrine, we should exhibit orthowitness, ortholove, and orthodeeds, by the Spirit's power. Thus, orthopractice is as important to pursue and to defend as orthodoxy.

Think about your home church and your denomination (or other larger fellowship). How much energy do people devote to defending pure doctrine? How much energy is expended promoting Spirit-empowered obedience and world evangelization? Every church will have its own characteristic emphasis. Perhaps you can relate to Missionary Paul Brink's verdict as he challenges his denomination:

> When will the Missouri Synod wake up to the fact that the *main issue* that it is facing today is not the doctrine of the office of the pastor, nor the charismatic movement within our church, nor abortion, nor our relationship with [the] ELCA, but that 3/5 of the world (3 billion people) are headed for hell?

> When will we stop considering ourselves to be primarily DEFENDERS of an endangered Gospel and start being primarily COMMUNICATORS of the saving Gospel?

> What *steps* need to be taken in order for the Lord of the Church to *reshape* us into a dynamic, sacrificial and committed force for the evangelization of the world? (Brink 1989, 2).

Ouch! Questions like these really pinch. Although we would just as soon ignore them, the Lord would have us wrestle with such questions, just as Jacob wrestled at Peniel (Gen 32:22–32), so that he might bless us.[4]

A Last Glance at the Big Picture

Paul follows his warning about right teaching and right living with a beautiful promise: "The God of peace will soon crush Satan under your feet" (Rom 16:20). In this verse and its preceding context, Paul's imagery takes us back to the Garden of Eden, thus giving us another glimpse of the big picture.

"By smooth talk and flattery they deceive" (Rom 16:18) brings to mind the crafty serpent who smooth-talked Adam and Eve out of their state of innocence.

"I want you to be wise about what is good and innocent about what is evil" (Rom 16:19) reminds us of the tree of the knowledge of good and evil.

Then comes the *piece de resistance:* "The God of peace will soon crush Satan under your feet. The grace of our Lord Jesus be with you" (16:20). In twenty words Paul includes every element of the Gospel chain. There is an obvious allusion to Gen 3:15, the very first Gospel promise in the Scriptures. Jesus Christ and his grace are prominent. Paul blends together obedience, mission, and glory in the phrase "crush Satan under your feet." His wording is artful. Gen 3:15 states that the descendant of Eve will crush Satan's head. Jesus Christ attained this victory through his crucifixion and resurrection (Jn 12:31; Col 2:15). And yet, says Paul, Satan will be crushed underneath *our* feet. How will this be accomplished?

Believers can crush Satan by offering the parts of their bodies to God as instruments of righteousness (Rom 6:13). As they do so, the nations will be liberated from Satan's deception as the Lord shows himself holy through us, his people, before their eyes (Ezek 36:23). By proclaiming Christ's glory among the nations, believers will break the serpent's sway over humankind (Is 66:19). Satan is crushed as we lift Jesus higher, as a succinct African folksong states:

> Cast your burdens onto Jesus,
>   for he cares for you.
> Higher, higher, higher,

lift Jesus higher!
Lower, lower, lower,
step Satan lower!

Looking at the Big Picture, we know that we were created to live before God in holiness, love, and purity. Obedience is not a burden but a blessing. When the Evil One snatched that blessing from us, we fell short of the glory God intended for us. But Jesus Christ, the King of Glory, while we were still powerless, died for the ungodly. Through faith in his abundant provision of grace, we are reconciled to the God of peace. As if that were not enough, we also receive the gift of righteousness, the ability to count ourselves dead to sin and alive to God in Christ Jesus.

By equipping us for obedience through Jesus Christ, God allows us to participate actively in the defeat of the devil. The image of crushing Satan under our feet implies progress. We march with determination to all the ends of the earth to rescue people from the dominion of darkness and bring them into the kingdom of the Son of God in whom we have redemption, the forgiveness of sins (Col 1:13–14). The gates of hell will not prevail when Christians blow them apart with the Gospel, the dynamite of God for the salvation of everyone who believes: first for the Jew, then for the Gentile (Mt 16:18; Rom 1:16).

Two years ago the authors began a biblical study of obedience because they knew too many Christians who never even think of crushing Satan under their feet. They are content to serve God primarily with their rear ends, by polishing pews on Sunday morning. Noting this weakness, Dr. Kent Hunter observes that the Father "did not shed the blood of his Son to organize a cult of pew sitters. He calls everyone to action." Rather than answer that call, many practice the " 'sacrament of the seat'—observed by the masses of lay people stuck on their ecclesiastical backsides" (Hunter 1985, 77). We have written this book to help Christians realize that God cannot crush Satan under their feet while they are sitting down on the job. As singer Keith Green quipped during a concert I [Phil] attended, "You say you don't feel led to serve the needy or to share Christ with the lost. You don't feel led, huh? Oh, you feel lead, all right. It's just in a different place!"

There are times when all of us need to get the lead out. Yet, no matter how lazy or lethargic the sleeping giant of the church has been in the past, Paul's promise assures us that when God lifts us up off our backsides, he will complete his mighty work of crushing Satan under our feet, yours and ours.

So, up and at 'em!

Gospel Chain II

Paul is about to end the Bible's definitive book about obedience, mission, and glorifying God. How shall he conclude? What else need he do but summarize the Gospel chain—Scripture, Christ, obedience, mission, glory—in a powerful doxology?

> Now to him who is able to establish you by my Gospel and the proclamation of Jesus Christ, according to the revelation of the mystery hidden for long ages past, but now revealed and made known through the prophetic writings by the command of the eternal God, so that all nations might believe and obey him—to the only wise God be glory forever through Jesus Christ! Amen (Rom 16:25–27).

As you believe these five truths and put them into practice, the Holy Spirit will make your life a doxology.

In this book's opening vignette, Pastor Ralph Kramer and layman Dave Schmidt shared their frustration about the spiritual lethargy and indifference in their congregation. They wondered how to preach about obedience and witnessing without legalistically browbeating the people. How they longed to arouse the giant of the church from its spiritual sleeping sickness! And what is the answer to this common problem?

In the past thirteen chapters you have discovered the answer: to link the Gospel with its goal. The Gospel is the power of God for the salvation of all who believe. And the goal of the Gospel is its powerful results in the lives of those disciples of Christ who understand why he has saved us by grace through faith. When we continually speak the Gospel in connection with its goal, the sleeping giant that is the church will arise.

Separate the links of a chain, and they are silent. Link them together, and they will rattle up a storm! That's what we hope we have done for you through this study. We've tried to rattle the links of the Gospel chain loudly enough to wake up the sleeping giant. At the very least, we hope we have aroused you to a new enthusiasm about your life in Christ. We pray that you will now join us in rattling the Gospel chain, so that many more Christians can be awakened, motivated, empowered, and equipped to obey the will of God and to carry the good news of Jesus Christ to the ends of the earth, all for the glory of his name. For that is, indeed, the goal of the Gospel!

Digging Deeper

1. Spend two minutes pondering Isaiah 53, especially vv. 4–6. Meditate on what these words mean for you personally. Share your reflections with another person.
2. Now spend two minutes pondering Is 52:7, 10, and 15, taking into account that the good news to be proclaimed is the saving sacrifice of Christ described in Isaiah 53. How do you think these verses motivated Paul to be a missionary? How do you think the Lord wants these verses to stimulate you and your church? Share your thoughts with another person.
3. Has a missionary ever visited your church and requested financial support? If so, what was the response? Do missionaries have the right to make such a request?
4. Has a missionary ever visited your church and urged members of your congregation to become missionaries too? If so, what was the response? Do missionaries have the right to make such a request?
5. If Missionary Paul of Tarsus were to visit your church, what requests and challenges do you think he would direct toward you?
6. Is your church busy about the Father's business, or just busy? Are *you* busy about the Father's work, or just busy? Try to explain your answer.
7. The section entitled "A Mission for All Seasons of Life" speaks of various generations of Christians: veterans, baby boomers, young adults, teens, and children. Which are you? What special experiences and resources do you bring to God's global mission enterprise? How can you put them to use?
8. Think of the generations in your congregation: veterans, baby boomers, young adults, teens, and children. What special ex-

periences and resources do you all bring to God's global mission enterprise? How can each of these age groups be encouraged and equipped to follow Paul to the ends of the earth?

9. Make an honest appraisal of your church's education curriculum. Is a conscious and significant effort being made to give Christians of all ages a heart for the world?

10. Consider this observation made by a missionary: "When will we stop considering ourselves to be primarily defenders of an endangered Gospel and start being primarily communicators of the saving Gospel?" How do you feel about this question? How much energy does your church expend in defending and in communicating? Which receives greater emphasis? What should be the proper balance between the two?

11. Take a new look at the Lord's Prayer (Lk 11:2–4). Can you identify the links of the Gospel chain in the prayer Jesus taught his disciples?

12. Compare Rom 16:20, "The God of peace will soon crush Satan under your feet," with Mt 16:18b, "On this rock I will build my church, and the gates of hell will not prove stronger than it." Do these promises imply a passive defense or an active offense?

13. What is your final verdict regarding the authors' opinion that the Gospel chain—Scripture, Christ, obedience, mission, the glory of God—is the organizing principle of Paul's letter to the Romans?

14. What is your final verdict regarding the authors' opinion that the Gospel chain—Scripture, Christ, obedience, mission, the glory of God—is the organizing principle of the Christian life? Or, to put it another way, do you believe that obedience, mission, and the glory of God are the "GOal of the GOspel"? Why or why not?

Notes

1. While Isaiah is universally acclaimed as the "Evangelist of the Old Testament," we could also rightfully call him the "Apostle of the Old Testament," because he repeatedly foretold the worldwide expansion of God's kingdom.

2. Isaiah 52–53 and Psalm 22 are universally recognized as the most significant prophesies of the sacrificial death of Christ. Just as Isaiah 52–53 strongly em-

phasizes worldwide proclamation, so the last six verses of Psalm 22 stress the global impact to result from Christ's one perfect sacrifice. Thus both these great messianic texts speak of both the Gospel and its mission goal.

3. The Persian Gulf War of 1990–91 was a much smaller military action than World War II. Even so, that experience has taught a new generation that victory demands sacrifice. Following World War II and the Korean conflict, a wave of Christian ex-GIs became missionaries. The Holy Spirit used their cross-cultural military experience to show them the needs of the world. Now is the time for us to be praying for a similar wave of new missionaries to bring the love and grace of Christ to the one billion Muslims who believe they can be saved by their own good deeds.

4. Dr. Erwin J. Kolb has written an excellent, highly-readable, theological article that wrestles with the tension between being defenders of the Gospel and communicators of the Gospel. "The Primary Mission of the Church and Its Detractors," which appeared in the April–July 1990 *Concordia Theological Quarterly,* merits the attention of all Christians.

Resources and Suggested Reading

Aldrich, Joseph C.
1981
Lifestyle Evangelism. Portland: Multnomah Press.

Arn, Win, and
Charles Arn
1982
The Master's Plan for Making Disciples. Pasadena: Church Growth Press.

Barclay, William
1957
Commentary on Romans. Richmond: John Knox.

Barry, Alvin L.
1990
"The State of Gospel Communication Today," *The State of Gospel Communication Today.* Eds. Eugene W. Bunkowske and Gregory L. Robertson, 10–22. Fort Wayne: Great Commission Resource Library.

Bickel, Philip
1989
Joy to the World: God's Global Mission for Local Christians. St. Louis: Concordia Publishing House.

Bonhoeffer, Dietrich
1959
From *The Cost of Discipleship.* Translated from the German by R. H. Fuller, with some revision by Irmgard Booth. Copyright © 1959 by SCM Press, Ltd. Reprinted with permission of Macmillan Publishing Company, New York, NY.

Brink, Paul
1989
"Reflections From Manila," *Brink Newsletter,* August 12, 2.

Bunkowske, Eugene
1989
"Cross Cultural Perceptions," *Inter-Connections.* May 1989. St. Louis: The Board for Mission Services, The Lutheran Church—Missouri Synod.

Bunkowske, Eugene W., and **Richard French**, eds.
1989
Receptor-Oriented Gospel Communication. Fort Wayne: Great Commission Resource Library.

Card, Michael
1989
"Jubilee," from his album *The Beginning.* Copyright © 1989 Birdwing Music. All rights controlled and administered by the Sparrow Corporation, P. O. Box 5010, Brentwood, TN 37024–5010. All rights reserved. International copyright secured. Used by permission.

Collins, Steven
1988
Christian Discipleship. Tulsa: Virgil W. Hensley, Inc.

Coltman, William G.
1943
The Cathedral of Christian Truth—Studies in Romans. Findlay, OH: Fundamental Truth Publishers.

Donfried, Karl P., ed.
1991
The Romans Debate. Peabody, MA: Hendrickson Publishers.

Elliot, Elizabeth
1981
Through Gates of Splendor. Wheaton: Tyndale.

Franzmann, Martin
1968
Romans. St. Louis: Concordia Publishing House.

Gallup, George Jr.
1990
"Gallup Finds Religion-Life Link Failing," *Journal of the American Family Association,* August 1990. Copyright © 1990 Princeton Religion Research Center, Princeton, NJ. Used by permission of George Gallup Jr.

Glasser, Arthur F.
1981
"The Apostle Paul and the Missionary Task," *Perspectives on the World Christian Movement.* Eds. Ralph Winter and Steven Hawthorne, 104–112. Pasadena: William Carey Library.

Green, Keith
1978
"Asleep in the Light." From his album *No Compromise.* Copyright © 1978 The Sparrow Corporation, P. B. Box 5010, 101 Winners Circle, Brentwood, TN 37024. Used by permission.

Hartman, Bob
1987

"Dead Reckoning." Records. Copyright © 1987 by Dawn Treader Musk and Petsong Publishing. All rights reserved. Used by permission.

Hoover, David, and **Roger Leenerts**
1979

Enlightened with His Gifts. St. Louis: Lutheran Growth.

Hunter, Kent
1985

Your Church Has Personality. Nashville: Abingdon.

Jack, Bob, and **Betty Jack**
1986

Your Home a Lighthouse. Colorado Springs: NavPress.

Kauflin, Bob
1989

"There's Not One." From the Glad album *Romans.* Copyright © 1989 LifeSong Music Press/BMI, Organon Key Music/BMI. All Rights Reserved. Used by permission of The Benson Co., Inc., Nashville, TN.

Keller, Phillip
1978

From *A Shepherd Looks at the Good Shepherd and His Sheep.* Copyright © 1978 by W. Phillip Keller. Used by permission of Zondervan Publishing House, Grand Rapids, MI.

Koeberle, Adolf
1964

The Quest for Holiness. Minneapolis: Augsburg.

Kolb, Erwin J.
1990

"The Primary Mission of the Church and Its Detractors." *Concordia Theological Quarterly,* April–July.

Kolb, Robert
1984

From *Speaking the Gospel Today.* Copyright © 1984 Concordia Publishing House, St. Louis, MO. Used by permission.

Lewis, C. S.
1953

The Silver Chair. by C. S. Lewis (approx. 104 words). HarperCollins Publishers Limited, London.

Mattson, Ralph, and **Arthur Miller**
1982

From *Finding a Job You Can Love.* Copyright © 1982 Thomas Nelson Publishers, Nashville, TN. Used by permission.

Mattson, Ralph, and **Arthur Miller** 1977
The Truth About You. Old Tappan, NJ: Revell.

McQuilken, J. Robertson 1981
"The Narrow Way," *Perspectives on the World Christian Movement.* Ralph Winter and Steven Hawthorne, eds., 121–134. Pasadena: William Carey Library.

Menconi, Al 1990
From February 1990 appeal letter. Al Menconi Ministries, PO Box 5008-T. San Marcos, CA. Used by permission.

Nee, Watchman 1963
The Normal Christian Life. Fort Washington, PA: Christian Literature Crusade.

O'Connor, Elizabeth 1971
From *Eighth Day of Creation.* Copyright © 1971 Word, Inc., Dallas, TX. Used by permission.

Peace, Richard 1985
Small Group Evangelism. Downers Grove: InterVarsity Press.

Petersen, Jim 1980
Evangelism As a Lifestyle. Colorado Springs: NavPress.

Petersen, Jim 1985
Evangelism for Our Generation. Colorado Springs: NavPress.

Pieper, Franz 1951
From *Christian Dogmatics.* Copyright © 1951 Concordia Publishing House, St. Louis, MO. Used by permission.

Pippert, Rebecca 1979
Out of the Saltshaker and Into the World. Downers Grove: InterVarsity Press.

Pollard, Mike 1990
"Middle East Meets West." In *ACMC [Association of Church Missions Committees] Newsletter.* Winter 1990.

Rosen, Moishe 1990
From "What's Wrong with Being Nice?" In *Jews for Jesus Newsletter.* January 1990, 3:5750. Copyright © 1989 Jews for Jesus Newsletter. Used by permission of Moishe Rosen.

Rudnick, Milton L. 1977
Lutheran Education Association Yearbook, *Authority and Obedience in the Church.* River Forest, IL: Lutheran Education Association.

Rudnick, Milton L.
1984

From *Speaking the Gospel Through the Ages: A History of Evangelism.* Copyright © 1984 Concordia Publishing House, St. Louis, MO. Used by permission.

Saint, Rachel
1991

From "The Family Room," *Guideposts.* January, 1991:45. Carmel, NY: Guideposts Associates, Inc.

Schaeffer, Edith
1978

Affliction. Old Tappan, NJ: Revell.

Schaeffer, Francis A.
1971

True Spirituality. Wheaton: Tyndale.

Schrenk, Gottlob
1971

"Dikaiosuna," in *Theological Dictionary of the New Testament,* Vol II, edited by Gerhard Kittel, translated by Geoffrey W. Bromiley. Copyright © 1964 by Wm. B. Eerdmans Publishing Company, Grand Rapids, MI. Used by permission.

Tan, Paul Lee, ed.
1979

Encyclopedia of 7700 Illustrations. Rockville, MD: Assurance Publishers.

Tappert, Theodore G., ed.
1959

From *The Book of Concord.* Copyright © 1959 Fortress Press, Philadelphia, PA. Used by permission of Augsburg Fortress, Minneapolis, MN.

Thorson, Paul
1978

"I Am." Copyright © 1978, Campus Crusade for Christ. All rights reserved. Used by permission..

Vicedom, Georg F.
1965

From *The Mission of God.* Copyright © 1965 Concordia Publishing House, St. Louis, MO. Used by permission.

Wagner, C. Peter
1979

Your Spiritual Gifts Can Help Your Church Grow. Ventura, CA: Regal Books.

Wagner, Stephen
1985

Heart to Heart. Corunna, IN: Church Growth Center.

Walther, C. F. W.
1928

From *The Proper Distinction Between Law and Gospel.* Copyright © 1928 Concordia Publishing House, St. Louis, MO. Used by permission.

Watkins, Morris
1987

Werning, Waldo
1986

Winter, Ralph D.
1981

Yancey, Philip
1977

Seven Worlds to Win. Fort Wayne: The Great Commission Resource Library.

From *Supply Side Stewardship.* Copyright © 1986 Concordia Publishing House, St. Louis, MO. Used by permission.

From "The New Macedonia: A Revolutionary New Era in Mission Begins," in *Perspectives on the World Christian Movement.* Ralph D. Winter and Steven C. Hawthorne, eds., 293–311. Copyright © 1981 William Carey Library, Pasadena, CA. Reprinted by permission of the publisher.

Where Is God When It Hurts? Grand Rapids: Zondervan.

Mission Organizations

All Nations Mission Education Materials, P.O. Box 5491, Fort Wayne, IN 46895.

Association of Christian Ministries to Internationals, 233 Langdon, Madison, WI 53703.

Association of Church Missions Committees, P.O. Box ACMC, Wheaton, IL 60189, or 1620 S. Myrtle Ave., Monrovia, CA 91016.

Evangelical Lutheran Church in America, Division of Global Mission, 8765 Higgins Rd., Chicago, IL 60631.

Evangelical Lutheran Church of Canada, Division of World Mission, 1512 St. James St., Winnipeg, Manitoba, Canada R3H OL2.

Evangelical Missions Information Service, Box 794, Wheaton, IL 60187.

Global Church Growth Book Club, 1705 Sierra Bonita Ave., Pasadena, CA 91104.

The Oswald Hoffmann School of Christian Outreach, 275 N. Syndicate, St. Paul, MN 55104.

Intercristo Christian Placement Service, P.O. Box 33487, Seattle, WA 98133.

Jews for Jesus, 60 Haight St., San Francisco, CA 94102.

Lutheran Association for Maritime Ministry, 2513 One Hundred Sixty-second Ave. NE, Bellevue/Seattle, WA 98008.

Lutheran Association of Missionaries and Pilots (LAMP), 9335 Forty-seventh St., Edmonton, Alberta, Canada T6B 2R7, or 3505 N. One Hundred Twenty-fourth St., Brookfield, WI 53005-2498.

Lutheran Bible Translators, 303 N. Lake St., Box 2050, Aurora, IL 60507-2050, or Box 934, Station C, Kitchener, Ontario, Canada N2G 4E3.

Lutheran Braille Workers, Inc., P.O. Box 5000, Yucaipa, CA 92399.

Lutheran Church—Canada, Box #55, Sta. "A" Winnipeg, Manatoba, Canada R3K 1Z9.

The Lutheran Church—Missouri Synod, Board for Mission Services, International Center, 1333 S. Kirkwood Rd., St. Louis, MO 63122-7295.

Lutheran Evangelism Association, P.O. Box 10021, Phoenix, AZ 85064.

Lutheran Immigration and Refugee Service, 360 Park Ave. S., New York, NY 10010.

Lutheran Institute for Jewish Evangelism, 20 Fawn Drive, Lebanon, NJ 08833.

Lutheran World Relief, 360 Park Ave., S., 15th Floor, New York, NY 10010.

National Council of Churches of Christ in the U.S.A., Division of Overseas Ministries, 475 Riverside Dr., New York, NY 10027.

The Tentmaker Training Center, P.O. Box 919, Oak Park, IL 60303-0919.

U.S. Center for World Mission, 1605 E. Elizabeth St., Pasadena, CA 91104.

Westminster Theological Seminary, P.O. Box 270090, Philadelphia, PA 19118.

Wheat Ridge Foundation, 104 S. Michigan Ave., Suite 610, Chicago, IL 60603.

Wisconsin Evangelical Lutheran Synod, Board for World Missions, 2929 N. Mayfair Rd., Milwaukee, WI 53222.

World Mission Prayer League, 232 Clifton Ave., Minneapolis, MN 55403.

World Vision International/Missions Advanced Research and Communication Center (MARC), 919 Huntington Dr., Monrovia, CA 91016.

Zwemer Institute of Muslim Studies, P.O Box 365, Altadena, CA 91003-0365.

About the authors...

Philip M. Bickel is Professor of Religion and
Evangelism and the Director of the Oswald
Hoffmann School of Christian Outreach at
Concordia College, St. Paul, Minnesota.
He is the author of *Joy to the World*.

Robert L. Nordlie is Pastor of Immanuel Lutheran
Church, Hillside, Illinois.